# PROVIDENCE
# THEIR GUIDE

# THE
# LONG RANGE
# DESERT GROUP
# 1940–45

# PROVIDENCE
# THEIR GUIDE

# THE
# LONG RANGE
# DESERT GROUP
# 1940–45

by
Major-General David Lloyd Owen
CB, DSO, OBE, MC

With a Foreword by General Sir Hackett
GCB, CBE, DSO, MC
and introduction by
Sir John Keegan

Pen & Sword
**MILITARY**

First published in Great Britain in 1980
by George G. Harrop & Co Ltd
Republished in revised edition 2000,
Reprinted in 2001 and 2008 by
PEN & SWORD MILITARY
an imprint of
Pen & Sword Books Ltd
47 Church Street
Barnsley
South Yorkshire
S70 2AS

ISBN 0 85052 806 2

Printed and bound in Great Britain
By CPI UK

Pen & Sword Books Ltd incorporates the Imprints of
Pen & Sword Aviation, Pen & Sword Family History,
Pen & Sword Maritime, Pen & Sword Military, Wharncliffe Local History,
Pen & Sword Select, Pen & Sword Military Classics, Leo Cooper,
Remember When, Seaforth Publishing and Frontline Publishing

For a complete list of Pen & Sword titles please contact
PEN & SWORD BOOKS LIMITED
47 Church Street, Barnsley, South Yorkshire, S70 2AS, England
E-mail: enquiries@pen-and-sword.co.uk
Website: www.pen-and-sword.co.uk

# Dedication

Officers and men from the British Army, from the Second New Zealand Expeditionary Force and from Southern Rhodesia served with the Long Range Desert Group during that unit's five years existence in the Second World War. This book is primarily dedicated to them.

But none of us will forget the many brave and generous people, in the countries where we operated, who so often gave us much needed help at frightful risk to themselves.

# Contents

# Foreword

## by General Sir John Hackett

Nothing throws a clearer light upon the characteristics of a nation than the way it goes to war, and what is revealed there is likely to be reflected to some degree in everything else it does.

The British way in war was the product of geography. The mongrel inhabitants of these off-shore islands, separated by salt water from the Continent of Europe, were forced ages ago to look to the sea, first for their very survival, and then for their prosperity. Defence, trade, the projection and advancement of the national interest as these islanders moved on towards the establishment of the world's greatest empire, all depended on the use of the sea. Wherever there was blue water there was an open flank, first for military exploitation and then for the introduction of the trader and the empire-builder. The British way in war is not that of continental nations, whose natural tendency is generally towards massive frontal action. It lies more in looking for the open flank and then making use of it, often by distant action and deep penetration. The British method lies predominantly in the oblique approach, in going round or under or over whatever stands in the way, whether in terms of physical obstruction or military forces.

In World War II the Mediterranean theatre offered an almost embarrassing choice of open flanks. There was not only the sea, offering enormous stretches of coastline often backed by useful mountains, with a plethora of islands. There was also the desert. The land battle for Africa, and for control of the southern shore of the Mediterranean, was essentially fought along a narrow coastal strip, a couple of thousand miles long but rarely more than fifty deep. To the south of it lay vast stretches of desert wasteland, little visited and largely unexplored. In these deserts there came into being one of the most remarkable of the small specialist forces spawned in such numbers and variety by the British in the Mediterranean theatre of war for the exploitation of its open flanks. This was the Long Range Desert Group. When the war in Africa came to an end and we had run out of desert the LRDG was to be used with great effect on sea-coasts, islands and mountains. But the deserts of Northern Africa were its cradle and its original habitat. It was here that the LRDG found the disciplines and the challenge under which it grew into a unit which in its professionalism, its level of attainment in specialist skills, its internal coherence, its very high morale and its avoidance of the public eye was in my experience unique.

David Lloyd Owen had long wanted—as had so many others—to join the Long Range Desert Group, and was taken on in July 1941. He was to finish the war in 1945 as its commander. This book of his about the LRDG, under so apt a title, is written with a restraint, and with a degree of generosity and modesty, as characteristic of the writer as of the unit he writes about. It is an enthralling document. I read it with deep enjoyment and a heightened understanding of men and events of which I already knew a good deal, and I am now grateful to be allowed to write this foreword.

It all started in the thirties, when travel by motor-car in desert places began for several young Army officers to become almost an obsession, and Ralph Bagnold, that ingenious and inventive officer of the Royal Signals, was developing better means of setting about it. Many others who served in Egypt in those years will welcome a glimpse in these pages of people some of us knew well—Teddy Mitford, Rupert Harding-Newman, Pat Clayton and Bill Kennedy Shaw (though these last two did not, I think, become soldiers till war came) and of course Guy Prendergast, whose modesty, and even shyness, made him not an easy man to get to know.

When war broke out and the early Patrols were set up out of detachments from the Brigade of Guards, the Yeomanry, Rhodesians and New Zealanders, there could hardly have been brought together men of more varied backgrounds. Of these the New Zealanders were the first, and the equally redoubtable Rhodesians came in soon afterwards. The development of high comradeship, intense loyalty to the unit and an almost fierce dedication to the task in hand—all characteristics uniformly found throughout the LRDG—was the result of careful selection from an enormous number of applicants (Lloyd Owen once had to select 12 from 700 volunteers), meticulous planning and the discipline of the task itself. Patrols worked and lived in small groups, very often hundreds of miles from each other, in a hostile environment and under frequent threat of discovery and destruction. Every member of a Patrol not only knew his own job perfectly and was able and willing to help every other man with his: he also knew exactly what was expected of him, and what he could expect from the others. The expectations were high, and were very rarely disappointed. To fall below them might mean being RTU, or 'returned to unit'. This was a dreaded punishment. In a unit where exacting requirements had to be most precisely met, the threat of it was the only sanction ever needed. It is little wonder that in spite of the efforts of Guy Prendergast (its commander from August 1941 to October 1943) and of others to keep the LRDG away from notice, this was probably the most difficult unit to get into—as well as possibly being the most efficient—in the whole theatre.

I found myself mentioned in this narrative, and enlarge a little here because that enables me to say something more about its author. In early September 1942, after the battle of Alam al Halfa, I was brought rather reluctantly in from the desert (where I had been in the summer of 1942 having a delightful time in tanks on rearguard columns, and then as 2 I/C of an armoured regiment), to set up a new General Staff section co-ordinating the operations in the whole theatre of all British raiding forces in the Middle East. I arrived in GHQ Middle East when the disastrous combined raid on Benghazi and Tobruk (see Chapter 10) was already under way and beyond modification, let alone recall. It was too big and too complex, as both Prendergast and David Stirling had not been slow to point out. Security was bad, and (a point on which Montgomery was critical) it was commanded not by a field commander but by a committee of senior staff officers. My first big task was to pick up the pieces.

One of the pieces was David Lloyd Owen. He had been wounded in the back and arm in the last stages of the raid, and was convalescent in Cairo when I got to know him. We shared a common predicament. The manpower-planners in Whitehall had worked out a plan by which Servicemen who had been abroad for more than four years (as far as I recall) were 'entitled' to repatriation. The so-called 'entitlement' was nearer to compulsion. I had already been serving abroad for seven years, and David for nearly four. Thus we were both highly vulnerable, but neither of us wanted in the very least to be sent away from where the war was going on to where it wasn't. I pulled strings in GHQ, and, as a recently appointed Staff Officer in what was regarded as a critical appointment, got myself exempted. To get David in turn off his hook I asked for him as a GSO3 in my own staff section, and when he was appointed said he could not be spared. It worked, and he stayed, soon to go back to where he longed to be—with the LRDG in the desert. The company of this very engaging person was delightful, when I had the chance to enjoy it. He did not, however, do much staff work. In his own recollection he only drafted one signal from me, and he claims I tore it up. We had, however, achieved what we had set out to do, which was to outflank his 'entitlement'. He makes no mention of all this in his narrative. What he also omits to mention is that for his gallantry in action he had been awarded a Military Cross.

The reader of these pages will meet some great people—Olivey, Timpson, Browne, Tinker, Wilder, Croucher, Lawson, the Signals Officer Tim Heywood to whom a unit in which communication was vital owed so much, the towering figure of Jake Easonsmith and in the background the quiet, tireless, devoted personality of Guy Prendergast. The author's praise of David Stirling and his prestigious exploits with the

SAS is both well earned and generous. In the early days, after their one and only parachute raid (which was a disaster) and before they acquired their own mobility, the SAS were carried in and out by the LRDG. But these were two very different sets of people. The SAS were raiders. The LRDG were specialists in deep reconnaissance. The SAS could act as information-gatherers too, and the LRDG, as Guy Prendergast explained to me, were the better for 'an occasional beat-up', but their rôles were different and their operations had to be kept apart. The 'Stirlings', as Guy called them, would dash in and destroy enemy aircraft on their landing-grounds, or some other equally tempting target, and wake the whole area up. When they had gone—usually leaving the desert strewn with what they had jettisoned—the enemy's patrols would come out in strength in an energetic search for them, sometimes to find and flush out instead the beautifully sited and carefully concealed observation posts of the LRDG. These two groups had enormous respect for each other, but it was better if they did not operate in close proximity. I remember behaving rather like a late-medieval Pope dividing up the maritime world between two rival sea-powers along a meridian in the Atlantic. I chose a meridian in the desert. To the west of it the LRDG was to operate, the SAS only to the east.

It was in deep reconnaissance, among many other distinguished activities, that the LRDG shone with truly unrivalled brilliance. In my opinion the Road Watch was their most remarkable achievement, and I expect that most who know what they did would agree. A circuitous journey, often over a thousand miles long, would bring a Patrol up through a deep forward base, already situated well inside hostile territory, and thereafter through a series of dumps to a point where a couple of men with binoculars would be hidden a few hundred yards from the main Axis supply road. There they would stay, counting every vehicle, in any category, which went up or down and reporting the tally back to GHQ. The value of this information in the attempt to divine the enemy's intentions was quite incalculable. The skill and boldness with which it was obtained take the breath away.

War is a hideous business, brutal, cruel, ruthless and unforgiveably destructive. Like all human activities conducted on a grand scale at a high level of intensity, however, it is not without opportunities for elegance. The LRDG displayed this quality of elegance at every point. In the whole concept under which it operated, in the devising of the means to carry it out, in the exquisite precision of operational and logistical plans, in the skill and restraint with which these were executed—and above everything else in the structure of human relations built up within the unit itself—I find an elegance unique and admirable. Fortunate are those with memories of service in the LRDG, who can be reminded of it in these pages.

# Introduction

## by Sir John Keegan

It is a great pleasure to write the introduction to this new edition of Major General David Lloyd Owen's memoir of the Long Range Desert Group. Part of the pleasure is personal, for I owe the author a debt of gratitude. When I joined the staff of the Royal Military Academy Sandhurst in 1960, David Lloyd Owen was a very senior Sandhurst figure and I was not only the most junior but also the youngest member of the instructional staff, not long out of Oxford and, having been found unfit for National Service, knowing nothing of the army at all. The General, as he now is, nevertheless took the trouble to be kind to me and to make me feel welcome. Such kindness is never forgotten.

More important, however, his invitation to contribute an introduction provides the opportunity to recall the achievements of an extraordinary organization that not only contributed greatly to the victory of the British army in the epic struggle against the Axis in the Western Desert but also helped to establish the foremost role of Special Forces in the modern military world.

Special Forces are an essentially British conception. They were born in an era of mass armies, which often wasted their valuable manpower in frontal assaults and attrition battles. The British, perhaps because they are a maritime nation, which must find entry into operational theatres by sea, or later by air, have a tradition of husbanding their quite limited manpower for operations against the enemy's flanks and weak points. Marlborough was the master of such operations. So, famously, was Wellington. His deployment of small forces against the flanks of Europe led eventually to the decisive victory of Waterloo.

The concept of indirect operations, in the aftermath of Britain's sole commitment of a mass army in the First World War, had been forgotten in this country. It was revived in the struggle against the Axis in Egypt and Libya during the crisis of the Second World War. Among several Special Forces raised to carry war to the enemy's flanks and weak points, the Long

Range Desert Group was pre-eminent. Today, when Britain's mastery of Special Operations is universally acknowledged, it is appropriate to recognize the pioneering achievements of those who raised, led and served in the Long Range Desert Group.

# Preface

It seems extraordinary to me that it is now almost 60 years since the Long Range Desert Group was first formed in June 1940. I am only too delighted that Pen and Sword Books are publishing this revised edition of *Providence Their Guide* to mark this anniversary.

It was back in early 1974 that I happened to be in touch with a collector of medals named Christopher Jary, then aged seventeen. He had acquired a Military Medal won by a soldier in the platoon I was commanding in Palestine in 1939 and had written to me for some details of the action concerned.

Somehow the subject of the Long Range Desert Group had been introduced into our correspondence. I suppose I told Christopher that I was currently working on an account of the five years during which the unit existed during the Second World War. He in turn told his father, Sydney Jary, who wrote to me and said that he would love to read my manuscript because, while serving in Libya with The Hampshire Regiment after the war, he had become greatly attracted to the desert. He had previously fought as an infantry platoon commander from the Normandy beachhead to Bremen. Rather delightfully, I thought, he added that he had a modicum of experience of the book trade, as he was a publishing consultant. From that moment I was spurred on by father and son Jary to complete the story for them to read.

Without Christopher Jary's interest in the first place, and his father's vibrant enthusiasm throughout, I am quite sure this book would never have seen the light of day. Christopher's early interest was by no means his only contribution. He later undertook to compile the index for me; and I am greatly in his debt for the painstaking and meticulous care with which he did it.

Sydney Jary lavished on me, quite without stint, the benefit of his knowledge as a professional and as a friend. I could not have been more appreciative of his willing co-operation.

The preparation of any work for publication involves much exacting reading and tedious checking of detail. My youngest son Christopher not only devoted hours of his free time at weekends helping me to plough through drafts and proofs, but he also came up with many sensible and original ideas for enhancing the presentation of the book generally. His wife, Antonia, was very long-suffering and patient throughout.

Among many old friends who also assisted me in various ways were two brigadiers under whom I once had the privilege to serve. Both feature in this book – Ralph Bagnold and George Davy.

None of us who knew Ralph Bagnold in the LRDG will dissent from the view that his flair, imagination and scrupulously careful eye for detail laid the foundations for our success. Even Rommel once claimed that the LRDG caused his forces more damage than any other unit of comparable strength.

Brigadier George Davy was Director of Military Operations in Cairo at the time of the raids against Benghazi, Barce and Tobruk in September 1942. His senior Staff Officer, responsible for special operations in the Mediterranean theatre of war, was Lieutenant Colonel 'Shan' Hackett. It remains a special joy to me that these two old friends each helped this book along.

For this edition my Publishers and I decided to retain General John Hackett's Foreword which we feel could not be bettered. I am very grateful to John Keegan, for whom I and so many readers of military history have enormous respect, for agreeing to write an Introduction placing the role of the LRDG in context.

The Trustees of the Imperial War Museum have again kindly permitted me to make use of a large number of hitherto unpublished photographs from the LRDG collection in the Museum.

The portrait of Ralph Bagnold was taken in 1944, and I am grateful to the National Portrait Gallery for allowing me to include it.

Messrs Cassell kindly gave me permission to quote a passage from *The Campaigns of Wavell* by R M Woollcombe, which was published in 1959.

I wish to acknowledge the use made of other published works. I have listed the main ones in a select bibliography; many of the authors were friends of mine, but to all of them and their publishers I am grateful.

Agreement on the spelling of place names is always difficult. It is especially so when some of them are not to be found on pre-War maps, others are too small to merit inclusion and some names have been changed after countries achieved independence. I have used those which were in common usage at the time.

Soon after this story was first published, an Officer of the Royal West Kent Regiment got in touch with me because he was concerned that I had made no mention of the fact that his Regiment had taken part in the battle for Leros. I was unaware that they had been there because I left the island five days before the German invasion on 12 November 1943, but I undertook to look in to the matter and to correct any omission of the part played by that Regiment if ever the book was reprinted. In fact the main body of the Second Battalion was sent to the island of Samos in the Aegean on 23 September and there it remained until the night of 14 November when it was ordered by GHQ in Cairo to Leros. It was then thrown in to battle in order to try to save an already forlorn situation which resulted in the surrender of the island two days later.

Over forty years ago I began to write another story for my three sons – Michael, Piers and Christopher. I hoped that it might be of some interest to them and I prayed that they would never know the ugly horror of war. Michael now has two sons of his own, Harry and Tom, and Christopher has Edward. One day, perhaps, they might gain some inspiration by reading of the spirit of those who suffered much to win victory over evil. It was certainly worth fighting for. But they must think how tragic it was that we failed to win peace in later years.

In the Long Range Desert Group our lives often depended on the need for foresight, which Bagnold, and Prendergast after him, instilled in us. But there were few of us who did not also recognize that Providence, in the guise of the benevolent care of God, often watched over us. In those huge open expanses of desert where we operated, it did sometimes seem that the world was all before us. And we were fortunate that, more often than not, we could choose our place of rest. It is for these reasons that I took the title of this book from Milton's *Paradise Lost*. I quote the last five lines of that great work:

> Som natural tears they drop'd, but wip'd them soon;
> The World was all before them, where to choose
> Thir place of rest, and Providence thir guide;
> They hand in hand, with wandring steps and slow,
> Through *Eden* took thir solitarie way.

Norfolk, *February 2000*                                David Lloyd Owen

# Chronological Table of Events
## 1939–1945

**1939**
3 Sept.    War declared between Britain and Germany.

**1940**
11 May    National Government formed under Churchill.
27 May
– 4 June  British Army evacuated from Dunkirk.
10 June   Italy declares war on Great Britain and France.
23 June   Bagnold given authority to form the LRDG by General
                Wavell.
5 Sept.    First LRDG Patrol leaves on operations.
11 Dec.   Wavell begins rout of Italians in the Desert.

**1941**
30 Mar.   Rommel advances in Western Desert.
27 Apr.   Germans enter Athens.
18 Nov.   Eighth Army's first offensive.
9 Dec.    Tobruk relieved.
24 Dec.   Eighth Army enter Benghazi.

**1942**
20 June   Tobruk captured by Rommel.
13 Sept.  Raids by LRDG and SAS on Barce, Benghazi and Tobruk.
23 Oct.   Eighth Army offensive at Alamein starts. German retreat
                begins 4 Nov.

**1943**
23 Jan.   Tripoli occupied by Eighth Army.
12 May    German resistance in N. Africa ends.
10 July   Allied invasion of Sicily.
7 Sept.   Italy surrenders.
17 Nov.   Germans capture Leros.

**1944**
22 Jan.   Allied landings at Anzio.
18 May    Cassino captured.
4 June    Allies enter Rome.
6 June    Invasion of Europe.
14 Oct.   British troops enter Athens.

**1945**
2 May     German armies in Italy surrender.
8 May     End of war against Germany.
1 Aug.    LRDG disbands.
14 Aug.   Japan surrenders.

# PART ONE

# NORTH AFRICA
## JUNE 1940 – APRIL 1943

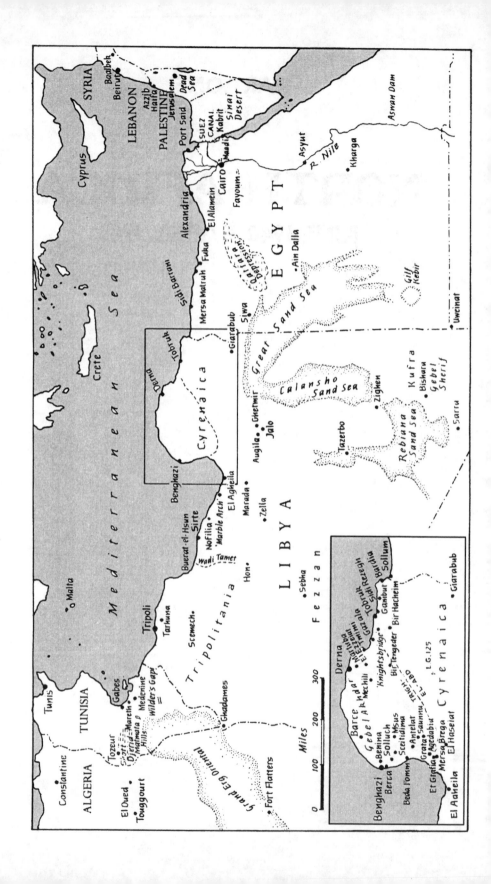

CHAPTER 1

# Ralph Bagnold

In 1971 Arthur Barker Ltd published a book called *Hidden Heroes*. It was written by a New Zealander called Trevor Constable, who had been a resident of California for twenty years. The blurb on the dust jacket of this book describes the contents as being 'the story of individual courage of a high order. Dealing with little-known achievements of heroes of the two World Wars, most of the deeds of daring involve a high element of danger . . . it tells of the tremendous efforts of little-known heroes, who served in less spectacular roles but with substantial influence on events'.

One of the subjects covered by Constable in this book is Ralph Bagnold. Bagnold's only claim to fame might otherwise have been the fact that he is the brother of that well-known authoress Enid Bagnold. (And this in spite of the fact that he has himself published books.)

I am so glad that at last something of Ralph Bagnold's genius has been given due credit. I have no doubt that, because of Bagnold's exceptional knowledge of deserts, and also of the Army, General Wavell was able to take some risks which he might not otherwise have been able to take, since he had Patrols of the Long Range Desert Group to cover him.

I do not doubt either that the success of the early Long Range Desert Group operations gave a fillip to Wingate with his Chindits, Bob Laycock with his Commandos and David Stirling with his Special Air Service. These very remarkable men became famous for their exploits. But as Trevor Constable so rightly comments, 'missing from among them [the famous men] is the brilliant progenitor of all these private armies of modern times—the soldier-scientist, who conceived and built the most successful of them all—Ralph Bagnold'.

I think that Constable's comment is a very true one. But it is interesting to consider why Bagnold, and the Long Range Desert Group, are so unknown. I believe that this was because the Group, and those who served with it, were inclined to shun publicity. There were two reasons for this. One was that the need for strict security made it very undesirable for more

3

than the absolute minimum to be known of the unit and its activities; and the other was because of the personalities of its commanders.

Bagnold, Prendergast and Easonsmith had certain characteristics in common. They were all to some degree reticent, undemonstrative, dedicated to their duty and imbued with a natural modesty that would have made it anathema to them to have received the plaudits of the public. I think too that their example made all of us practise the art of British understatement to a very marked extent.

As I tell this story I suspect that the reader may sense this himself when I try to describe the kind of man who volunteered and was selected for this work behind the lines. I only hope that my own fascination with the subject—coupled with a desire to do it proper justice, without being influenced by bias—will not detract from the courage, endurance, patience and strength of mind of those whom this story is about.

I did not myself join the Long Range Desert Group until the end of July of 1941, and so I do not have first-hand knowledge of the early days when Bagnold raised the unit, nearly a year previously. I have therefore had to rely a great deal on the memories of those who were with him at the time, and also once again on Trevor Constable's book.

When I wrote to Ralph Bagnold asking him if he would record for me any facts about the founding of the Long Range Desert Group which had not been related elsewhere he replied in a typically modest way, that

> the fullest account is that given in *Hidden Heroes*. I hesitate to mention this book because of the immoderate references to myself. You must discount these [his letter continued], as being necessary to the author if a book of this kind is to have any reasonable sale . . . the facts are correct as far as my memory goes and Constable went to a lot of trouble to get them right. He asked me for a lot of the detail including my talks with Wavell.

That statement authenticates the facts as far as these can ever be established after such a gap in time.

In the late twenties and thirties Ralph Bagnold and a small group of like-minded enthusiasts who were inspired by the magic of the desert spent a lot of time and money in exploring the areas of sand between the Mediterranean and the Sudan. Among this band were Pat Clayton, Bill Kennedy Shaw, Guy Prendergast and Rupert Harding-Newman, all of whom rejoined Bagnold when he needed them in the Long Range Desert Group. Their expeditions in those days were really very remarkable achievements, for they explored areas which had never before been crossed; and from their experiences many of the everyday items of desert equipment for the Army in the Western Desert were designed, perfected and later developed.

Bagnold was the leader and driving force behind these trips. His inventive brain produced the answers to the many problems that arose. He designed a simple sun-compass to make navigation easier; he perfected the condenser, first invented by the Light Car Patrols of the Great War, to conserve the water in car radiators which would otherwise be lost through overheating; he thought up the ideas of sand mats and iron channels, which could be laid under the wheels to help extricate a car stuck in soft sand; and he appreciated the necessity for properly balanced rations, in order to keep healthy under extremes of heat, thirst, fatigue and strain.

Over the years these men had built up a wealth of experience, knowledge and lore about travel in the desert which was unrivalled anywhere in the world. It is a little surprising, therefore, that the man with so much practical wisdom about deserts, who had established (by sheer necessity) the four fundamentals essential for successful travel in them, was sent soon after the outbreak of war to Kenya in some routine post.

This man was Major Bagnold of the Royal Signals, who had been recalled to the Army to turn his unique energies towards scientific work connected with sand-formation. His treatise *The Physics of Blown Sand and Desert Dunes*, published in 1941, must establish him anyhow as one of the world's experts on the subject.

But he had also learnt more than this. He had such a shrewd understanding of the capabilities and limitations of human nature that he knew that he would only get the best out of it by devoted attention to what I described above as the four fundamentals essential to successful desert travel, which are also the secret if any small behind-the-line force is to triumph.

These four tenets are: the most careful and detailed planning, first-class equipment, a sound and simple communication system and a human element of rare quality. Ralph Bagnold had learnt these things the hard way in his pre-War desert ventures, and he was not the sort of man to forget them when it came to applying them to war. It was his teaching of the men who served with him in the Long Range Desert Group that made us ever mindful of every minor detail in order to ensure success.

Such qualities, of course, are not so glamorous as those of flair, élan and eye-catching strokes; but I believe that they are more enduring, and are more likely to contribute towards the achievement of continued success.

When Bagnold was on his way by troopship to Kenya a fortuitous accident in which his ship was involved in the Mediterranean sent the passengers ashore at Port Said while the badly damaged vessel was repaired. Italy had not yet come into the war, and there was little sense of urgency or tension in Cairo in those days.

But it was not to the flesh-pots of Cairo that Bagnold took the first train; it was to make contact with old friends in the Army and perhaps to find out what was going on, and whether anyone foresaw any use for his special talents and expertise. It would probably be at least a week before his troopship was overhauled, and he continued his journey through the Suez Canal to East Africa.

Bagnold went one morning to see an old friend of his—Colonel Micky Miller, who was then the Chief Signal Officer at Headquarters of British Troops in Egypt. Miller was obviously delighted to see him, having been asked to trace him by General Wavell. The latter had been appointed Commander-in-Chief of the new Middle East Command, and had read about Bagnold in a gossip column of *The Egyptian Gazette*.

An intelligent and observant reporter had noticed Bagnold in Shepheard's Hotel, and happened to know a good deal about his pre-war desert journeyings. He put two and two together and assumed that

> Major Bagnold's presence in Egypt at this time seems a reassuring indication that one of the cardinal errors of 1914–18 is not to be repeated. During that war, if a man had made a name for himself as an explorer of Egyptian deserts, he would almost certainly have been sent to Jamaica to report on the possibilities of increasing rum production, or else employed digging tunnels under the Messines Ridge. Nowadays, of course, everything is done much better.

That quote was published in a column headed 'Day in Day Out' and was read by General Wavell, who then decided that he would like to see Bagnold.

It must have been a strange interview between these two taciturn characters—each a genius in his fashion, and each having the confidence necessary to overcome most difficulties placed in his way. I suppose that they both had something of the mystique of the visionary, for they were each able—as no other man at that time was able—to see the possibilities of exploiting the natural forbiddingness of the desert.

This first meeting between the two men was just long enough for Wavell, with his one good eye, to peer into and size up the material of which Ralph Bagnold was made, and for him to be convinced that there was more than might be apparent at first sight. Wavell made up his mind to have Bagnold's posting to Kenya changed so that he could keep him in Egypt, and make some proper use of his experience.

This was quickly effected, and Bagnold was posted to a Signals appointment in the 7th Armoured Division, based on Mersa Matruh, which was commanded at that time by that very great exponent of armour Major-General Percy Hobart—or 'Hobo', as he was known in military circles. Bagnold was fortunate in that he was to find himself with a commander who was as full of original and unconventional ideas as himself; and he began to think about the alarming possibilities if Marshal Graziani decided to march into Egypt with his quarter of a million men. He knew too that the Italians had garrisons at Kufra (about six hundred miles due south of the port of Derna) and at Uweinat (some two hundred miles farther south-east of Kufra, and where the borders of Egypt, Libya and the Sudan meet).

Bagnold realised that from Uweinat it was not beyond the bounds of possibility for a strong mobile force of the enemy to move on farther east and to seize the Aswan Dam or wreck the docks and railway workshops at Wadi Halfa, thus cutting the tenuous communications between Egypt and the Sudan. At Uweinat there were landing-grounds and a good supply of water. It would only take a force three days to reach the Nile from there. Wasn't it therefore terribly important that the British should know exactly what was going on deep in the vastness of the desert south of the Great Sand Sea? And in those days there were no aircraft capable of covering these approaches to the Nile.

Bill Kennedy Shaw, who later joined Bagnold as Intelligence Officer of the Long Range Desert Group, in his admirable book covering the desert operations (*Long Range Desert Group*) writes also of the approach to Chad Province from Kufra. In Chad were immensely important airfields, which helped to sustain the Takoradi-Cairo air route along which so many aircraft were flown when the Mediterranean route was no longer safe. He goes on to guess how hard it would have been to dispose of an Italian force moving from Kufra and from Murzuk to the west down into Chad to capture Fort Lamy, and thus woo the hesitant French to their side in June 1940. All this reinforced Bagnold's burning desire to know exactly what was going on.

So he decided to analyse the problem on paper, and he came up with a solution based on the formation of specially equipped patrols capable of penetrating into these seemingly impassable wastes. He set out the organisation that he thought was necessary, and prepared three copies of his proposals. He gave the first to General Hobart in November 1939, and with the latter's prescient understanding of the situation, it is not surprising that he agreed to send Bagnold's ideas on to Headquarters in Cairo.

But Hobart was not confident that the project would be well received, and Bagnold's plans were turned down. Of course, I do not know why this was, but I imagine that it was on the grounds that there was so little available in the Middle East in the way of men or equipment that it would be foolish to dissipate what little there was in penny packets. And there always had been a rather odd aversion to anything unconventional among the majority of Regular officers.

It is interesting to read in Constable's book that the real reason why the Staff turned down Bagnold's submission was because of their ignorance about—and resultant fear of—the desert, and that they thought that this curious major in the Royal Signals was propounding theories which were either ridiculous or mad!

In January 1940, after General Hobart had been removed from command of 7th Armoured Division, Bagnold put forward his ideas to his successor. Once more they were sent on to Cairo and rejected.

It is very easy to be critical of the Staff, and to express the opinion that much valuable time in creating a Long Range Desert Group was thus lost.

It is very easy to rail at the apparent stupidity of those who were unable to see how urgent it was to have intelligence of Italian intentions. However, I have always thought that the most likely explanation for failing to do more at that time was that there was no absolute certainty that Italy would actively invade Egypt, let alone the Sudan; and anyway, even if they did surely nobody honestly believed that the Italians would venture into the unknown desert, most of which was commonly believed to be quite impassable? Bagnold knew otherwise because he had experience of it; but very, very few others had even one iota of his insight.

On 10 June 1940 much was changed for those living comfortably (as I was myself) in the peace-time luxury of the Middle East. Italy declared war after France had collapsed, and so the Mediterranean was well nigh closed to shipping. Overnight the whole strategic picture had changed immeasurably, and the dangers which Bagnold had seen so clearly were now something that had to be faced up to squarely.

On 19 June he presented his proposals once again, and it is a reflection of how much the strategic picture had altered—together with the realism that had thus been injected into the Headquarters Staff in Cairo—that on 23 June Bagnold was summoned to see General Wavell.

What a triumph this was! For so long Ralph Bagnold had been convinced that it was necessary to do something. It was not only the need to know more of what the Italians might do: he had also been evolving ideas as to how he could create a threat to their lines of communication to Kufra and Uweinat, and thus leave them jumpy, jittery and disinclined to move far from the safety of their fortified bases. Now, at last, he had the ear of the Commander-in-Chief, who fortunately was a man who understood Bagnold's arguments.

This time the two men spent longer together, for Wavell was interested in how Bagnold thought he could carry out his plans; which were to get into Libya to watch the routes to Kufra and to Uweinat. He knew that by reading the tracks of enemy vehicles he could tell exactly what sort of traffic was using the routes, and thus he would be able to deduce the volume of troop movement involved.

Bagnold's plan was based on an approach from the least expected quarter. He told Wavell that he intended to go slap through the Great Sand Sea, by a route Clayton had discovered in 1932, to the west of Ain Dalla.

Wavell quizzed Bagnold about the dangers of using a route which was shown on maps which were published, and openly obtainable in the shops in Cairo. He asked him too about how he intended to cover up his own wheel-tracks in order to avoid the chance of the enemy following up such a party. The Commander-in-Chief then inquired of him what he would do if he found no signs of undue enemy activity. The latter suggested rather tentatively that his force might profitably take some aggressive action, and carry out some piracy against enemy convoys.

It was then that Wavell must have become convinced of Bagnold's ability to do what he promised, for he suddenly asked him if he could be ready in six weeks. He was told that this deadline could be met, providing Bagnold was given absolute authority to select the men that he wanted, and to collect the very special items of equipment that he knew he must have.

What happened next in this meeting between these two men was probably the most significant factor in those formative days of the Long Range Desert Group. Wavell was obviously clear in his mind that Bagnold could give him what he wanted, and that he was not risking his money on an outsider. He therefore dictated a memorandum to the heads of all directorates and branches in his headquarters, telling them that they had his full authority to meet any demand made personally by Bagnold, and to meet it quickly and without question. He even told Bagnold that as soon as the latter was ready to start operations he was to write out his own orders for carrying out his intentions, and to bring them personally to the Commander-in-Chief.

Bagnold was virtually given a free hand, and, of course, without it he could never have been able to raise and train the Long Range Desert Group as quickly and as thoroughly as he did.

I have also written to Lt-General Sir Arthur Smith, who was Wavell's Chief of Staff at the time in question, as I was interested to find out what he might be able to remember of the meetings between the Commander-in-Chief and Bagnold some thirty years earlier. He replied that it was difficult to remember details of events which happened so long ago, but added that the account given by Woollcombe in *The Campaigns of Wavell* is accurate as far as he knew. He went on to write that the Long Range Desert Group 'was certainly the sort of enterprise that appealed to Wavell, and, incidentally, to myself. I seem to recollect difficulty in getting the necessary equipment, but that was a persisting headache not confined to the Long Range Desert Group.'

The following extracts from Woollcombe's book are, I think, of interest:

> Impressed with the risk of mechanized raiding parties being sent by the Italians from the far interior of Libya across to the Upper Nile, to block our communications between Cairo and Khartoum, Major Bagnold before the end of 1939 had put forward proposals through normal military channels to Headquarters, British Troops in Egypt. These were for training a cadre of men for experimental long-range motor patrolling through the great sand seas to the inner deepness of the desert, the Libyan Desert, which was virtually the Sahara.
>
> It appears that at that time Headquarters, British Troops in Egypt were in awe of the vast desert reaches; their minds were focused upon regular precautions inside Egypt and the war with Germany. They had a

solitary map of Libya, printed in 1915, carrying information which dated from 1873. Bagnold's proposals were turned down. He tried again in January 1940 with the same result. But then the personality of Wavell emerged from those modest rooms in Cairo, as Commander-in-Chief—and Bagnold was himself now serving in an appointment at the new GHQ. It was a simpler matter for him, when Italy entered the war, to press his case yet again. He placed the third and last copy of his plan before the Chief of Staff, Major-General Arthur Smith, who took it straightaway to Wavell.

Bagnold was sent for, and he writes that the Commander-in-Chief grinned at the scheme. Its acceptance illustrates a further feature of General Wavell's character: his gift for adapting the ideas of subordinates to his own purposes, and for allowing his subordinates full scope to carry them out, sustained by his backing but untrammelled by interference.

He signed what amounted to a blank cheque empowering Bagnold to order anything he wanted as an absolute priority from any department in Egypt, with no questions to be asked. Bagnold was instructed to be ready within six weeks and henceforth had personal access to Wavell at any time.

The cupboard of Middle East Ordnance was nearly bare. Nothing of this kind had been catered for. Specialized equipment and vehicles designed to particular specifications had to be improvised from the slender means that existed. Much had to be begged second-hand from the Egyptian Army, while a theodolite for navigation came from as far afield as Nairobi. Bagnold gathered his band: kindred spirits to lead the patrols were flown to him and commissioned on the spot, and the rest of the personnel were recruited initially from New Zealanders. There was some hurried navigational training, and at the end of August, seen off by Wavell himself, the Long Range Desert Group comprising three patrols each of two officers and twenty-eight other ranks moved in secrecy out of Cairo.

Bagnold's original fear of Italian activity directed against the Upper Nile was soon dispelled, but the patrols were brought into fresh alignment with General Wavell's aims. Their task was to harass the Italians by making trouble in any part of Libya they chose to select, to draw Italian troops and their transport, of which they were short, away from the coastal region to the defence of scattered garrisons in the deep interior. For Marshal Graziani had by this time begun his invasion of Egypt and his forces were ensconced, and seemingly mesmerized, at Sidi Barrani.

It was an extraordinary deception plan, conceived by the Commander-in-Chief and remarkably carried out, whereby the Libyan wastes became a liability to the enemy, and the few score men of the Long Range Desert Group in their trucks caused Marshal Graziani to reinforce remote standing garrisons, consume transport, provide escorts for his inland supply columns, and to be unable to discern whether his own reports of Wavell's shortage in men and material were accurate or a trap. For this reason the work of the long-range patrols has been assessed as a main factor contributing to the failure of the Italian offensive into Egypt. [This was also the view of Brigadier Shearer, who had been Wavell's Director of Military Intelligence at GHQ in Cairo.]

A touch of the gambler . . . if there was any doubt as to what General Wavell really implied in attributing this quality to the great commanders, perhaps a panache which he himself scarcely seemed to typify, there is now an answer. After the Long Range Desert Group had been equipped there remained three machine-guns in reserve for the whole Middle East.

There have been so many dramatic and exaggerated accounts of what the Long Range Desert Group did in the desert, or of what it was reputed to have done, that I think it important to be quite clear what the role of this original and unusual new unit was. It was raised (and so remained throughout the five years of its existence) chiefly for the purpose of gathering information about the enemy behind his lines. It was never primarily intended to carry out offensive operations, which so often ruin the chance of effecting successful reconnaissance. (This is not to say that the Long Range Desert Group was not capable of taking part in harassing tasks, and the unit, of course, carried out many of them. But this was only a secondary role, when such work could rate a greater strategic priority than the gathering of intelligence.)

Bagnold raised the unit with an offensive capability in mind, and he was sage enough to know that it would probably never be easy to keep men continually operating behind the lines just watching the enemy, without ever giving them the thrill and relief of 'having a go' at him every now and then.

I have purposely rather laboured the point about the primary role of the Long Range Desert Group because I think it important to bear in mind when one comes to consider the other 'private armies' that later came into being. It has also a considerable bearing on the insistence by Bagnold—and Prendergast after him—that the Long Range Desert Group must operate only under the direction of the highest formation controlling operations in the desert. This was essential, because only at that level could the Long Range Desert Group be fitted into the overall strategic picture, and the correct priority between offensive action and intelligence work be weighed up. On top of this was the difficulty of trying to co-ordinate the work of such deeply penetrating patrols with the long-range attacks of the Royal Air Force.

With the best will in the world, there were bound to be mistakes when our Patrols were attacked by their own side from the air; but at least the risks of such disasters could be minimised if control of both elements was kept at the highest level.

When some new organisation such as the Long Range Desert Group is created—and especially one whose success is going to depend very considerably on the secrecy of its employment—another difficult problem arises. This is how to convince the commanders and staffs of lower formations as to the necessity for such a concern, and to explain what its task is to be, when broader strategic issues must seem fairly remote to those involved in the day-to-day business of fighting the battle.

In the first place, there is probably quite a bit of understandable jealousy that any newly formed unit should be given priority as to men and equipment; and secondly, it is only the normal reaction of any good Commanding Officer to resent having his best men attracted to such 'crackpot' outfits, when his own inherent pride in his Regiment has always led him to believe that it is the best, and second to none.

For these reasons too it is very necessary to retain control of any unit such as the Long Range Desert Group at top level. Whenever this principle was broken during the last war Long Range Desert Group patrols were either grossly misused or they suffered unnecessary casualties in both men and equipment. It was fortunate that Bagnold was able to secure the application of this fundamental doctrine from the very start.

To appreciate the real size of Bagnold's contributions to the success of the Long Range Desert Group I believe that one must look at the problems facing him when he left the Commander-in-Chief's office on 23 June 1940. He had Wavell's full blessing and unstinted backing; and he knew that he had to produce a force in six weeks' time capable of moving across generally unknown expanses of desert in order to provide information of the enemy's intentions towards the Nile.

But there was rather more to it than this. Bagnold's force had to be self-contained, and capable of finding its way across regions of which no maps existed, and where very little indeed was known about the conditions.

To be self-contained and capable of finding the way across the areas envisaged was, in itself, a formidable demand in those days. The distances involved a normal capability of covering about 1,500–2,000 miles. It depended on what kind of vehicle was found to be both available and suitable as to what the petrol consumption might be. But Bagnold was probably working on 5–6 miles per gallon and this would mean each vehicle being able to carry over 350 gallons of petrol.

These trips might take anything up to three weeks, so food and water had to be carried. The force had to be able to protect itself, so arms and ammunition were required. How were they to navigate, and what equipment was needed? What measures were to be taken to deal with casualties? What communications was he going to need? What were the men to sleep on? How were they to keep themselves reasonably fit?

Bagnold, of course, knew the answer to many of these problems from the trips that he and his friends had made before the war. He knew much about desert travel, navigation, proper food and extricating vehicles from soft sand, and he knew a great deal about communications because of his training in the Army.

But the hardest problems to solve must have been where he was going to find the vehicles suitable for carrying the considerable loads envisaged, and where he was going to find the sort of men that he wanted, and who would be capable of standing up to the strains he proposed to impose on them. Everything depended on the solution to these two major questions.

Bill Kennedy Shaw recalls how Bagnold came to see him in Jerusalem in June 1940 and asked him to join his new unit. Bill was helping to censor newspapers in Palestine in the service of the Colonial Office. He was absolutely thrilled at the prospect of returning to the desert which he loved so much, and to be able to do something more active to help in the war effort. He had tried as soon as the war started to obtain some job in the Middle East, which he knew extremely well, but it was thought more important to leave him censoring the newspapers. Bagnold had to waste no time in persuading Kennedy Shaw to join him, and within two weeks he was a captain in the Army, and was to remain as the Intelligence Officer of the Long Range Desert Group throughout the campaign in the desert.

Pat Clayton was doing some survey work in Tanganyika, and was fairly soon contacted and brought to join Bagnold. He was another of Bagnold's pre-War friends who had tremendous experience, and he had spent nearly twenty years with the Egyptian Survey Department. Rupert Harding-Newman was serving with the Military Mission to the Egyptian Army, and he was released from his job there. Prendergast was in England, and he could not join the others until the end of the year. But Bagnold knew that Teddy Mitford was in the Middle East, and he was one of the few people who had been to Kufra. He was soon co-opted into the new force which Bagnold was to call The Long Range Patrols when they were first formed. Six months later this name was changed to The Long Range Desert Group, and I have used this name throughout in order not to confuse the reader.

So already things were looking up once Bagnold had collected a quorum of the men who had worked with him on his journeys of exploration before the war. None of them were young, but all of them were men who had gained great knowledge of the desert, and how to overcome some of its disagreeable features. They would be of incalculable value to Bagnold in helping to train, mould and lead his raw material—the men he was going to select, and on whose quality would depend the success of them all.

Mitford and Harding-Newman were both Regular officers in the Royal Tank Regiment, and they at least had some military background with which to blend their local knowledge. Clayton and Kennedy Shaw were civilians. The fact that all these men did so much to help Bagnold in those early days speaks a volume for his personal drive, encouragement, determination and strength of character. He must have inspired them with a deep conviction that he could do everything that was expected of him, and a great deal more, once he had made a start.

But this was so typical of Bagnold. I remember Guy Prendergast telling me once about the trips that he, Kennedy Shaw and others had together with Bagnold before the war. In those days too it was always Bagnold who had the ideas, and he was a fount of knowledge on all subjects: historical, climatic, anything to do with cars, navigation, wireless. He seemed to know the answers to everything.

Guy told me too about how after Ralph Bagnold had been posted from Cairo to India he used to send Guy comprehensive orders concerning the next trip in exact detail. And he even once drove his truck from India to Cairo before the proper journey began!

He was a perfectionist in every way, and both set himself and expected from others a very high standard of physical fitness, attention to detail and sense of duty. He did not suffer gladly those who failed to measure up to his expectations; and there were often good-natured mutterings about his frugal habits and his inexhaustible stamina, which seemed never to fail him. It was these great qualities that were to prove so invaluable when he came to raise and build up the Long Range Desert Group.

But where was Bagnold to find the men that he wanted? And what sort of men did he hope to find? Certain things were clear. He would need drivers and fitters, wireless operators and gunners. He would probably need medical orderlies as well. But besides these basic tradesmen he had to have men who had something more.

He would require them to suffer the pangs of thirst and of hunger, and there would be long periods when they would be exposed to the burning heat of the desert at the middle of the day in the summer, when this might reach 120°F in the shade, and the temperature of the metal in the vehicle was enough to strip the skin off a man's hand. He would also require them to tolerate long periods of tedium, just watching and waiting and reporting; and at other times they would be expected to work frantically to get some vehicles through the softest patches of sand. They must be capable of dealing with any unforeseen attack by the enemy on the ground as well as from the air; and they would have to get used to exceedingly uncomfortable travel, lying on top of a lorry laden with petrol, rations, water, ammunition and other hardware. Above all, there was the most tangible strain, to which every man would be subjected—the sheer stress of men who would inevitably find themselves for weeks on end behind enemy lines, and liable to be hunted.

The Commander-in-Chief had spoken to General 'Jumbo' Wilson about Bagnold's plans, and they had concurred that the best sort of men to meet all these requirements might well be found among the New Zealand Expeditionary Force. This Force had arrived in the Middle East having lost a good deal of its equipment at sea, and so was not yet ready to take its place in the Western Desert. General Wilson arranged for Bagnold to meet General 'Tiny' Freyberg, who was commanding the New Zealand Division. Bagnold went out to see Freyberg at Maadi, just outside Cairo, and told him what he was looking for.

He was looking for a couple of officers, to lead two of the three patrols of about thirty men and eleven trucks apiece, which he had decided would be the ideal size. Freyberg appreciated that here was a great opportunity to get his men doing something really well worth while, but it also meant that his Commanding Officers might lose some of their best men, for Bagnold obviously wanted nothing less. He wondered also as to how the men would react to being under the command of those whom they were pleased to call 'Pommie-Bastards'. He must have been struck, nevertheless, as Wavell had been, by the sincerity of the tough, wiry little major who had come to ask for his help.

Freyberg decided to recommend to his Government release of the necessary men. On 1 July 1940 Government consent was given, and Lt Bruce Ballantyne, with 2/Lt Don Steele, were chosen by Freyberg as the first two officers. They were then given the task of sifting through a thousand applicants who had answered the call for volunteers for an undisclosed but dangerous mission.

This decision of General Freyberg's began an association between New Zealanders and the Long Range Desert Group which was to last throughout the war. It started with New Zealand soldiers coming under the command of British officers and it finished with the happy position of some New Zealanders commanding British soldiers in the later stages of the war.

I have an immense and enduring admiration for the Kiwis. Once one has got through a rather suspicious cloak of reserve with which some of them are inclined to surround themselves, there are some very warm hearts, much true courage and men with great mental and physical toughness. I have always been happy that I can count a number of them among my very greatest friends.

While Bagnold had been finding these splendid New Zealanders Harding-Newman had been doing what he could to find the trucks which had been selected. These were the Chevrolet 30-cwt commercial two-wheeled-drive vehicle.

The Army in the Middle East had absolutely nothing that was remotely suitable; and it still strikes me, nearly forty years later, as being a trifle bizarre that Bagnold had to go around to the Chevrolet company in Alexandria, where he obtained fourteen of the trucks he wanted, while Harding-Newman managed to talk the Egyptian Army into providing the remaining nineteen.

A great deal had to be done to these vehicles, and it must have been Wavell's support which spurred on the Middle East Base Workshops to design and carry out the many modifications which were required. The chief problem to be overcome was how to carry the heavy loads without making the trucks so impossibly overladen that their engines could not drive them through the terrain to be encountered. Obviously, everything that was unnecessary had to be removed—doors, cabs and windscreens could easily be scrapped, and some weight would thereby be saved.

Some suitable method of carrying the wireless sets, the sand channels, the sun-compass, the machine-guns, the spare wheels and a whole lot of other equipment had to be devised. An effective camouflage, that would suit most types of desert, had to be perfected, and such things as condensers to conserve the amount of water used in the radiator, or recognition signs for indicating our nationality to the RAF, or some way to carry the maps—all these had to be invented or modified to suit the special requirements of the Long Range Desert Group.

But whatever one did to these splendid 30-cwt trucks, they were still more than likely to be loaded with up to two tons of weight. This could only be done if the springs could be given extra leaves to carry the additional load. And, of course, the other essential thing was to know exactly what type of spares would have to be carried to meet the most likely contingencies. It is no exaggeration to say that Bagnold and Harding-Newman did a superb job in working out the answers to all these problems, and their solutions taken in July 1940 stood the test of time throughout the desert campaign.

Men and vehicles had been chosen. These were, I feel sure, the crux of the problem, and the fact that Bagnold found the most sensible answer set the Long Range Desert Group on a solid foundation from which only a major upheaval was likely to shake it. I pay this tribute at this stage because I found myself commanding the Group in November 1943, after the débâcle of the Aegean campaign, and when it seemed in danger of collapse.

There was quite a lot more to be done in those six short weeks. The rudiments of navigation had to be taught to a number of selected men, who would specialise in this art. (I will endeavour a little later on to describe what had to be learnt, and how the technique of land navigation was perfected. Suffice it to say at this stage that Bill Kennedy Shaw and L/Cpl Dick Croucher, who had held a mate's ticket in the Merchant Navy, undertook the instruction of those selected.) They taught them to use the wonderfully simple sun-compass which Bagnold had himself invented, and which the British Army had failed to adopt in favour of some horribly complicated contraption called the Coles sun-compass. (Mercifully, the Egyptian Army had taken Bagnold's compass, and a small supply was obtained from that source.)

Maps and theodolites for fixing the position by the stars at night had to be collected. The former were hardly a problem, for those that did exist were so inaccurate that they were not worth carrying; and the latter were in such short supply that the only three in the whole of the Middle East were found in the Army's stores, in the Egyptian Desert Survey Department and in Nairobi.

There was a mass of small details to be attended to. 'Chaplis', or leather sandals, were found to be much more suitable for movement in the hot, soft sand than the Army-issue leather boot; the headdress worn by the Arab was obviously more sensible than the Service Dress Cap designed for the British Army to wear on ceremonial and most other occasions; Air Almanacs were needed to work out positions resulting from the theodolite readings of the stars, and a wireless receiver which could give accuracy to within one second of time for the perfection of those readings; a wireless set capable of communicating over great distances had to be found, and a secure method of transmitting information had to be devised; Bofors guns for anti-aircraft defence, Lewis guns for automatic sustained machine-gun fire and pistols for close combat all had to be drawn, and the operators trained in their uses.

Once everything had been assembled, men and materials, in the barracks at Abbassia just outside Cairo there was still much to be done to practise everyone in the use of the equipment with which they had been provided; and then to shake everything down so that the loads travelled properly, and the essential pieces of equipment were ready to hand.

In July and August 1940 the first two trips were carried out under the eagle eye of Major Bagnold. These were purely training runs, but at the end of them the Major reckoned that his force was ready for operations, and thus he reported to General Wavell.

When the latter came personally to wish Bagnold's Patrols well, before they departed on their first active task, each of those great men must have felt some satisfaction in what had been achieved so far—Bagnold in the fact that he had been given such unbounded support in realising his dreams, and General Wavell in the knowledge that the young runner he was backing looked a pretty healthy prospect.

To Bagnold I have given a lot of credit for his personal magnetism, perspicacity, thoroughness and dedication to a cause; and I would not modify one word of it. But I feel also that due regard must be given to the wisdom of General Wavell, who saw the opportunities that Bagnold's ideas might open up to him, and also to those of his Staff who were ready to give unlimited support to the brain-child of that great man.

Kennedy Shaw recalls rather charmingly how very few of the Staff of those days were very desert-minded, and how some of them found many of the requests of the Long Range Desert Group difficult to understand. I am sure that it is in fact quite remarkable that any of them were able to envisage the returns from giving the last reserves of important equipment to a novel, untried and unorthodox organisation, led by a fanatical major whose interest in sand was almost pathological!

# CHAPTER 2

# The Patrol Structure

It might make some of the subsequent narrative simpler to understand if I now write a little about the organisation of Bagnold's early Patrols, the methods they used to find their way about and the communications by which they kept in touch with their base. I am also assuming that not all those who will read this book will know anything at all of the desert in which these Patrols were to operate behind the lines from September 1940 until two months after the fall of Tripoli in January 1943—a period throughout which there were always one or more Patrols at work.

The basic sub-unit of the LRDG was the Patrol. This consisted of one 15-cwt Chevrolet and ten 30-cwt trucks of the same make. The one light load-carrier was for the Patrol commander, who had a driver and a gunner with him, the idea being that this lighter vehicle would range around, finding the best route through any difficult country so that the heavier vehicles might follow. One of the 30-cwts carried the navigator and the wireless operator, together with a driver. The remaining nine trucks were organised into three troops, each of three vehicles. Each truck had a team of three men—a driver, a gunner and one other man, who was also trained as a gunner, and might have been a fitter or a cook or a medical orderly as well.

All the trucks were unarmoured, and their offensive weapons at that time consisted of eleven Lewis machine-guns, four Boys anti-tank rifles (a more useless military weapon has never been invented, either before or since) and one 37-mm Bofors gun. Each individual was armed with a rifle or a pistol, and a number of hand grenades were always carried.

The total lack of armour made the Patrols very vulnerable to attack from the ground, and especially so from the air; but the extra weight involved would have reduced the range of an armoured vehicle to an unacceptable degree. The Patrols had to rely on their superior speed, faster reaction and their wits! There is no doubt that you soon learn to sharpen every faculty when you realise that your life depends on them.

The absolute lack of normally easily recognised features such as roads, hedges, streams, railways, villages or even trees makes the desert a pretty arid and featureless place. It is therefore in some ways very similar to the sea; and in order to find one's way across great distances one has to use similar methods of navigation.

Even if maps had existed the amount of information on them would have been unlikely to have been of much assistance. It is a fact that when the LRDG was first formed Bagnold was only able to find in Cairo one small-scale map which extended westward beyond the frontier of Egypt. This was dated 1915, and contained little more up-to-date information than that discovered by Rohlfs in 1874. Few people realise that in 1940 there was only one tarmac road in the whole of Libya, and that ran mostly along, or within fifty miles of, the coast for the whole way from Tunis to Alexandria.

In one or two places tracks were marked by tall iron beacons every few kilometres. Otherwise there were no recognised roads as such. So the LRDG navigator had, like the sailor, to rely on the sun, the stars and the compass to keep his position.

The compass we used was invented by Bagnold, and the advantage that it gave us over the sun-compasses used by the rest of the Army lay in the fact that it showed the true bearing of the course followed at any moment, whereas the other types only made certain that if the sun's shadow fell on the correct time-graduation the truck was following a set course. This meant that if one had to change course for any reason (and this happened all the time in rough country or sand dunes), the truck had to be halted and the compass set again. This was all very time-consuming, and I have never understood why the Army did not adopt the Bagnold sun-compass, which was far simpler to operate, absolutely 'soldier-proof' and, I would have thought, cheaper to produce.

Without going into details of exactly how the sun-compass worked, the principle can be briefly described as keeping the shadow from the sun of a vertical needle (which projected from the centre of a small circular table graduated into 360 degrees) on to the appropriate reading in order to maintain the direction required. If one was forced off this bearing it was still possible to read the direction in which the truck was then travelling. There were problems connected with the sun's azimuth at various times of day and seasons of the year, but these too were overcome by the inventive genius of Bagnold.

Roughly how the Patrol navigated was as follows. At the start of the day the leader would decide that he wanted to travel due west (270°) for the first hundred miles. He would set his compass, as also would the navigator travelling in the truck behind the leader. The compass was mounted between the driver and his front passenger so that the driver could see it to steer his car on the bearing laid down.

The navigator would note the speedometer reading at the start, and as soon as there was any major diversion off the correct bearing he would note the speedometer reading and the new direction. This simple method of dead-reckoning enabled the navigator to work out fairly accurately where he was at any moment, and a well-trained, experienced navigator was unlikely to find himself more than a mile or two out at the end of a day when the Patrol had covered two hundred miles or so. But, of course, no speedometer or such a rough-and-ready method can be really accurate, and so a theodolite was used to get an astrofix at night. As I have mentioned earlier, the LRDG had some difficulty in getting hold of these, as there were so few of them in the Middle East.

The job of navigator was a demanding one, and it called for a man with special ability and powers of concentration. He could seldom relax, and even when the Patrol was halted for the night he still had a great deal of work to do in shooting the stars before working out his exact position. It was for this reason that War Office approval was given for the trade test of Land Navigator, and those who passed it were rewarded with an extra shilling a day. Riches then!

Throughout the time that I was in the desert with the LRDG I was wonderfully lucky in having expert navigators. I never even considered the possibility that we might get lost; and this was always a very comforting assurance when there were quite enough other anxieties.

Providing the Patrols were constantly in touch with base, they could not only report back the information which they had gained but they could also receive fresh instructions themselves. So a suitable wireless set with first-class operators and a secure method of communicating were very essential. Not only was there a requirement for a set to communicate with the Patrols—which might be anything up to a thousand miles from base—but the latter had to keep in touch with the higher formation under whose command LRDG HQ was working.

The set selected was the No 11, High-powered. It turned out to be ideal for LRDG purposes. The greatest distance over which satisfactory communications were established in the desert was 1,400 miles, and the sets proved remarkably robust under all the conditions experienced. Sky-wave signalling was relied on almost exclusively, as also was key operating. No word of plain language or speech was ever transmitted.

Security was the most vital factor in LRDG communications, and the methods adopted at the start were sound enough to be used with success throughout the campaign in the desert. In brief this was achieved by such devices as changing the frequencies at least twice every day, and altering call signs at the same time; all signal instructions were carried encoded; international commercial procedure was used, and the known call signs of local commercial stations were employed whenever possible; and the controls of the set were always set to zero after every transmission was completed, thus avoiding the risk of compromise if the set were captured. A simple low-grade type of cipher was used in an unusual way so that security could be obtained. All these devices achieved the object of the exercise, and there was never any reason to suspect that any of the communications within the LRDG were ever compromised.

Power for the set was obtained from the vehicle 6-volt generator and battery, with the addition of another 6-volt battery. Both batteries were charged by the vehicle generator. Windom aerials were used for communicating over longer distances, but often a six-foot rod aerial was quite adequate for distances of 500 miles or so.

The control station at base was on continuous watch for Patrols so that they could come up on the air at any time they liked in an emergency. But they normally worked on a schedule system whereby each Patrol was allotted three times in the day when it could communicate if it was possible to do so. One of these was in the early morning, one at midday and one in the evening after the Patrol had been expected to halt for the night.

It was not possible to operate the set while on the move, and it took some time to erect the aerial and to encipher or decipher messages. For these reasons the midday calls were not always possible to make, and most Patrol commanders would skip them if they possibly could. This was unfortunate, as it was very often the best time of day for good communcations.

I have said what first-class men the LRDG had as navigators, but the same is true of the wireless operators. They too were volunteers, just like everyone else, and their work often kept them up late at night transmitting or receiving messages. On top of this they had to have technical ability well above the average if they were to keep their equipment working for weeks on end without any assistance from outside. Much of the success of LRDG operations was due to the immensely high standards of communications that the wireless operators achieved.

What was this desert like where there were apparently so many problems? I have mentioned its comparative lack of salient features, but this does not mean to say that there were none. A pile of stones or even the carcass of some long-dead camel might stand out on open, hard, level plain for miles, while the fact that some of the sand dunes could reach a height of six hundred feet is also not without significance. But the distances were immense: the Libyan Desert has been described as being roughly the same size as India, covering some twelve hundred miles by a thousand.

Some of the fascination of the desert lies in the extremes of intense, searing heat by day and near freezing temperatures by night; while there is the additional contrast of sufficient rain along the coast producing a certain amount of vegetation as against the total lack of it deep in the south, sometimes for as long as ten or twenty years. These too create conditions which are not easy to master at once.

The coast areas, more especially those comprising a quite broad strip in Tripolitania and the Gebel Akhdar in Cyrenaica, are almost European in cultivation and life generally; but beyond this to the south, where the LRDG was mainly to work, there were colossal expanses of Sand Sea. In those days these regions were taken to be impassable to any form of motor transport. This was almost hostile country, and savage in its utter emptiness of life and even sound. Yet those arid, barren stretches of waste were not without their attraction, although one was occasionally reminded of the respect one had to pay to their dangers by the whitened remains of a camel lying desolate and forgotten on the sand.

There were certain essential rules for survival in this forbidding country; and if one failed to regard them one was taking risks which were foolish and almost always quite unnecessary. It was a maxim that one vehicle should never be allowed to go off alone from the main party, for, if it were to break down without assistance the passengers might well be faced with a walk beyond their ability and resources.

Similarly, no individual must ever walk off alone beyond the limit of his vision, but must keep his base always in sight. However, the LRDG eventually worked out for themselves the necessity for having dumps of food, water, spare sandals, maps, etc., every two hundred miles along the route they normally used to go westward from their bases at Siwa and Kufra. The idea behind these was that if men were forced for any reason to abandon their vehicles and walk, then at the worst there would probably be little more than a hundred miles to cover before finding much-needed replenishment.

The almost total lack of water—save that found in the few oases— meant that every drop had to be carried, conserved and cherished for the survival of the crews and the refilling of vehicle radiators. The LRDG worked normally on a gallon per day per man and his vehicle for all purposes; and this was not much when it was used for cooking as well as for cooling the Vickers machine-gun (adopted in 1941). The solution to the loss of water from the radiators of the cars was found by Bagnold in 1927, and he describes what they decided to do in his book *Libyan Sands*:

> We realised that cars do not use much water by actually boiling it off in steam, but that the steam blowing violently down the narrow overflow pipe, provided in all radiators, carries with it a great quantity of water splashed up by the boiling. All this could be saved if the overflow were led into a special tank even if the steam itself were lost. So we blocked up the overflows of the radiators, and in their place soldered large copper pipes to the filler-caps, joining them by other tubes down into two-gallon cans bolted on to the running-boards of the cars, so that the only outlet from the radiator was at the end of a pipe immersed in cold water at the bottom of a can. When the water boiled in the engine a mixture of water and steam was carried over into the can where all the water was saved, and so, until at last the water in the can itself began to boil, the steam was condensed and saved.

This was the principle of the condenser adopted for the Chevrolet trucks by the LRDG; and we almost took it for granted without realising how much water it was saving all the time.

In every age there have been explorers or tourists or, perhaps, escapists or cranks who have fallen under the spell of the desert. They have succumbed to its lure; and sometimes I find it difficult to explain just what is so magnetic about it. Kennedy Shaw wrote that the attraction for him was that it was so clean, and also because it was so quiet; and, he said, 'it was beautiful too, not at midday when the hills look flat and lifeless, but in the early morning or late evening when they throw cool, dark shadows and the low sun makes you marvel at the splendid symmetry of the yellow dunes.' He has probably covered most of the things that people have found so alluring about the desert; but perhaps there is one more sense, and that is the sensation of freedom.

Somehow one feels unfettered by any of the harsh, restricting influences of human existence as we live it these days. There are no buildings, no roads, no street lights, no artificial or even natural noises, no hustle and bustle, no need for anyone to shout or to have money or to pretend about anything; those human beings who are with you are probably fairly well known to you, and are there for the same reason that you are—they know the dangers and delights of solitude just the same as you do, and they will react to the unblemished and staggering loveliness of a huge expanse of desert sky, deep blue by day and of a marvellous purple at night sprinkled haphazardly with hundreds and thousands of stars silently lighting up that great canopy of night-time that drifts down with the close of day. I personally think I know of nothing more restorative than lying on the soft sand—cool now after the retirement of the day's sun—and just staring at the miracle of such a sky. And then you fall asleep, rolled up in a sleeping bag against the considerable fall in temperature as the night goes on, perhaps waking an hour or two before dawn for just long enough to notice that those little stars are still there—as bright as ever—and do not even look as though they are getting ready to be extinguished by the advent of another day. It is a lovely, comforting feeling when the world around you is quite still; and there is no sound anywhere to penetrate the delightful peace that surrounds you.

When the dawn comes, and the stars have all gone away, there is something sharp and exhilarating about the smell in the air. It is fresh and clean and tantalisingly different to the atmosphere which will pervade the day once the sun has come up over the distant horizon. Then there will be no escape from its merciless and desiccating heat, which drains you of energy and leaves you burned and incapable of any prolonged activity. And the bright reflection of the sun off the light-coloured sand can be piercing and painful to the eyes. There is probably not even a tiny breeze to move that sullen, sultry air, and there can be no relief from its effects until once more, and inevitably, the great ball of fire that is the sun will slide slowly below the land and allow it to grow cool.

It would be foolish to pretend that all of those who served with the LRDG saw the desert in the way that I have described it, all or even much of the time. But I am quite sure that when their minds were not diverted by rather more pressing considerations concerning the enemy, there were few who were not moved by the beauty of the sky at night. They all spent quite a number of hours on sentry duty, when, alone with his thoughts and in such surroundings, no man can be oblivious of such a miraculous revelation.

I have a feeling that it was a combination of those two influences—the awareness of danger and the awe-inspiring grandeur of the desert—that always marked the good relationship between those who served in the LRDG. By the very nature of their work the Patrols had to live a life isolated from others for long periods of anything up to six weeks. Even at the end of that they would only return to base at Siwa or Kufra for a short spell to repair trucks and to replenish their stores before getting further orders for another job.

There were other soldiers in these oases, and, of course, the local inhabitants; but there were no bright lights, and nothing to do besides talk or attempt to read by the light of a hurricane lamp after dark. As a result everyone became adept at looking after himself, amusing himself, restraining his temper, and controlling the wanderings of his mind—the fears, the lusts, the loves, hatreds, dreads and imaginings. If he had not done so there would have been no limit to his unsettling fantasies.

Together the men had to help each other withstand such pressures—everyone had to, for unless they did, and if tensions had been allowed to build up, something was bound to crack sooner or later. Both officers and men were in the same situation, suffering the same privations, the same exhaustions, the same exhilarating thrill at the success of some operation, and the same agonising distress at some tragedy or disappointment, the same fears to a greater or lesser degree when threatened by enemy action, the same strong determination to survive, the same anxieties about their families and their friends, the same pleasure in savouring a thick stew of bully beef and tinned potatoes when it had been ladled out of a blackened dixie on to a chipped tin plate; and the same peace of mind when the day's work was done and one could lay one's tired and shaken body on the sand in the lee of a truck's wheel, to fall almost instantly asleep to rest before the onset of another day.

There was no officer's mess to which the leaders could betake themselves. Everything was shared—even the sentry duties and the washing up of the cooking utensils after the consumption of each meal. (This, incidentally, was done with the pure, untarnished sand, of which there was never any shortage, and which is just as effective as any of the detergents which abound today.) If a truck became stuck it was its crew that had to extricate it, for the others were not going to stop unless they had to do so. Everyone therefore worked as a team, for they soon learnt that their own future was in the hands of others.

A unique relationship, trust and respect for each other thus grew up between officer and man. The Patrol itself became to every man much more important than the individuals in it. Each man knew that his fellows were doing no more and no less than he was himself, and getting no more and no less; and each knew that if he failed in any way it would affect them all.

The officers had to be just as good as the men at all the normal activities, for unless they were they would only become a burden to the Patrol. They knew that the men would react to their leadership if they showed from the very start that they understood, and would share, all the joys and hardships of their job. In such an atmosphere, of course, there developed a natural confidence between leader and led which was certainly different to anything that I had ever experienced until I served with the LRDG.

I think it is clear that the sort of relationship that I have described is only going to evolve where there are comparatively few men and they are not too diverse in character and make-up. The brash and boastful, the volatile, the jealous, the burningly ambitious, the sullen and humourless, the nervous, the fastidious, or the man liable to be lacking in moral fibre are hardly likely to fit into the pattern.

It was the ordinary man whose emotions and reactions were moderate and whose other characteristics were never extreme who was the perfect choice for the LRDG. Those who did not meet these criteria were soon found lacking, and they did not fit into the life, nor did they like it. Those who did would not have wished for a better, and it brought out the best in them.

Bagnold began with New Zealanders, and how well he chose, for on the whole their way of life had made them tough, dependable and of an equitable temperament. There were, of course, some who were unsuitable, and they were quickly exchanged for others who were keen to join.

As time went on, and the success of its early operations made it necessary to enlarge the LRDG, other sources of manpower had to be tapped to fill the ranks. It was doubtless primarily for reasons of availability that the call went out to units of the Brigade of Guards, to the Yeomanry Regiments and to the Rhodesians serving with the South African Division.

It would be difficult to imagine three more dissimilar types of men, but it was merely that the outward and visible signs of these men's background, training and traditions were not the same.

# CHAPTER 3

# First Sorties

Pat Clayton was the first to cross the frontier into Libya, and during August 1940 he carried out two preliminary reconnaissances before the first operations proper were launched. The most important of these was aimed at examining the Jalo-Kufra track in order to estimate the amount of traffic that was using it.

With some load-carrying assistance from six trucks of the Egyptian Frontiers Administration, which came with him for the part of the journey until the frontier was crossed, Clayton moved on across the eastern finger of the Sand Sea. He then went on over about a hundred miles of good gravel going until to his surprise he ran into another formidable series of sand dunes, which were unknown to him. (This was the Calansho Sand Sea, and he was unaware of its existence.) He eventually came through to the western edge and reached the Jalo–Kufra track, which ran to the outside of this sand barrier, and was marked with beacons.

Clayton did not want to prejudice future operations by leaving his own tell-tale tracks to show where he had come from, and so he sent off a patrol on foot to see what information they might glean from the incidence of traffic along the beaconed route. It was disappointing that they found nothing save some old tracks, which had obviously been made some months previously.

Not until some time later did the LRDG discover that in fact the Italians *were* moving up and down between Jalo and Kufra, but were doing so some distance to the west. This was because the continual movement of supply lorries along the route marked by beacons had cut up the surface badly, and so every trip they tended to travel a little farther to the west. In some places movement had gone twenty miles from the original route.

Although Clayton did not find the information that he hoped for, he nevertheless brought back intelligence that was to be of inestimable value to future operations, and the route that he had discovered was used very often in the future.

His second venture at this time was notable only for the remarkable stratagem he used to discover what the Italians were doing at Uweinat. He knew enough about the area to see that he would not be able to approach the garrison without being observed if he motored up in transport.

To walk was out of the question at that time of the year, so he resolved to obtain a camel in Kharga, pack it somehow into the back of a truck with two Arab acquaintances of his and take it to within reasonable distance of Uweinat. This he did, and his two Arabs duly spent a week in the oasis finding out what they could, before returning to Kharga after a round trip of nearly a thousand miles with the camel in the back of a lorry.

These two journeys proved that the men, and their equipment, were going to be suitable for the ploys that Bagnold was hatching for his Patrols. Their discovery of the western finger of the Sand Sea was a major one for the future.

While Clayton was doing this Kennedy Shaw had taken out the large 6-ton Marmon-Harrington lorries which had been acquired from an American oil company, in order to establish a dump of supplies on the eastern edge of the Sand Sea. It had become clear that without such support the distances they were going to cover from the base in Cairo would be far too great.

Everything was now ready for the first real sortie, and the three Patrols into which Bagnold had now organised his force were longing to see some action. On 5 September 1940 they left Cairo, just eight days before Marshal Graziani was to pour his forces east across the Egyptian frontier and entrench himself as solidly as he could at Sidi Barrani. It was further suspected that he might do something enterprising farther to the south against Egypt and the Sudan, through his garrisons at Kufra and Uweinat. For this reason Bagnold was sent to carry out a thorough scrutiny of the tracks leading to these two places, and to capture some prisoners to provide further information. He was also told to destroy any enemy dumps that he might run across.

Kennedy Shaw and Teddy Mitford went off across the Sand Sea to visit two of the enemy landing grounds on the Jalo–Kufra route. They destroyed the fuel dumps and wind indicators, before running into two Italian 6-ton lorries not far from Kufra a day or two later. This was a supply convoy, and one short burst of Lewis-gun fire brought the LRDG its first capture of the war—two Italians, five Arabs, a goat, 2,500 gallons of petrol and the bag containing the official mail! From then on the Italians felt it necessary to protect all similar convoys with an escort on the ground and in the air.

The other two Patrols meanwhile were carrying out more tasks of reconnaissance, and they eventually all met up to cover the approaches around Uweinat, discovered little untoward and returned to Cairo at the end of the month. On 1 October General Wavell wrote to Bagnold to congratulate him on the success of this first effort in desperately hot and unpleasant weather. He paid tribute to the tremendous skill with which Bagnold had planned, mounted and carried out this first operation, and wished him every success for the future.

When one remembers how little was known of the inner desert in 1940, and the unsuitability of the vehicles and equipment for desert travel, it is extraordinary to realise how many of the established prejudices about the desert had been exploded because of Bagnold's faith and previous experience. No longer was the Sand Sea impassable; no longer would men be expected to suffer from sunstroke unless they wore a solar topee; and no longer was it thought impossible to find the way in featureless desert.

I find it almost incomprehensible that when I was in Palestine in 1939 it was a crime to be found out of doors between the hours of 1.00 p.m. and 5.00 p.m. during the hot season unless one was on some essential and unavoidable duty. We no longer wore spine pads, but we were not allowed in the sun without wearing the absurd solar topee!

Bagnold's Patrols had covered 1,300 miles completely self-contained. They had impressed everyone, and even the most doubtful of their critics had begun to see what possibilities there were if the exposed southern flank—which was thought to be quite impenetrable—could be used with impunity by the LRDG. While they were still away in the desert the HQ of Middle East had sought permission from the War Office to double the strength of the LRDG, and to this suggestion approval was given almost at once. In the event an extensive reorganisation took place, and the Long Range Desert Group became a lieutenant-colonel's command, with a Headquarters and two Squadrons each of three Patrols.

However, at the same time as this plan was approved a body blow was dealt to the LRDG when General Freyberg demanded the return of all New Zealanders to the division which he was commanding. Obviously this could not be done at once, and General Wavell persuaded him to shelve his claim for long enough for Rhodesians and men from British units to be trained to replace them.

Meanwhile further harassing Patrols were laying mines and generally keeping the Italians on the hop everywhere where they had isolated garrisons in inner Libya. General Wavell had given Bagnold a free hand to do whatever he could to stir things up in this remote area, so he was turning over in his mind the possibility of persuading the French in Chad province to join him in a raid on Murzuk.

The French colonies in Central Africa had not all sided with Pétain when he signed an armistice after the defeat of France in June 1940, and some were still sitting on the fence wondering which way to go.

Bagnold has given me a most interesting, and hitherto unpublished, account of events at that time. His record of it all is as follows:

Murzuk was far beyond our self-contained range; but a raid on it seemed possible geographically if we could get some extra supplies from the

French Army in Chad. We could get no information from our Intelligence people in Cairo as to which side the Chad government was on. All the other French dependencies were pro-Vichy.

So I flew to Khartoum to consult Douglas Newbold, then the permanent head of the Sudan Government. He told me that he knew the Governor of Chad, a little negro from Martinique called Eboué. Newbold thought that Eboué was a shrewd little man, who might well come in on our side, but he warned that there was dissension between him and his military commander, who was either pro-Vichy or was sitting on the fence. However, he thought that the younger officers were itching for action.

Newbold told Bagnold that he himself could do nothing, as relations with the French dependencies were top-level stuff being discussed between Mr Churchill and General de Gaulle.

Newbold then said that as Bagnold himself had no diplomatic standing why didn't he go to Fort Lamy and see what he could do by talking to Eboué; and he offered to fix up an aircraft for him.

This was the kind of man that Newbold was, and Bagnold, of course, was not slow to take advantage of such a suggestion. His story goes on:

So I flew on to Fort Lamy not knowing what to expect. But my arrival could not have been more dramatic for I collapsed on the airfield of a sudden violent fever. A little later I came to in a neat French bedroom, watched over by a charming little negress—Madame Eboué.

There then followed a very odd bedside conference in French. The Governor came in first followed by a tall red-haired Lieutenant-Colonel in the flowing robes of the French Colonial Camel Corps, who was introduced to me as Colonel d'Ornano and who was commanding the troops. His second-in-command was a Corsican and when d'Ornano came into my room he asked Eboué if the latter was coming to the meeting as well. The latter replied that he would not come.

The conversation that followed, and as Bagnold remembers it, was of historic significance, for it shows how Bagnold's appearance in Chad at that time must have had the effect of bringing that French colonial territory in on the side of the Allies.

'Good', said d'Ornano, 'if he's not here then I will speak for the French Army'. He then turned to me and enquired 'You haven't come here for nothing. What do you want of us?'

I told him frankly exactly what I wanted—petrol, rations and water to be carried by camel through the Tibesti mountains to a point near the Libyan frontier, where we would rendezvous with them. I handed them the details.

Then d'Ornano turned to the Governor, and said 'This is it. You must decide now—now', he said, thumping the table. 'I can't hold my officers much longer.' Eboué nodded thoughtfully. D'Ornano then spoke to me. 'I'll do all you ask but on one condition. You take me with you to Murzuk with one of my junior officers and one NCO and we fly the French flag alongside yours'.

I agreed at once and d'Ornano wrote out a formal contract between the French Army of Chad and myself as Wavell's representative. We both signed it. The French had burned their boats. On hearing of their decision, de Gaulle, who was then in Gabon, immediately sent Colonel Leclerc to take over command in Chad Province in the name of Free France.

'D'Ornano', adds Bagnold, 'was as good as his word. The Murzuk raid was successful though d'Ornano was unfortunately killed during it.'

General Freyberg's threatened withdrawal of New Zealanders from the LRDG had never materialised, but the first of the new troops intended to replace them had begun to arrive in Cairo. These were officers and men from the 3rd Battalion, Coldstream Guards and the 2nd Battalion, Scots Guards. A new Patrol (called G Patrol) was formed under Michael Crichton-Stuart, Scots Guards, in December 1940. They had a very short period of training, and left a day or two after Christmas of 1940 with Pat Clayton and his Patrol of New Zealanders for the planned raid on Murzuk.

It all sounds so simple. However, the Guards contingent arrived in Cairo to join the LRDG only on 5 December, four days before General Wavell's advance in the Western Desert against Sidi Barrani, yet they were trained, equipped and ready to leave Cairo on 27 December.

Crichton-Stuart had Martin Gibbs, Coldstream Guards, as his second-in-command, and Bill Kennedy Shaw went with them as navigator for the tremendous journey on which they embarked. With Pat Clayton's party, there were a total of 76 men and 23 vehicles.

The success of this operation was very important, for it was hoped that the fact that the French in Chad had co-operated with the English would influence those in Niger Province, which was under the control of the Vichy government. Also, if news of a victory against the Italians deep in the Fezzan could be spread among the local people in Western Libya this might persuade them not to co-operate too willingly with the Italians. Much was at stake, therefore.

By 4 January 1941 the Patrols were south-west of Tazerbo. Crichton-Stuart and his Patrol had three days' rest here, while Pat Clayton went south to join up as planned with the French. On 6 January they heard that Bardia had fallen to the Army in the Western Desert, and a distance of very nearly seven hundred miles separated the two forces. Two days later they were approaching Murzuk, nearly 1,500 miles distant by truck from Cairo.

Clayton had collected the petrol—which the French had brought by camel—through the Tibesti mountains, together with Colonel d'Ornano, Captain Massu and eight others. These colourful allies were distributed among the two Patrols, and a couple of days were spent in finding out all they could and making plans for their attack on Murzuk.

On 11 January the force reached the road running to Sebha to the north, about ten miles away from the Oasis. They had almost attained their objective without having been spotted.

After stopping for lunch Clayton led his party along the track into Murzuk, and found no sentries or posts to obstruct them as they drove on towards the Beau Geste fort to the southern end of it. As they passed a group of Libyans by a well they were given the Fascist salute. A moment or two later Clayton came across Signor Colicchia, the postmaster, cycling with his bag of mail towards the fort. This unfortunate official was hauled aboard Clayton's truck and taken on as a reluctant guide.

As the New Zealanders approached the fort the members of the guard were seen to turn out as rapidly as they could, and were dispatched equally swiftly. The fort was a fairly formidable structure, and there was little hope of taking it without heavier weapons than were available.

Crichton-Stuart very sensibly decided therefore to lie off a few hundred yards in the palm trees and contain the garrison in the fort while some of the others went to deal with the aerodrome. They set the tower on fire, and kept the heads of the Italians as low as they could. But after a while the enemy was able to bring some machine-guns into action, and one of our men was killed and three others were wounded. In the middle of all this an Italian staff car drove up to the gate, and this contained the local commander and his wife, who had been out to lunch. They too were quickly killed by a shell from a Bofors gun.

Half the New Zealanders had gone to the aerodrome and had had quite a spirited battle there with the twenty or so of the garrison which was looking after the three Ghibli light bombers. These latter were destroyed and the hangar set on fire, but not before Clayton's own truck had run point-blank into a machine-gun post manned by some rather more than usually courageous Italians. His own gun, mounted on the front of his vehicle, had jammed, and they were unable to get it into action. Unfortunately, d'Ornano, who was riding on the back of that truck, was shot through the throat, and he died at once. But the garrison had by that time had enough, and they put up a white flag of surrender.

Clayton then went off to see how things were going at the fort, and wisely decided that as he had destroyed the aircraft and hangar, it would be prudent to withdraw before the enemy were able to send aircraft over from Hon, some 250 miles to the north-east. He therefore gave orders for the destruction of the fuel stores, ammunition and other equipment at the aerodrome before pulling his whole party out again along the Sebha track.

The estimated balance sheet at the end of this action in casualties was that the enemy lost ten killed and fifteen wounded, and two prisoners were taken; but the remainder who had surrendered were released, as there was neither transport to carry them nor rations to feed them. Kennedy Shaw recalls that this was much to the disgust of the French, who would willingly have slit their throats. We ourselves had lost d'Ornano and one other killed and three men were wounded—one Guardsman had a severe wound in his leg.

What else had been achieved? Three aircraft had been destroyed, with all their equipment, fuel and ammunition. The fort itself had been extensively damaged, and the peaceful existence of the Murzuk garrison shaken for ever. It must have had a very upsetting effect on the Italian high command that one of their isolated garrisons could be taken completely by surprise.

There was a lot of speculation about the place of origin of the attack, and it is even thought that the Italians believed that it had come from the Vichy French in West Africa. It was this sort of anxiety which must have had the most alarming effect on Italian morale: from that time on no garrison anywhere and no convoy of vehicles would ever be absolutely secure. I imagine that many of them slept pretty fitfully from that moment, waking at the slightest sound, and I suspect too that many a sentry fired at phantom shadows in the night, thus adding to the discomfort of the restless! The Italians were never anything but jittery at night, and the potential threat that the LRDG posed from then on was very considerable.

On 18 October 1941 *Il Popolo d'Italia* published an article on the war in the desert. This described how in September 1940 'though the enemy was far off, some of our trucks after leaving the Libyan coast did not arrive at their destination having been intercepted . . . no doubt this fast unit was composed of personnel expert in desertcraft and equipped with trucks specially adapted for the work'.

The Italian newspaper then gave an account of the raid on Murzuk, where 'the Italian reaction was prompt and vigorous', and it summarised the work of the LRDG as

> exploiting the element of surprise, a few 'coups' of this modern form of desert raiding had been partially successful. But our own men were quick to react. At a certain moment Clayton decided to embark on an even more daring and vaster enterprise, a really sensational coup. He made for French Equatorial Africa, where a few De Gaullist elements were beginning to make trouble, to prepare with considerable forces an attack on Kufra and eventually the general occupation of Southern Libya with the help of the French renegades.

In 1968 I had the opportunity to visit Murzuk. In the remains of the hangars there still lay the charred and twisted frames of those Ghibli aircraft; and I had the pleasure of talking to some of the older inhabitants about the raid.

I had read the story up before I went there; and as I left Murzuk to drive back up that track to Sebha I remember thinking of what must have gone through Clayton's mind as he left Murzuk at about four o'clock in the afternoon on 11 January 1941.

They had stopped about five miles to the north, and there they buried d'Ornano and Hewson, the New Zealander, in a common grave by the side of the road. They could hear the Italians still firing away at the fort—presumably at each other. They then turned south-eastward, and as dusk began to settle they camped for the night to consider their situation and to inform base in Cairo of the result of their day's activity.

I imagine Clayton must have been worried about how soon they would be spotted by enemy aircraft, and I expect the extra rum ration that he authorised for that evening was much appreciated by everyone. It was a cold night, but at least for a few hours they had the safety of darkness to give them some uninterrupted rest before they had to move on the next day. Everyone was tired, a little dispirited at the deaths of d'Ornano and Hewson, hungry too and apprehensive about the morrow. Yet they must have been elated at their success; and I can imagine that weary, unshaven, dusty collection of men climbing into the warm comfort of their blankets to indulge in well-earned rest after a good day's work.

Clayton decided to lead his party southward towards Chad, dealing with any small Italian garrisons that he knew of en route. Some thirty miles away from Murzuk was a small post at Traghen, and when they got near this the next morning they ran across two Libyan policemen mounted on camels, who were out on patrol. These two were gathered in, and they soon confirmed to Kennedy Shaw that there was no wireless in the garrison housed in another small fort in the centre of the village.

Clayton sent one of the policemen and an Italian in on foot to tell the garrison that they must surrender within twenty minutes or they would suffer the most horrific bombardment! Kennedy Shaw describes what happened:

> A quarter of an hour had almost passed . . . when a confused hum of noise arose on the edge of the village. Was this a garrison of unexpected size massing for a sortie? Then a small crowd left the western gate. Gradually it came nearer across the open ground, an extraordinary procession. With banners flying and drums beating, the Mudir (the Mayor) and his elders were coming out to surrender the village in traditional Fezzan manner. Trailing behind the crowd were a few sheepish-looking Italian carabinieri.

They captured two machine-guns, rifles and ammunition, a flag, a typewriter and a vast quantity of documents. They set fire to any of this that was of no further use, and turned their trucks towards the next garrison at Umm el Araneb, some twenty miles away to the north-east. This was a place with a bigger fort, and they did not know until they arrived that the garrison had been warned in advance of the marauding

Patrols. When the luckless postmaster from Murzuk was sent in to demand the garrison's surrender he soon beat a hasty retreat when machine-guns opened up on the truck which was carrying him.

Sensibly, Clayton decided that there was no point in risking his unarmoured trucks against a well-sited fort, whose occupants were obviously alert. So they turned south towards Gatrun. But at last the Italian Air Force had taken to the air, and one heavy bomber had made an ineffective effort to bomb Clayton's men. He therefore decided to leave the area and go south to Zouar on their way to Faya, which he reached on 24 January.

After the death of d'Ornano another great Free French officer, Colonel Leclerc, took over as commander at Fort Lamy. Bagnold had flown down to discuss with him possible operations against Kufra. It was agreed that Clayton's two Patrols should come under Leclerc and operate as the advance guard for his French column. They left Faya on 26 January and thereupon went via Sarra and Bishara, where they were spotted by enemy aircraft.

On 31 January they had got to Gebel Sherif, sixty miles south of Kufra—or, more accurately, half the force had done so, the Guards Patrol being left in reserve at Sarra. Realising he had been spotted earlier on, and there was some sort of cover where he was, Clayton tucked his eleven trucks in among the rocks. In the early afternoon enemy aircraft came again, and were obviously directing a ground force—an Italian Auto-Saharan company—on to Clayton's party. This arrived at 2.00 p.m., and had four 20-mm Breda guns to bring to bear, as well as the three aircraft flying overhead.

Heavy and unusually accurate fire was poured into the LRDG trucks, and before long three of them were on fire, while one of our men and two of the prisoners taken at Murzuk had been killed. Clayton saw that the sooner he got out of it the better, and so he gave the order to pull out in order to sort themselves out for a counter-attack. But at this point the three aircraft came in with machine-guns blazing and they dropped their bombs too. Clayton was wounded, his truck damaged and he was taken prisoner.

Il Popolo d'Italia reported that 'the capture of Clayton was a real master stroke, the enemy had lost an irreplaceable element for its experience of the desert and with him many precious documents had fallen into our hands'.

The remainder of the New Zealand Patrol withdrew southward towards Sarra, where they met Crichton-Stuart and his Guards Patrol. They all joined up and left to meet Leclerc, who quickly realised that everything had now changed, and that he could not carry out the operation against Kufra quite as he had planned it.

The LRDG had lost their commander, several trucks and quite a lot of ammunition and stores. One man had been killed, and so, as it turned out, had the unhappy postmaster from Murzuk, whose misfortune it had been that he had happened to be bicycling into the fort soon after lunch on 11 January 1941. He certainly had never dreamed of seeing the amount of action that he did!

Leclerc decided to release the LRDG patrols, so they travelled back to Cairo, where they arrived on 9 February 1941, having covered about 4,500 miles since they had set out two days after Christmas. However, they left one truck with Colonel Leclerc to help him navigate his force during the reconnaissance that he planned to make of Kufra.

Clayton had not had time to destroy his papers, and so Crichton-Stuart knew that his codes were almost certainly compromised. This did not worry them, however, as someone thought of the ingenious ruse of inventing a new one based on the regimental numbers of various Guardsmen. This was used until they no longer had need for communication with their base in Cairo.

At the Gebel Sherif action when Clayton was captured four other men were missing, and it was assumed by Bruce Ballantyne (who was in command of the New Zealand Patrol) that they too had been taken in the confusion. However, this was not so, and what actually happened to those four, together with a fifth man (one of the Italian prisoners), is an epic of courage and endurance that must be told fully, for I personally often used to draw great strength from the story when I later joined the LRDG.

The crew of one of the trucks destroyed consisted of Trooper Moore, Guardsman Easton, Guardsman Winchester and Fitter Tighe, RAOC. When the ammunition on their burning vehicle began to explode they took cover among the rocks. The Italians were not very keen to investigate the scene of the battleground, for they did not return to have a look around or think about burying any of the dead—even their own. They merely set off at once for Kufra with Clayton and the two other men who had been on his truck.

That night—and it was a very cold one—Moore and the others discussed what on earth they could do. It seemed that there were only two courses open to them. Kufra was almost seventy miles away, and they could try to find it and surrender to the Italians there. Or they could follow the tracks of their Patrol to the south and hope that they would be picked up.

Moore was a strong personality, and he was not even going to countenance the first alternative. I know that Alf Tighe would not have done so either, for I got to know him very well indeed later on, when he was the fitter of the Patrol I was to command; and he won a splendid Military Medal before he was killed by a mine in Greece early in 1944.

The four men decided not to surrender.

Moore was wounded in the foot; Easton wounded in the throat; Tighe, Winchester and the Italian were unscathed; but Tighe was troubled by an earlier internal injury. They had a 2-gallon tin of water with a bullet-hole near the top, and it had about 1¾ gallons of water in it. They had no food, and only the clothes that they stood up in; everything else had been destroyed in the trucks when they went up in smoke.

They started to walk south on 1 February 1941. During that day the Italian left them, and he was later picked up by his compatriots. The others kept going for the next three days, but on 4 February Tighe began to tire. They also found a pot of jam and some lentils, which had been left behind on the way north by their Patrol. The lentils were bad, and made Winchester ill.

On 5 February Tighe could not keep up, so the others agreed to leave him with his share of the little water that they had. They had no food to give him.

Next day there was a sandstorm, and this made it hard for them to follow the tracks. However, they reached Sarra, 135 miles from Gebel Sherif, whence they had started. The well there had been filled in by the Italians, but they found some waste motor oil in a few old mud huts around the well. They bathed their feet in this but found nothing else except some wood with which they were able to make a fire to warm themselves that night. Tighe reached Sarra after they had left the next day and found one match, which the others had dropped; he too was able to light a fire. He stayed there the following day as well.

On 9 February just before dark a party of French, with a British liaison officer, came to Sarra from the north on their way back from a reconnaissance of Kufra. They had also been to Gebel Sherif, where they had buried the dead. They found Tighe in a hut, very weak but conscious.

Tighe was able to tell them of the three others, and the French set off to try to find them that night, but could not follow their footmarks in the dark. Moore and the other two were struggling on. Easton had been forced to drop behind, but during that day a French aircraft had seen them and realised the straits that they were in. It could not land as the country was too rough, so the pilot dropped some food and a canvas bag of water. Moore and Winchester never found the food, and the cork fell out of the water bag when it landed. However, they got a mouthful each.

On 10 February a French plane flew over again and a rescue party left Sarra, following the traces of the three men's footsteps. After a time one set wandered off to the west, and at the end of these they found Easton lying on the ground. He was alive, and was 55 miles from Sarra. Luckily, the French had a doctor with them and they took the exhausted and wounded Easton back to Sarra, where they did all they could to save his life. But that evening he died, and he was buried near the well at Sarra.

The British liaison officer told a wonderful story of Easton's courage and sense of humour right up to his end. He was suffering terribly from his wounds, and his body was almost withered. Yet when the French made him some tea, weak and sweet, he drank it and smiled, saying, 'I like my tea without sugar.'

Moore and Winchester had gone on together until the latter could continue no longer. Moore gave him half the remaining water, which was just one mouthful, and he pushed on alone. The French found Winchester, ten miles farther on beyond Easton, and he was almost insane, but he was able to stand up when he heard their transport.

The French found Moore another ten miles farther south, and he was then some 210 miles from Gebel Sherif and going steadily southward. He was quite confident that he would reach the nearest water at Tekro, eighty miles away, in the next three days; and the British officer with the French records a rather delightful observation that he was slightly annoyed at not being allowed to prove that he could do so! He was very soon back in Cairo, and was awarded a Distinguished Conduct Medal for his leadership on that great march. Winchester and Tighe were taken to hospital in Khartoum, and they both eventually recovered.

After their reconnaissance of Kufra the French were determined to attack the place. Colonel Leclerc began to invest it, and the Italian Auto-Saharan Company there felt that their mobility was designed so that they could escape, while leaving their compatriots in the fort to withstand the French siege. This was really the moment at which Leclerc knew that success would be his, for the only threat to him had scurried off towards Tazerbo.

From then it was only a matter of time, and eventually Kufra fell to the jubilant French after the garrison had attempted to treat for surrender terms. On 1 March a white flag flew above the fort and the Italian rule over Kufra that had been so mercilessly imposed in 1931 collapsed with the surrender of 64 Italians and 350 Libyans, together with a large quantity of arms and ammunition.

Kennedy Shaw tells of the final moments of the Italian endeavour to protect this far-flung outpost of their African empire, and how in the signal room at the fort a copy of the commander's last message to the outside world was found. This read, in the accustomed grandiloquence of Italian surrender dramatics:

'We are in extremis. Long live Italy. Long live the King-Emperor. Long live the Duce. Rome, I embrace you.'

Kennedy Shaw comments somewhat sardonically, 'Positions are not held on such stuff as this!'

# CHAPTER 4

# Spring and Summer, 1941

Colonel Leclerc's capture of Kufra was to be a great boon for the LRDG, who used it in the following two years as a base and forward supply point. It was an attractive straggling oasis of date palms; it had an excellent supply of water and useful areas for the landing of aircraft. It also had some wonderful deep blue salt lakes, which were a joy to the Patrols of the LRDG when they returned there after weeks away in the scorching hot sands to the north of them. It was so cool and peaceful to lie in the shade of the palms after days on end when the only relief from the sun came when you could crawl under your truck.

But as yet the headquarters of the LRDG was still at the Citadel in Cairo, where the reorganisation mentioned earlier was taking place. The next new Patrol to be raised was called S (Southern Rhodesia) Patrol, and this was created at the end of January 1941.

At the same time General Freyberg made it known that he and his Government were no longer insisting that the two New Zealand Patrols should return to their parent division. Instead they were to remain, and be kept up to strength. I do not know why this decision was taken, but I can only assume that it was because of the success of the Murzuk operation, and the excitement that it had caused in Cairo when news of it began to leak out. Whatever the reason may have been, I know that it would have been a tragedy if those fine experienced men had been withdrawn just at the moment when the LRDG was beginning to prove its value.

On 25 February 1941 the Yeomanry (or Y) Patrol came, under the command of Pat McCraith of the Sherwood Rangers, to join the LRDG. It was formed from units of the 1st Cavalry Division in Palestine, which—believe it or not—had been sent out from England complete with all their horses. Even the most unarmoured-minded blimp in 1940 must have thought the use of a horsed formation to be a trifle anachronistic on the battlefield against the armed and armoured might of the Nazis. I still do not understand how they can ever have been fitted into any battle envisaged anywhere at that time; and what a waste of splendid horseflesh!

By this time Guy Prendergast had come out from England to join Bagnold as his second-in-command, and a properly constituted Group headquarters was organised together with two Squadrons. Teddy Mitford commanded A Squadron, with the Guards, Yeomanry and Rhodesian Patrols, while Don Steele was given command of B Squadron, comprising the New Zealanders.

The faithful Chevrolet 30-cwt trucks were beginning to get rather tired, and it was unprofitable to waste time on repairing them, so they were replaced by a similar load-carrying Ford vehicle with four-wheel drive. They were heavier than the Chevrolet, and by no means ideal for the job, but there was simply nothing else available in the Middle East.

On the coast at this time Western Desert Force had taken Benghazi in early February, and the Italians were driven back westward over the frontier of Cyrenaica. This made the Germans appreciate that if the whole of Tripolitania was not going to be lost by their allies they would themselves have to come across in considerable force. However, it was not until April that Rommel had advanced across the whole of Cyrenaica and occupied all of it except for the fortress of Tobruk.

Bagnold saw that distances from Cairo were becoming too great, and so it was decided that Kufra would be a much more suitable place from which the Patrols could operate. This appeared to be a thoroughly sound move, and the whole of the LRDG was moved there except for the Guards and Yeomanry Patrols, which were based on Siwa for operations directly under the control of Western Desert Force.

Bagnold was made commander of Kufra Garrison, where there was still a French force, and he was responsible for denying the oasis to the enemy. In order to ensure its safety two LRDG Patrols had to be used on static observation duties at Tazerbo (about 160 miles north-east of Kufra) and another at Zighen (about 120 miles to the north of the oasis).

But there were many problems connected with the maintenance of this force some 800 miles from Cairo, and over some really dreadful desert country. An acute shortage of petrol resulted, as by the end of such a long journey there was little left to supply the Patrols who were needing it so badly.

In the event, therefore, the LRDG at Kufra spent much of the summer months necessarily on garrison duties ensuring the safety of its base—for there were no other troops to do this—and also in keeping itself supplied with petrol and rations. It was not until the middle of July 1941 that the Sudan Defence Force arrived to take over the former role and the LRDG could revert to its proper job of long-range reconnaissance. One asks now why the LRDG could not have been relieved of such a static commitment earlier, but the campaign in Abyssinia was not yet ended, and there were no other troops to spare.

However, the Guards and Yeomanry Patrols were kept busy from their base at Siwa. They were keeping an eye on the country to the south of the Gebel Akhdar, which is the fertile hilly area of Cyrenaica. In April the German arrival enabled the Italians to move forward once again to the Egyptian frontier.

Teddy Mitford was operating in a close reconnaissance role with the Guards and Yeomanry Patrols during the enemy advance in early April. They had a number of skirmishes with the opposition round Msus and Mechili. The episode of Trooper Cave's capture at Mechili and subsequent escape is another tale of the triumph of personal determination and courage.

The Yeomanry Patrol was in Mechili just before the Germans reached it, and one of the trucks had had a damaged radiator. Trooper Cave was left with it while it was being repaired in the workshops of an Indian motorized brigade, while the rest of his Patrol went off to inflict what damage they could on the advancing enemy columns.

On 7 April the Germans launched their attack on Mechili with infantry and tanks. The Australian, British and Indian troops were overrun after a strong resistance, and Cave, along with 1,500 other Allied troops, was taken prisoner.

A week after that Cave was back with the Yeomanry Patrol in Siwa. His escape had involved him in walking over two hundred miles, and he felt it good to be back where there were trucks to convey him in future.

While Cave had been living through the days and nights of his escape the others under Teddy Mitford had got away from Mechili and made their way first to Giarabub, which an Australian force had captured a month or two before from the Italian garrison. They then went on to Siwa, which was to become well known to LRDG Patrols in the months ahead.

Meanwhile the Western Desert Force (which later became the Eighth Army) had been driven back to the Egyptian frontier, where it was holding firm east of Sollum. Tobruk was still in our hands, and it was unlikely that Rommel would attempt any major advance while the garrison there could pose a threat to his long line of communication. Tobruk was the key to the battle in the Western Desert that summer of 1941, and despite every effort to raise the siege the Allies were quite unable to alleviate the drain on their resources which its very necessary maintenance involved. If Tobruk had fallen I do not believe that the Commander-in-Chief could have prevented Rommel from reaching the Nile—yet Rommel failed to do so a year later, when that disaster did occur. But the circumstances then were rather different.

With Group Headquarters in Kufra and Teddy Mitford with A Squadron based in Siwa, the necessity for rapid communication between these two places—some four hundred miles apart, even by the most direct route—and between GHQ in Cairo and the LRDG, became very evident.

The RAF were either unable or unwilling to provide aircraft for this purpose. They were certainly rather hostile to the idea that the LRDG should have some under its direct command. They took the view (very understandable, I suppose, looking back on it) that all military aircraft must be under their control. Ralph Bagnold was also rather impatient of the fact that the RAF never seemed able to find their way to some of the outlandish places that he seemed to want them to take him.

So never being the sort of people to be put off by minor difficulties of Service dissension, Bagnold and Prendergast managed somehow to obtain permission to buy two single-engined cabin aircraft which were each able to carry two men—or three at a push.

These planes had previously, I believe, belonged to rich Egyptian Pashas and were called WACOs (having been made by the Western Aircraft Corporation of Ohio). Guy Prendergast, who had a lot of private flying experience, flew one and Trooper Barker, who had at one time flown with Kingsford-Smith, took the other. One had a cruising speed of 140 mph and the other one of 115 mph, and this difference made the very necessary manoeuvre of flying together a little complex to execute.

The LRDG air force was a remarkable unit, and it did magnificent service while it existed. Prendergast and Barker did the routine maintenance between them, two navigators were trained and they helped too, while major repairs and engine changes were done by an Egyptian civil company—Misr Airways—in Cairo.

The RAF just did not want to know! They even refused to give the aircraft numbers or to allow us to paint their roundels on the wings—and it was made quite clear that without them the aircraft would inevitably be shot down! It took rather more than the usual channels to get this sorted out, and an appropriate word in the proper ear of the RAF high command had the desired effect. From then on they gave the LRDG every assistance to operate their private air force.

The WACOs were a most useful acquisition, and they were kept fully employed in carrying passengers between the various HQs, recovering wounded, delivering spares, bringing orders and even much-needed and longed-for letters from home to the Patrols in the desert. The standard of navigation and maintenance insisted on by Guy Prendergast and Trevor Barker was, of course, the reason why neither aircraft ever got lost or gave serious trouble, in spite of the vast and inhospitable tracts of country flown over in those little single-engined machines. What a joy it was to hear those small aircraft come into earshot at the expected time, several hundred miles behind the lines, and then to greet the shy, reassuringly calm face of Guy Prendergast, who might have come with news and revised orders.

It was in exactly this sort of role that both WACOs landed at Siwa soon after Teddy Mitford had brought the Patrols there. Guy Prendergast had been to get orders, and he passed these on before flying across the Sand Sea to Kufra. The Army wanted to know whether the enemy was planning any movement to the south of the main area of contact, so the Guards Patrol was sent to Giarabub to maintain a watch on the approaches to the oasis. Michael Crichton-Stuart and Martin Gibbs did this unexciting work through some exceedingly hot days of May.

The area of Giarabub at the best of times is not very attractive, and its water-supply was always brackish and unpleasant. The failure to clear up any of the mess after the defeat of the Italian garrison there made the fly population some of the most virulent ever encountered.

All these factors were probably contributory to the near-disaster which beset Gibbs and his Guardsmen. For two days an all-pervading, energy-draining Khamsin had been blowing, and, with a shortage of water, Gibbs's Patrol had begun to suffer severe exhaustion because the intense heat had prevented their bodies from functioning as they should have done. They were in some distress, and Gibbs may have left things a little too long before he realised what had struck them.

I only suggest this because he himself was badly affected by the conditions, and when this happens it is the hardest thing of all to grasp, because one just cannot believe that one can succumb oneself. Others, yes; but no, not me! I am not likely to be affected! When this sort of hallucination strikes one all sense of judgment has already gone.

Gibbs knew later on that he had become, as he described it, a bit potty when 'I followed the moon that night, lost the way and got into Siwa very late indeed.' He also recounted how he and his navigator on the way there had stripped stark naked to cool off in the salt lake to the east of Giarabub, and were seen playing boats with tin plates at the water's edge!

Poor Martin Gibbs. Heat exhaustion can be a very nasty experience, and it is merciful that he was able to see the funny side of it. He later wrote how he was evacuated to hospital in Cairo and put into a mental ward under observation for a fortnight. 'I was in a bed next to an old man, who was under the impression that he had lost three Mobile Bath units.' It was two months before he really regained his strength.

I owe Martin Gibbs a lasting debt of gratitude, for it was while he was recovering from this misfortune that I met him in Cairo. I was then an instructor at the Middle East Officer Cadet Training Unit, hating every moment of it half the time and having a tremendous amount of fun in Cairo for the other half.

I hated it because I knew that I ought not to be enjoying the luxury, the night life, the complete safety of the Egyptian capital; I ought to have been doing something much more active, like so many of my friends who were fighting in the Western Desert. There was I in Cairo, admittedly posted there, and forbidden by my Commanding Officer—Callum Renton of the Rifle Brigade—ever to make mention of a request to be transferred until I had served my time as a company commander in charge of cadets.

But back to Martin Gibbs. The OCTU where I was then serving was at Kasr-el-Nil Barracks on the Nile, and the officers were giving a party in the Mess. I got talking to Martin, and he was being very secretive about what he had been doing recently, and so I continued to press him for information.

After a bit he told me that he was a member of a special unit, which had been raised with General Wavell's backing, to work behind the lines and to gather information about what was going on. He told me that he had come back exhausted by the ghastly conditions that they had run into near the Great Sand Sea, and that several of his men had had to be brought back with him. I had little idea of the scale or scope of these operations, but when he began to talk of the hundreds of miles that they had been working behind the lines a sense of excitement in me began to stir just a little.

I asked him more. 'Who are the chaps involved in these fantastic trips?' I asked.

'We've got a mixed lot. Mostly Kiwis to start with, and goodness, they really are tough. They just don't seem to be frightened by anything, and they don't give a damn for anyone.'

'Who else? I mean, how did you get involved with it?'

'We've got a Guards Patrol from the Coldstream and the Scots Guards. And there are some Rhodesians from the South African Division and a Yeomanry Patrol. For God's sake, keep all this to yourself, for we are still kept pretty secret.'

'But, Martin, tell me what is the chance of someone like me getting into it?' I asked.

'Oh, I wouldn't think there's a hope. You aren't a New Zealander, a Rhodesian, a Guardsman, or in the Yeomanry. But I don't know exactly what is going on at the moment as I have been away for a bit and I'm out of touch. I don't think I'll be going back either.'

'Can you tell me', I asked him, 'who runs this show? Or is that the sort of question I should not ask you?'

'I can answer that, because we are allowed to mention just a few things. We obviously aren't allowed to talk about what we are going to do or give any details of where we have been. But the boss is called Colonel Bagnold. He's in the Signals, and I don't see much of him. He's not easy to get to know, and I've only met him two or three times. But he's very shrewd, and you daren't put a foot wrong while he's around. He knows his stuff about the desert better than anyone else.'

Thus it was that I first heard any details about the LRDG, and it was from that moment that I had made up my mind to get into it if I possibly could. I was going to defy one of the two great bits of advice that my father—a naval officer—had given me when I joined the Army.

These were, firstly, to make friends with the Quartermaster, and, secondly, he told me never to volunteer for anything, but just to do what I was told to do. Very excellent advice this was, and I have made lifelong friends with many of the magnificent Quartermasters with whom I was lucky to serve; and it has been so worth while. Not only were those who reached that rank men of very remarkable stature and ability, whom I have been proud to call my friends, but the help that they gave me throughout my time in the Army has been immeasurable. One of the many superbly generous human beings among them was 'Shorty' Barrett, Quartermaster of the LRDG in 1941 when I joined it and thirty years later an archdeacon and Vicar-General of his diocese in New Zealand.

I think that my father was essentially right in telling me never to volunteer for anything, but instead to do just what I was told. For then no muddle I happened to find myself in could be anything but my own fault. I suppose this was the line of argument, and, on the whole, I think it a pretty sound one.

But in my father's days in the Royal Navy I imagine that there were practically no such opportunities to volunteer for the unorthodox. Perhaps expeditions such as those that Captain Scott led to the Antarctic called for volunteers, and my father may have felt some regret about his absence from it, since he and Scott were close friends and much of the last great expedition was planned in my father's house. All I know is that when I did volunteer to join the LRDG it was a decision that I was never to regret.

While Martin Gibbs and many of his Patrol had to be rested, Michael Crichton-Stuart was still operating, and he was next ordered to work with the 11th Hussars in patrolling to discover what Rommel's intentions might be.

While he was on his way to meet the 11th Hussars at the appointed rendezvous he saw in the distance a number of armoured cars and two tanks. He imagined these to be the British party and drove towards them, giving the accepted recognition signal. The armoured cars were by no means friendly forces, and both the machine-guns and the main armament of the tanks opened up on our Patrol. Mercifully, the shooting was poor, and only one Guardsman was hit apart from Michael Crichton-Stuart's own truck. He had to abandon this as one of the tyres had been punctured, and the enemy followed them up in a more than usually determined way. They were chased for another thirty miles, and lost another truck in the process.

Crichton-Stuart knew that Italians would not follow them as resolutely as these armoured cars had done; and he was still uncertain at this stage whether it was the 11th Hussars or the Germans who had given him such a thoroughly unpleasant time. However, a few days later it was confirmed to him that our own armoured cars were not involved. This did not alter the fact that this was a bad misuse of the LRDG, which was neither trained nor equipped for close-range patrolling, where it was liable to come up against enemy armoured cars.

As a result of this little episode the Guards Patrol had been reduced to an unacceptably low number of men and vehicles and was obviously unfit for further operations until it could be reorganized, rested and given new equipment. It was therefore pulled back to Siwa, while the

Yeomanry Patrol took over its tasks around Giarabub.

Pat McCraith had been wounded earlier on when one of the diabolical thermos bombs exploded under his truck, and so Jake Easonsmith took command of the Yeomanry Patrol for a time. Much more will be heard about this very remarkable character. Kennedy Shaw later wrote of him as being 'the finest man we ever had in the LRDG', and I can think of no possible grounds on which to challenge that view.

GHQ in Cairo took steps to prevent the further misuse of LRDG Patrols, and started to employ them for the dropping of agents in the Gebel Akhdar, for the collection of their information, and for the topographical study of the 'going' on their journeys to and from these missions.

During one of these trips in June, Jake Easonsmith had to take two Arab agents as close as he could to the airfield at Gambut. This he duly did, leaving them only five miles from where they wanted to go. He then went on to see what enemy traffic was moving on the main Tobruk-Bardia road, and he came across sixteen heavy lorries dispersed and probably halted for the night as the light was beginning to go. He decided to lay into them and take advantage of the LRDG's best weapon on such occasions—surprise. This he did, and there was so little resistance that he was able to do considerable damage to twelve of the trucks and to take two prisoners.

Jake seemed to have a sort of sixth sense which made him by far the most successful Patrol leader the LRDG ever had. Throughout June and July 1941 he was moving freely in and out and around the various enemy posts and patrols and convoys dotted around the Gebel Akhdar and to the south of it. He had an almost uncanny knack of knowing where he would meet danger, and his supreme confidence in his own force's superiority over that of the enemy was of course very quickly transmitted to the men he led, who would follow him anywhere without question or demur.

His next venture was to pick up a French fighter pilot who was reported as being looked after near a certain well. Jake eventually found a dry well-shaft from which a faintly surprised Bedouin emerged. He was obviously extremely suspicious of Jake and his bearded collection of bandit-looking thugs and, thinking that they were probably Germans, he denied all knowledge of any pilot. But the latter, overhearing the conversation from his hiding-place at the bottom of the well, soon clambered out and introduced himself as a French pilot officer. He and the Arab were taken safely back to Siwa.

A day or two later Jake was sent out again to the Gebel to drop a British intelligence officer with two Arabs. He was also given other tasks of reconnaissance around Mechili itself. This he accomplished successfully on foot, but had some bad luck when two of his men were examining an abandoned British vehicle which had been booby-trapped. One man was killed and the other wounded. Jake then carried on to keep a rendezvous with the British officer, who duly turned up as planned, and also had with him two men of the Northumberland Fusiliers who had been looked after by some Bedouin after their earlier escape.

Several similar trips were carried out by Jake, who was scarcely ever allowed back to base for longer than it took him to replenish his supplies before setting out again. Then Michael Crichton-Stuart caught malaria, and Jake even had to take out Tony Hay, who had arrived to relieve Martin Gibbs, in order to show him the ropes.

Unfortunately, Michael never got any better, and after a further attack of malaria and a temperature of 106° he had to be taken back to Cairo. He was never to rejoin the LRDG with whom he had done so much.

Michael writes of this period as being a thoroughly frustrating and even wasted summer. Bagnold, and his headquarters, with the splendid New Zealand Squadron and the Rhodesian Patrol, were tied down in the static defence of Kufra until July, when the Sudan Defence Force took over. After that our Patrols were released for reconnaissance tasks in the area of Sirte, and between Jalo and Agedabia, and the information they provided was to be of tremendous use later on.

Only the Patrols based on Siwa were being used for much of this time, and they were being employed on tasks for which they were ill suited. But obviously everyone learnt some excellent lessons from all this, and the LRDG were seldom again used on tasks best carried out by reconnaissance aircraft or by armoured cars.

Because of all this the LRDG itself came to the conclusion that the size of the Patrols was too large. They were both unwieldy to control and difficult to conceal, either when halted or when on the move. As surprise was so surely the most potent weapon in the LRDG armoury, it was essential that this should not be compromised if humanly possible.

Once again a reorganisation took place, which resulted in the doubling of the number of original Patrols and a halving of their size. On 1 August 1941 Ralph Bagnold was promoted to the rank of colonel, and Guy Prendergast was given command of the LRDG.

Bagnold was called back to Cairo to become the Inspector of Desert Troops, which was presumably a 'cover' for the job for which he was really required. It had been decided that there was scope for the employment of up to five formations similar to the LRDG in the Western Desert and in Syria. Bagnold was to raise, train and ultimately control them all from a special section of the Operations Branch in Cairo.

In the event a decision was speedily taken that because of the shortage of men and equipment no increase in LRDG-type units could be implemented. But Bagnold had gone; although the mark of his personality would remain indelibly on all the LRDG's future operations.

I supposed no better tribute could be paid to Ralph Bagnold than that recorded for history in General Wavell's official dispatch sent to the War

Office in October 1941, of which General Arthur Smith (Wavell's Chief of Staff) sent a copy to the LRDG. It read:

*Appreciation of Services*

I should like to bring to notice a small body of men who for a year past have done inconspicuous but invaluable work, the Long Range Desert Group.

It was formed under Major (now Colonel) R. A. Bagnold in July 1940, to reconnoitre the great Libyan desert on the Western borders of Egypt and the Sudan. Operating in small independent columns, the Group has penetrated in to nearly every part of desert Libya, an area comparable in size with that of India.

Not only have patrols brought back much information but they have attacked enemy forts, captured personnel, destroyed transport and grounded aircraft as far as 800 miles inside hostile territory. They have protected Egypt and the Sudan from any possibility of raids and have caused the enemy, in a lively apprehension of their activities, to tie up considerable forces in the defence of distant outposts.

Their journeys across vast regions of unexplored desert have entailed the crossing of physical obstacles and the endurance of extreme temperatures, both of which a year ago would have been deemed impossible. Their exploits have been achieved only by careful organisation, and a very high standard of enterprise, discipline, mechanical maintenance and desert navigation.

The personnel of these patrols was originally drawn almost entirely from the New Zealand forces; later officers and men of British units and from Southern Rhodesia joined the Group. A special word of praise must be added for the RAOC fitters whose work contributed so much to the mechanical endurance of the vehicles in such unprecedented conditions.

For his part in these achievements Bagnold was awarded an OBE. I think it superfluous to comment further, except to say that at the end of 1941 the award of a DSO (which takes precedence over the OBE) was 'for meritorious or distinguished service in the Field or before the enemy'. It was not until later in the war it was laid down that the DSO could only be awarded for distinguished service in the face of the enemy.

Chapter 5

# Easonsmith and Prendergast

With the increase in the number of Patrols, the change of Commanding Officers and the creation of the Eighth Army in September 1941 in order to take the offensive, it is not surprising that the scope and methods of employing the LRDG were bound to alter to some degree.

The Guards and Yeomanry Patrols had been withdrawn to Cairo for a rest and for a refit, as also was one of the New Zealand Patrols. Another invaluable addition to the unit during the autumn of 1941 was an RAOC light repair section as an integral part of the LRDG. Without some such addition the problem of the maintenance of the vehicles and the supply of spare parts would have become too great, and it was essential to make proper provision for repairs if the LRDG was going to take on ever-increasing responsibilities.

At the same time the Signal Section was strengthened under the brilliant Tim Heywood, who remained with the LRDG from this time until the end of the war. His insistence upon an impeccable standard of security, procedure and training ensured continuous and unfailing long-range communication between the Patrols and Group HQ.

While all this was going on Don Steele and the rest of the New Zealanders were operating from Siwa while the Rhodesian Patrol under John Olivey worked from Kufra. Their tasks were largely concerned with gaining information concerning 'going' and enemy intentions and movement, and were all closely connected (although they themselves were unaware of this) with the forthcoming offensive being planned in Cairo.

Olivey was ordered in September to go up to the coast road west of El Agheila from Kufra with the object of finding out exactly what kinds and quantities of guns, lorries and armoured vehicles were using the road. Very detailed reports were required, and these were all spelt out by the Intelligence staff before Olivey left in the middle of September.

In order to appreciate what was demanded of John Olivey and his Patrol of Southern Rhodesians one only has to look at a map to see first of all that a point on the coast road west of El Agheila is about 550 miles from Kufra and around 350 miles as the crow flies west of the enemy front line, then still on the frontier at Sollum.

He probably reckoned on being out for two to three weeks, and that he would cover up to 1,500 miles on the round trip. Rations, water, petrol, ammunition, spare parts and tyres all had to be decided on, collected and stowed in the five trucks that he was to take, with about fifteen men to man them. Much time and energy could be saved by the methodical stowage of such large quantities of stores; some sixty-four 4-gallon tins of petrol alone were needed for each truck, quite apart from all the other equipment.

Olivey was also given strict instructions not to let his presence be known if he could possibly avoid it, even though he was also told that he had to keep the only tarmac road along the coast under observation night and day for a certain length of time. Knowing John Olivey's wonderfully puckish sense of humour, I can imagine his caustic comments when he was asked to do such an absurdly difficult job. Yet he knew that he could do it; and he doubtless provided every iota of information requested by the Staff, together with such comments as 'the religious denomination of the tank drivers was unfortunately not established and only one of the Gunners was wearing a monocle!'

He and his party watched the road continuously for a week. Olivey himself spent much of one day only two hundred yards from the road in order to take a really close look at the traffic along it. Every vehicle, motor-cycle and gun was carefully noted, classified and timed so that the information obtained could be passed back to the Intelligence Staff in Cairo. Such information must have been invaluable to them; in fact, in October the LRDG were asked for a repeat performance.

This time Gus Holliman, an officer of great skill and daring from the Royal Tank Regiment, took another party of Southern Rhodesians to the same area used a few weeks earlier by John Olivey.

The information required of Holliman was even more particular in detail. Naturally, every possible bit of identification and armament of tanks and armoured cars was required, but he was also asked to report on the details of headdress worn by the enemy seen in all vehicles. Were they wearing German or Italian helmets, or even feathered hats? The fact that the majority of them were actually observed to be wearing a forage cap must have indicated pretty considerable German reinforcement.

Holliman also spent a week observing the road, and he did this from a shallow sort of sand pit about five hundred yards from it, with his trucks hidden behind some rising ground about a further two miles to the south.

Just before Holliman returned safely to Kufra with his invaluable information the redoubtable Jake Easonsmith left Siwa to carry out yet one more of his wonderfully successful patrols. He was detailed to look very carefully at some country over which the Eighth Army shortly hoped to advance; to pick up John Haselden, who had been working in the Gebel with some Arabs, and to plant some doctored Italian ammunition where it was likely to be found and put to use by the enemy.

Jake had two alternative rendezvous with Haselden, and not finding him at either, he decided to go off on foot to have a really thorough search for him. While doing this he came across a large enemy camp about twenty miles to the north-west of Mechili, and noticed that a great deal of traffic was moving on towards the latter place. He felt that he must find out what was going on, so he decided to lay an ambush in order to get a prisoner.

Jake worked out a typically daring plot in which he inevitably took the lead. He had three trucks and decided to station two of these on rising ground commanding a track along which he felt it likely that some enemy transport might travel. He would take the third truck, acting as though broken down, and would stop the first vehicle that came along for help.

He set the scene beautifully, and when they heard a vehicle approaching Jake and his driver stuck their heads beneath the bonnet, and the gunner hid himself under a tarpaulin on the back of the truck. As he had hoped, the lorry ground slowly to a halt as Jake held up his hand. Feeling a little foolish, and trying to conceal a tommy-gun behind his back with one hand, he opened the door of the driver's cab with the other. At this moment the driver saw what was happening, leapt out and started to tackle Jake. Meanwhile an officer, who was the passenger in the front seat, gallantly drew his pistol and emptied it at Jake and the driver, who were by now fighting it out on the ground. Luckily, all the shots missed.

The officer decided that discretion was the better part of valour and bolted up the side of the hill away from the fray, only to be mown down by machine-gun fire from Jake's men. Then the driver got free, but Jake brought him to the ground with a quick burst of fire.

At the same time the rest of the convoy of twenty vehicles appeared on the scene, and, presumably seeing that all was not well with the leading truck ahead of them, they stopped too. Some men were brave enough to open fire in return for the damage that Jake's men were doing to them with a Lewis-gun while others took cover under their vehicles.

So far he had not got a prisoner. There were only two dead Italians. Jake decided that he must go and get his man. So with as many hand grenades as he could carry he went down the enemy convoy, hurling bombs under the trucks and bolting the unfortunate Italians like rabbits from their burrows!

He got his prisoners all right and, although one of them died that night, the other gave Jake all the information he needed concerning the move of the Trieste Motorised Division to Mechili.

Haselden had meanwhile found the rest of Jake's Patrol, and he was brought safely back to Siwa.

What a charmed life Jake Easonsmith seemed to lead! Every job he did never failed to go well, and yet he was apparently such a modest, quiet and unassuming man. The New Zealanders loved him to a man.

The last of these independent operations was when Anthony Hunter was sent north to carry out a reconnaissance south of Tobruk in early November 1941. Once again this was in preparation for the offensive which General Cunningham was soon to launch. While Hunter was moving about near Bir Hacheim he bumped into a motor-cycle patrol of five men, and as always when the LRDG was saddled with prisoners and extra mouths to feed he very wisely decided to take them and the information they would have back to Siwa, rather than to carry them with him.

At this time Guy Prendergast and Bill Kennedy Shaw, his intelligence officer, had come to know that General Cunningham and the Eighth Army hoped to attack Sollum and begin a general move forward in the middle of November. And I had had the good fortune to join the LRDG. I have told how Martin Gibbs had whetted my appetite by telling me a little about it, but I had a wonderful stroke of luck a short time after this, when General Wavell arranged for me to meet Colonel Bagnold. I had no idea that he was actually looking for an officer to take over from Pat McCraith, who had commanded the Yeomanry Patrol until he had been wounded.

Thus the opportunity came my way, and after a not very satisfactory interview with Colonel Bagnold he asked me when I would be able to report. I never did understand why he took me, because I had none of the things for which he must have been looking. There never has been anyone less mechanically minded than myself; I could not speak Arabic; my knowledge of the desert was confined to a short spell with my regiment the previous year; and I really had nothing to offer. But I was desperately keen, and I wanted terribly to join the LRDG.

My Commanding Officer at the OCTU, Callum Renton, had been very understanding of my desire to get away, and once he had come to know something about the LRDG he was only too ready to help me in joining them. But there were frustrating delays in getting a relief for me, and I lived through agonising weeks with the fear that Colonel Bagnold would not be able to wait for me, and would be forced to find someone else instead. However, by the start of August 1941 I was at last relieved, and I went out to Abbassia Barracks to join up with the Yeomanry Patrol while they were back from the desert on a refit.

As the months with that Patrol went by and I came to know those splendid men so well, and to understand what made them the men that they were, they would never believe me when I told them with what awe I regarded them the first time I met them. After all, they were to me legendary figures, who seemed to think it perfectly natural to spend weeks on end behind the lines. Somehow I did not think it would be easy to spend an hour or two in that situation without a paroxysm of anxiety. They seemed to be utterly confident in themselves and in their weapons and equipment.

I was also immensely struck by the way everyone got on with the job without somebody telling them what to do and how to do it, but I soon came to know that every man had his job to do, and got on with it to the best of his ability. When one is behind enemy lines one's own life and that of the others may well depend on all tasks being done properly. When a job had been done I found that the men looked around to see if anyone else wanted any help.

I shall never forget how inadequate I felt. I had so much to learn—not only about the vehicles, the equipment and the navigation, but also about the desert, the inner desert deep in Libya, in which these men operated. On top of this I had to learn an entirely novel approach to discipline from that to which I was accustomed. I think this gave me more pleasure than anything else, for I had always disliked intensely the sort of discipline that relied on instant, unquestioning obedience and the fear of summary punishment. I had already discovered that you could get men to do anything you wanted if you let them know the reason, and if you showed them that you were going to do it with them.

Despite my very genuine feelings of being quite unequal to these men, they were kind enough to accept me as being an equal with them. They were watching me very closely, for they wanted to see what kind of officer had been inflicted on them. I could sense this; yet they took the line that I was probably all right until I had proved that there was reason to believe otherwise. Then they would know how to make life so difficult for me that the sooner I got out of it the better! This seemed a reasonable arrangement.

There was only one way to learn, and that was to get on with the job. At last that great day came in early October when both the Guards and Yeomanry Patrols were all ready to return to the desert. Eric Wilson, of the East Surrey Regiment—who had won a posthumous VC in Somaliland before turning up safely as a prisoner—had taken over from Teddy Mitford as Squadron Commander, and he was with the party as we set off up the Nile on the first leg of our journey to Asyut and Kharga.

At Kharga we would draw more petrol from the Shell Depot there, spend a night in the very comfortable guest-house and then set off westward across the desert to Kufra. I did that journey once again almost a year later, and I still have memories of the thrill of getting away from the heat and noise and hubbub of Cairo into the fertile green of the Nile Valley.

Traffic on the rough track which ran along by the river through little villages was almost negligible save for the occasional cart, loaded with water-melons or palm fronds, creaking its way wearily along with its stupefied owner asleep on top of it all.

And all along the way there were great dirty grey water buffaloes wallowing in the murky waters of the Nile or just rolling aimlessly, and apparently ownerless, along the track. Chicken and naked brown children scurried out of the way as we swept on down the road, raising great clouds of filthy dust, which permeated everything that we had.

How the locals must have hated us! We gave little thought, I am afraid, for their comfort, and, if the odd goat or cur got run over as we drove by we were not particularly worried. Nor did we care if we forced their carts off the road in order to make way for our convoy. Mostly, however, they were sensible enough to keep out of the way until we had gone by and the dust had settled again.

After some two hundred miles we would turn away to the south-west from the Nile Valley and follow a fairly well-defined track to Kharga—one of those wonderfully well-watered oases which were dotted all too far apart about the desert. This was about another hundred miles farther on, and we were glad, even after such a short trip, of the chance to lie under the shade of trees and to buy dates or eggs or water-melons from the locals.

When we left Kharga there were about five hundred miles to go to Kufra, which to me at that time was a place of great mystery and attraction, since I had little idea what it might be like, and it seemed so very remote. As I suppose it was, for very few Europeans had ever been there until the Italians first occupied it.

We arrived at Kufra on 20 October 1941, having covered eight hundred miles since we had set out from Cairo. I had learnt so much, and had been content to watch everything that the others were doing, for I knew that there was nothing that I could teach them about travel in the desert. But they had been wonderfully carefree days, with no possible threat from the enemy, either from the air or on the ground.

I had already been entranced by the expanse, by the cleanness, by the silence, the unbelievable beauty of the shadows and light at dusk, when the sun was sinking behind that far-off horizon of desert. I had been happier than I had been for months in the company of men who seemed to love the life as much as I did, and who were content to suffer all the inevitable hardships and anxieties because they believed that this was so very well worth while.

Each time I came back to Kufra I never failed to recapture the joy of reaching the shade and shelter of those thousands of palm-trees which for the last few miles of the journey had been dancing in the mirage above the horizon. We had got so used to the fierce heat reflected off the sand that it was almost a shock to think that we could at last escape it and lie on cool, clean white sand and wash in ample supplies of limpid water.

Now that we had arrived there was much to be done. We had brought a lot of stores with us. These all needed sorting out and cleaning up. The vehicles had to be overhauled and our weapons put in good order for whatever might lie ahead—and as yet we had no indication as to what we might be asked to do. These few days in Kufra were not wasted, and under the expert tuition of Bill Kennedy Shaw and Tony Browne—who had won such a fine DCM at Murzuk—I learnt with one or two others the art of shooting the stars, and from the resultant readings working out the complex formulae that would give latitude and longitude. I had never before seen a theodolite at close range, but I discovered what an important item of equipment this would be to us in the weeks ahead.

Although I had met my new Commanding Officer—Guy Prendergast—when I had been for my initial interview with Bagnold, this was the first time that I had a chance to get to know him. He met us the day we first rolled into Kufra, and the next morning I had to report to him officially for the first time. Eric Wilson, who had come from Cairo with us, had obviously not thought a great deal of me, for he had felt that I was not doing enough on the way, and that I had left too much to my Patrol sergeant. He had passed on all this to Guy Prendergast.

Guy was never the sort of person to beat about the bush and he made it quite clear that Eric had not reported very favourably of me. But he also made it equally clear that he was going to give me a fair run for my money, and that he hoped very much that I was going to make the grade.

It was not until two years after this, when Guy Prendergast had become a lifelong friend of mine, that he told me how near I was to being returned to my regiment. When Guy mentioned this to me over a drink he had moved on, and I was myself commanding the LRDG in his place. But it had been touch and go!

I know that Eric Wilson had been quite right, not only in the impression that he had gained of my performance, but in reporting what he had seen to my Commanding Officer. What he did not know was that I simply had not got a clue as to what I ought to be doing, and I was biding my time, watching everything diligently.

Any credit for any success that I might have had later on was due as much as anything else to Guy giving me some well-timed encouragement when I most needed it.

His was an interesting character, and I suppose the most striking of his traits was his transparent honesty. He had a thoroughly open face, with eyes that looked straight at you, and a slightly quizzically shy manner which made some people suspicious of him. I never understood this, because behind this deceiving façade there certainly lay a warm and generous heart longing to be friendly but not always quite sure how to make the first move. And, I suppose because of this, he had become a reserved and totally composed person, who was never moved either to heights of elation or to depths of despair.

He was so modest that he somehow imagined that nobody could ever wish to seek his views or opinions; and then when they did and they failed to pay any regard to them, he found it very hard to understand why they had bothered to ask him in the first place. So he usually kept himself to himself.

Nothing came before his duty, except perhaps his firmly held religious beliefs and the standards that resulted from them. He held convinced Catholic principles of faith, but he was not so dogmatic as to be intolerant of others who did not hold them too. I think, perhaps, he probably felt rather sad for them, because they were missing so much comfort in life.

I lived close enough to the men in the LRDG to know just about most things that they thought and felt. There was no question but that they held 'The Colonel' in very high regard. I don't think they had a lot of affection for him, for he was never really very good at talking with them; he used to feel that they didn't want to be bothered with him. But they had immense respect for him.

Soldiers admired the military qualities that he had. They admired him for the way he flew 'that old crate tied together with string and sealing-wax' all over the desert, never giving a thought for the dangers of being forced to land with engine failure, or by enemy fighters. They admired the depth of detail and care with which he planned every operation on which he sent the Patrols.

He knew exactly how much of every item would be required, for he would take the trouble to check that it was all there when, as he so often did, he came to wish a Patrol well before it set out. They never ceased to wonder at the infinite trouble that he would personally take to get them out of any difficulty that they might have run into, and they knew that he would never rest until he had found a solution to it.

But, most important of all, they knew that he would never commit a Patrol to any task from which they did not stand a reasonable chance of returning; and I think it is comforting in war for any man to know that he is unlikely to be sent to certain death!

I have always maintained that it was the personalities of the first two Commanding Officers of the LRDG which had such a direct bearing on the success of its operations. Both men were meticulous over detail, and both knew their jobs better than anyone else did. They were given a free hand to select the officers and men who were to work under them, and it is only natural that they should to some extent tend to look for people in their own image.

Earlier on I wrote of how Bagnold had appreciated the four fundamentals essential to desert travel. Prendergast too never failed to bear these uppermost in his mind: the most careful and detailed planning, first-class equipment, a sound and simple communications system and a human element of rare quality.

I have written just a little about this latter when I was describing the qualities for which Bagnold was looking when he was first raising the LRDG with the New Zealanders. I mentioned such things as the ability to withstand extremes of temperature and also boredom, discomfort and the constant strain of living behind the lines for considerable periods. These were just some of the qualities required, and I have said how necessary it was to exclude those who were unable to live equitably with their fellow-men under these conditions. I have said that it was the ordinary man who was required, and this is certainly true as far as temperament was concerned.

But in the men who were the most successful, the other characteristics needed certainly had to be of a higher standard than normal. They had to be more than usually intelligent in order to understand fully the meaning of the task that the Patrol was given, and to contribute effectively towards achieving it. They had to have plenty of initiative to operate independently of supervision and control; they had to have acute powers of observation; they needed a speed of reaction which was faster than most; and I think they also had to have an unusual sense of responsibility and balance to be able to make the best of the light rein on which they were led without taking advantage of it.

It was obviously not easy to choose the men who fulfilled all these requirements from the many volunteers for the ranks of the LRDG; and to pick the winners in the space of only a short interview was enough to test the judgment of anyone. I found that the best way to do this was to take two other members of the Patrol with me, and I remember involving both my navigator, Alan Denniff, and Titch Cave when I once had to sort through some seven hundred volunteers to select twelve of them.

I found that the views of these two were invaluable to me for they were going to have to live with the newcomers, just as I was, and they knew quite as well as I did the kind of chap who would fit in. I think they were probably rather better at discerning this, as they were certainly very quick to see through the man who did not particularly like discipline and who thought that he would find things rather easier in an unconventional unit.

# CHAPTER 6

# Supporting the November 1941 Offensive

At the end of October it became clear to Guy Prendergast that what was likely to be required of the LRDG in the coming offensive could best be achieved by operating from Siwa. Not only would this entail a shorter approach to the probable scene of operations, but it would also mean that he and his HQ would be nearer to that of the Eighth Army. So everything was moved from Kufra across the desert to Siwa. Rupert Harding-Newman was at this time on the Operations Staff at Eighth Army, and he was the link through which Guy Prendergast and Bill Kennedy Shaw used to get their instructions.

Six Patrols of the LRDG were to be used initially, and their roles were to observe and report on enemy movement and reactions in the area of Bir Hacheim and Mechili, as well as along the Trigh el Abd. The approaches to Jalo from the north also had to be watched.

An additional task was the collection of a party of fifty-five men, led by Captain David Stirling of the Special Air Service Brigade. These men were being dropped by parachute to destroy aircraft on enemy landing-grounds in the area of Tmimi and Gazala on the night selected for the long-awaited offensive—17 November 1941.

Jake Easonsmith was selected for the task of picking up David Stirling, and I will deal with that particular operation a little later on. It was the first meeting between Stirling and the LRDG, and from it resulted the very successful combination of the two forces, which did so much to harass the enemy in later months. Anthony Hunter was also given a separate role at this time, as he was sent out well in advance of the actual offensive to take John Haselden and several other agents to an area about twenty-five miles to the west of Mechili.

Hunter did exactly what was asked of him, as far as dropping Haselden off was concerned, and he was then moved to a position where he could assist in the main role given to the LRDG—watching enemy reactions. He had bad luck and, while out on foot, looking for one of his men who had failed to return from observation duty, he ran into a patrol of Italians from whom there was no possibility of immediate escape.

However, another Patrol was sent out later on to pick up John Haselden, after he had completed the work that he had been doing. They found him as planned, and were delighted to find Anthony Hunter with him. Hunter had managed to get away from his captors and join up with Haselden. The latter was very well known among the locals in that part of the desert and they had guided Anthony to him.

The other six Patrols were all in position as ordered, in readiness to begin their observation by the evening of 17 November. They had a very uneventful time on the whole for the first week of the Eighth Army's fighting. Mostly they saw practically no movement to report; but Frank Simms with one of the Yeomanry Patrols had an encounter with three RAF Beaufighters, from which they were lucky to escape with the loss of only their wireless truck, and without casualties. But the planes had run out of ammunition before they were able to inflict greater damage. The loss of the wireless truck was a serious blow, and made the Patrol quite useless in the circumstances.

While I was in hiding at Bir Tengeder we suddenly saw two trucks coming across the desert in our direction, and after watching them very carefully through a telescope we realised that they were two of ours. So I therefore moved out into the open to greet Frank Simms, who had come to find me in order to use my wireless set so as to contact Siwa and inform Group HQ what had happened to him. This was soon done, and Frank was ordered to return to Siwa. I was then moved across to the area which he had been given to cover.

Before he left he told me how he had been driving along quite happily at about eleven o'clock in the morning when three aircraft appeared in the sky and he recognised them as being our own. So he stopped and began to put out the recognition signals which we used.

We had some special recognition panels, as we obviously could not go about behind the lines with the usual identification signs painted on our trucks. Frank had just got these laid out when the RAF came in with all their machine-guns.

This was one of the hazards which we had to accept, and a very unpleasant one it was—being attacked by our own aircraft. It happened very rarely; but the risk was always there, for it was virtually impossible to warn every pilot flying of the exact location at any one time of all our Patrols. And no pilot can be blamed for assuming that a party of trucks a hundred miles or so behind the front at Sollum could be anything other than the enemy.

It was as a result of this incident that we later devised a trick which we found useful in the future. We designed and carried a plywood circle about eighteen inches in diameter and with a handle four or five feet long. On one side was painted an RAF roundel, which was the normal identification sign for vehicles in the Eighth Army, and on the other was a swastika as used by German transport. Depending on the nationality of the aircraft seen approaching us, we would hold out the appropriate side of our sign on the bonnet of our trucks.

Alastair Timpson with one of the Guards Patrols had a little excitement to alleviate the complete lack of movement that the rest of us were experiencing. He was at a position about fifty miles east of Agedabia when he saw an Italian aircraft make a forced landing a mile or two away near a well. It had had engine trouble, and I imagine the pilot knew the area well enough to use the well as a landmark for rescuers.

Timpson moved over to investigate with two trucks, and found the Italian bomber revving up its engines and obviously trying to get rid of a tiresome splutter. They could also see one of the crew manning a gun in the turret, and so before it had any chance to do them any damage Timpson decided to open up with his machine-guns. The pilot and one crew member were killed, and the Guardsmen took the other three men of the crew as prisoners.

He then poured petrol over the bomber and set it on fire. Soon the bombs aboard it began to explode, and he only just got his Patrol clear of trouble before another Fiat bomber came over—presumably in response to an emergency call from the first. Alastair Timpson was lucky to get away unseen.

Meanwhile there were the activities of David Stirling and Jake Easonsmith, who had been sent off to recover the Special Air Service (SAS) parties. Stirling became one of the best-known personalities in the desert campaign; and he was certainly a very remarkable character among all the unusual people who found themselves involved in so-called private armies during the war.

Educated at Ampleforth and Trinity College, Cambridge, he was one of four sons in his family, and his earliest ambition had always been to climb Mount Everest. This was typical of this extraordinarily tall young man—he was six foot five, and if he had ever stood properly upright, instead of with a very slight stoop, he would have looked even taller.

At the start of the war Stirling was in the Rocky Mountains, but he came home at once and joined the Scots Guards. When the Commandos were raised he immediately wanted to join them, and at the end of 1940 came out to the Middle East with a Commando force which it was planned to use for the capture of Rhodes.

In the event there were found to be no really useful tasks for the Commandos and they were disbsanded. Serving with them, however, were a number of interesting and enterprising officers who were all to make their mark in the desert later—Randolph Churchill, George Jellicoe, David Sutherland, Jock Lewes and Tommy Langton among them.

Soon after this David Stirling, whose mind had been turning over the possibilities that there seemed to be for raiding along the very exposed coast of North Africa, managed to obtain an interview with General Ritchie and talk to him about his ideas.

After a while General Auchinleck—who had taken over from General Wavell as Commander-in-Chief—became interested in Stirling's conviction that one could create immense havoc in the enemy's lines of communication if small parties of men were dropped across them by parachute. There was never a more convincing talker than Stirling once he had an idea in his head. On top of this he had a burning passion to fight the enemy, and unbounded confidence that given surprise he would always be able to destroy them, despite the odds with which he might be faced.

Stirling was given permission to recruit about sixty men from the remnants of the Commandos, and he was provided with a base in the Canal Zone at Kabrit where he was to train them for the future. Somehow he found the aircraft and the parachutes in time for the 17 November operations.

The intention behind this plan was for Stirling and fifty-five of his men to be dropped within striking distance of the Gazala and Tmimi airfields in order to destroy Rommel's forward air force. It was a bold concept, and if it had succeeded it might have had a very considerable effect.

In the event it was a disastrous failure because they were dropped in foul weather conditions, miles from their objectives and all over the place. As a result they never found many of the essential stores which had also been dropped for them, and were never able to concentrate in sufficient strength, or in time, to carry out the raids. In the end Jake Easonsmith brought back a total of only twenty-one of Stirling's original party of fifty-five. The rest were all missing and either killed or captured.

The rendezvous for Stirling and his men with Jake was not far away from my position. The first I saw of any of them was when Paddy Mayne came striding across the desert past my hiding-place. He told me the little that he knew of the rest of Stirling's detachment, and I guided him to where I knew that Jake was waiting for him.

In the early light of dawn on 20 November 1941 I met David Stirling for the first time. From our hide-out we saw two figures walking across the desert. I was expecting odd parties to come trickling in for the next day or two, and so I walked across with Titch Cave to find out who they were.

David introduced himself to me; and he decided to stay with me for a bit after I had told him that Paddy Mayne had come through with nine men the night before. We were in the top of a small wadi which was a few feet above the level of the surrounding desert, and so we could see for quite a way. David hoped to find others of his party from this vantage-point.

We sat down and had a mug of tea together while he told me the story of his heart-breaking failure and how from the start very little had gone right. But, of course, Stirling was not in any way downhearted; he was even then turning over in his mind all the mistakes that had been made and the lessons that he could learn from his first abortive attempt. He was so certain that he could succeed and nothing was going to stop him—if he was given another chance.

What a man! Failure meant nothing more to him than to generate fierce determination to be successful next time. He was convinced that he had only been thwarted by bad luck and certainly not by any lack of preparation or training. This intense enthusiasm, of course, spread down through him to every single man under his command and they all held him in great awe and admiration.

While he was telling me of the events of the last few days, and of his ideas for the future, I detected in him just the slightest doubt that parachuting was really the answer to getting to his objective without fail.

There were always, he told me, the limitations imposed by weather conditions quite apart from the problem of availability of aircraft. At that stage of the war the techniques of accurate dropping were certainly far from developed for either bombs or bodies, and there was no guarantee that anyone would be landed exactly as planned, even on the brightest of moonlit nights.

Suddenly an idea came to me. Surely the answer was for the LRDG to convey the SAS parties to within a few miles of their targets? We would then lie off while they were doing whatever they had in mind, and we could always return a day or so later to collect them again. There were no difficulties, and I assured David that we could guarantee to take them exactly where they wanted to go, and precisely when they required to be there.

It was quite clear to me that David was turning this idea over in his mind, and, as he had never at that stage travelled with one of the LRDG Patrols, he had no idea whether my claims were true. He did not know how very reliable were our methods of navigation, or how good were our communications. He had no idea then of how safely we could range across the desert and rely on our superior speed and knowledge to outwit the enemy. He had some doubts as to the validity of my claims.

But there can be no doubt that from that moment onward it is a fact that David Stirling never again attempted to reach the object of his attention by parachute; or of the success of the many future jobs which his SAS undertook after being taken to the spot by LRDG Patrols.

Meanwhile the great offensive by the Eighth Army was beginning to lose some of its impetus after our armour had swept over the frontier, got to the escarpment of Sidi Rezegh and fought their way to within ten miles of the besieged garrison in Tobruk. Relief seemed at last in sight, but Rommel realised the danger in time and fought back to retake Sidi Rezegh from us, before launching a typical all-out thrust across the Egyptian frontier with the object of forcing the Eighth Army to reduce its lines of communication by withdrawing. This was a boldly desperate stroke, which came a little too late, and which the Eighth Army was just able to contain. But it was a close thing.

These were very anxious days, and on 24 November HQ Eighth Army issued a further instruction to Prendergast, completely changing the role of the LRDG from that of careful and concealed observation of enemy reactions, to going directly on to the offensive against any enemy targets that we could reach.

I see now that this was a fairly desperate attempt to stem the tide of Rommel's advance, in order somehow to effect the relief of Tobruk at any price; for the cost of its continuous maintenance must have been mounting insupportably.

There were six Patrols available for this effort, and Prendergast informed them on 24 November that their job was to attack enemy transport, or any other target that presented itself. Two Patrols of the Yeomanry he allotted to the area of Gazala-Derna-Mechili; the two Patrols from the Guards were given the road between Benghazi and Agedabia to beat up wherever they liked, while two other Patrols were given the road through the Gebel.

The two Yeomanry Patrols joined together to attack targets, but found none worth while in the area they had selected. They therefore split up again, and the Patrol under Frank Simms eventually found themselves in the middle of an MT park of about thirty vehicles. They drove round, firing off all their guns and throwing a few hand-grenades into the enemy trucks, and did quite a lot of damage to fifteen of them before they felt that it would be prudent to withdraw. Somehow in the mêlée Lance-Corporal Carr, the Patrol's navigator, was separated from the others, and they waited for him for some time at the rendezvous arranged for such a contingency, but he did not appear.

Carr managed to hide in a wadi, and he was not captured. Knowing what Frank Simms had in mind for his next sortie, he moved across to the area where he hoped that he would meet up with his Patrol. But they never met. Instead Carr was looked after by some locals for the next two weeks until he was found by men of a field regiment which had reached the position where he was then in hiding. Three weeks after he had first been lost, he was reunited with his Patrol in Siwa.

Meanwhile the Yeomanry Patrol which I was commanding had much less luck than Frank Simms in our search for targets. We had one thoroughly frustrating day spent stuck in the mud. The story is just one illustration of the very different conditions that could be found in various parts of the immense area of the Western Desert.

It was on 27 November that I moved northward with the idea of seeing what was going on near Tmimi. The weather had been simply appalling, with heavy rainstorms, which were very unusual. The 'going' on the coast was bad, and some of the usually dried-up mud-pans were treacherously misleading.

I was certainly not used to working over the more cultivated soil of that part of Cyrenaica, and seeing a lovely flat, but slightly lighter-coloured, area of land I decided to lead my Patrol across it as we had run into some rough country and had made slow progress to date.

We tore across the first hundred yards of the mud-pan (for this is what it turned out to be) at a splendid speed, and I suddenly noticed that its colour was getting darker. What I did not then know was that this was a sign of damper ground, and very quickly my truck was brought to a reluctant halt. Titch Cave, up on the load behind me, was pitched forward between Brian Springford, my driver, and myself and he swore darkly and with the proverbial profanity of the trooper that he was!

Mickey Coombs was driving the truck behind mine, and there were two others level and on either flank of mine. I think that we were going so well that it had turned into a bit of a race. Anyway, Mickey was laughing so much when he saw the round little figure of Titch Cave hurled over the top of our truck that he himself was too slow to realise the cause of it all. One of the other two vehicles then joined the first two in being firmly embedded up to the axles in rotten mud; and so there were three very heavily laden vehicles totally bogged within about a hundred yards of each other.

We tried everything to extricate ourselves, but this merely resulted in us getting even more deeply into the quagmire. So I thought I would call up one of the two vehicles, which were still on hard ground, and with two or three tow-chains joined together I hoped to get it to tow us out. But that managed to get itself bogged also! So we now had four of our five trucks firmly stuck within fourteen miles of the landing-ground at Tmimi, from which German and Italian aircraft were flying over us constantly. It was not a happy situation.

There was only one alternative left, and this was to unload every single thing from each of the vehicles, and we would then be able to get them out. It was a very uncomfortable six hours that we spent in the process, so near one of the enemy's landing-grounds.

This taught me a lasting lesson never to take such a risk with more than one vehicle when we were so close to the enemy. The sheer physical effort of unloading and reloading over a ton and a half of stores—quite apart from the digging out of the wheels, and lifting the heavy steel sand channels—was a thoroughly exhausting performance, which none of us was ever keen to repeat.

We had been very lucky to get away with it. But we had wasted a whole day in the process.

We rejoined Simms the next day. He and I decided to spend it in hiding, as there were an awful lot of enemy aircraft about and we had no desire to get what we had deserved a day or so before. It was only later that we discovered that Jake Easonsmith with David Stirling's men had been attacked from the air on their way back to Siwa. The enemy was on the alert.

However, Frank and I decided to split up, and an hour or so before dark I led my Patrol again to the north. We had only been going for a short time when Titch Cave, up on the back of my truck once more, cried out 'Aircraft!'

I think all of us in the LRDG hated this warning more than anything else, for we knew that if the enemy identified us he could so easily pick off each truck in turn with machine-gun fire. Our load of petrol and ammunition, among other things, would be child's play to ignite, and soon the vehicles would go up in flames.

There was normally only one thing to do on these occasions and our automatic drill, once we were sure the aircraft was hostile, was that each vehicle should scatter to the four winds as fast as it could. The individual vehicle being attacked might be able to avoid the worst of the onslaught by judicious jinking at the last moment, provided the ground were not too uneven. But the odds were heavily on the side of the air. It was every vehicle for itself, and there was little that the others could do to help.

After each truck had scattered it drove as fast as it was able away from the scene, and eventually made its way back to the last major halting-place—that is to say, where the Patrol had stopped for lunch, if the attack was during the afternoon, or for the previous night, if the attack came during the morning.

However, on this occasion I decided to try to bluff it out with a different tactic. Why not try to pretend that we were friendly troops? So I halted our five vehicles in line ahead along a track and the Italian single-engined fighter came roaring in not very far above us. I was quite clear that it was an enemy aircraft, but he was not at all sure about us. He circled slowly round us twice at a safe distance while he made up his mind.

I got down off my truck and walked away a few paces so that he might see me clearly, and especially the very friendly wave that I was unctuously making to him. He took one more sweep around; and one or two of the others also got off their trucks when they felt that we were fooling the poor chap. They too waved at him.

It was a terrific relief for us all when we saw the pilot wave back cheerily out of his open cockpit, and fly home in the dusk to his supper!

Next morning we moved on again in the cold, unfriendly light of dawn, huddled in our overcoats for warmth after a damp and chilling night. Morale was pretty low, especially after such an early start under an overcast sky, while it looked as though we might get more rain during the day.

We hadn't been going for long when I suddenly noticed that Brian Springford—never at his most cheerful at that hour of the morning, for he hated my habit of starting off before breakfast—was looking rather more alert than usual.

'Titch', he shouted, 'do you see something moving over to our left?'

Titch moved from his prone position nestled among the bedding rolls on top of the truck, grabbed the handles of his best friend, the Vickers machine-gun, and peered out towards the west.

'It's a truck,' he replied calmly.

'Right, we'll stop a moment and have a look at it through glasses,' I said to Springford.

I soon saw that it was a Ford lorry, and I said so to the others.

'Can't be,' Titch observed.

'Damned well can be. They've captured lots of ours. Yes, I am sure it is, and I can see some men in the back. Let's get cracking and go and see who they are.'

So off we went, and I decided that we would encircle them. I also told Titch not to shoot, hoping that we would take them by surprise.

'Let's scupper them, Skipper,' Titch replied. 'We don't want any bloody prisoners.'

I saw the logic of this, but thought still that if we held our fire for a bit longer we would probably avoid any danger of being fired at ourselves, because I intended to open up on them when we had them cornered.

This is what we did, and the vehicle jammed on its brakes the moment its crew saw that the game was up. They stood up in the back with their hands high in the air—three Italian soldiers and two Libyan soldiers in a very useful new Ford 15-cwt truck.

This poor, sad little party was on its way for a few days' leave in Derna from a small outpost of the Italian Empire in a fort a few miles away. Some of the wags in my Patrol told them that they were sorry that we could not take them to Derna but that we would be very pleased to take them to Cairo. The one who spoke the best English thought this a splendid idea, as he had, he said, always wanted to see Cairo!

'You will, brother—if you're lucky!' snapped Titch.

'Thank you,' said the Italian. 'Thank you very much indeed.'

'OK! You be good then, and no monkey-tricks,' retorted Titch, still behind the machine-gun.

After a fairly protracted and frustrating conversation with the English-speaking Italian I understood that there were about twenty men with some machine-guns in the fort, and I resolved to attack it. I was encouraged in this plot by the Italian, who was pretty sure that the garrison would surrender fairly smartly if we frightened them enough.

I was confronted with quite an interesting military exercise, the solution to which I never learnt during my time later on at the Staff College. How does one attack a stone fort effectively with cavalrymen mounted in five unarmoured 30-cwt vehicles?

The answer in practice was an interesting one, for we found that the garrison was far more determined than we had imagined. When we had got to about two hundred yards from our objective the defenders opened fire on us.

I obviously could not endanger my trucks, and so I had to withdraw just a little before offloading my gallant little band of men. I had decided to assault the place on foot, and this is what we succeeded in doing. After an attempt to get the enemy to surrender before they (and ourselves!) suffered any more unnecessary casualties, we had the satisfaction of watching the dispirited garrison of seventeen men come running out of the fort in their eagerness to capitulate. We found the bodies of two others whom we had killed, and, after destroying their weapons and anything else useless to us, we drove away from El Ezzeiat with our prisoners, some of their food and all the 'plonk' that they had in the fort.

We disappeared into the desert as fast as we possibly could, for we had found that the enemy's wireless set was still switched on, and they had obviously been reporting our presence before throwing in the towel. I knew of some good cover about thirty-five miles away, and we were glad to get there and feel comparatively secure while we sent a signal to Siwa to tell Guy Prendergast what we had done.

I was fairly pleased with our success, and thought that the Colonel might feel the same way. So I was a little crestfallen and deflated when in reply to my news I deciphered a message from Guy which read:—'Your orders were to operate against transport offensively. Dispose of your prisoners and do what you were told.'

He was quite right, as I saw only too well when I analysed my morning's work. I then appreciated that it had done nothing whatsoever towards the main aim of disrupting the enemy's communications.

I had to find a solution to the problem of what on earth to do about the prisoners, as I could not take them with me; I could not possibly afford to leave a guard with them; and I could not risk letting them go. There were those who thought that the only thing to do was to bump them off. But I had to veto this suggestion.

In the end I had a brain-wave and we reached a compromise that would save our lives and our consciences. It would also allow us to go on with our task and do what we were told. We certainly had not enough food and water to keep them for any length of time.

I worked out that I would have a reasonable chance of getting away without my presence being reported if I could make certain that the prisoners did not reach any Italian garrison in less than five days. I did not have enough food or water to stay out any longer, and it had always been intended that we should return to Siwa in under three weeks.

So the answer was for the prisoners to be left at a point eighty miles from any possible help, which was about thirty miles farther to the south of us. I would also give them enough food and water to spur them on to survival and, as Bill Kennedy Shaw said in his book, 'the general direction for a march on Rome'.

Some months later I heard that these unfortunate devils had got safely to their own lines, for the German High Command was very incensed at what they considered to be savage treatment of prisoners at the hands of the piratical Patrols of the LRDG. They made sinister threats as to what would happen if this occurred again.

We were now free to get on with the job, and on 30 December we arrived within striking distance of the road between Derna and Tobruk. We left the vehicles concealed about three miles from the road, and a party of us walked on, to arrive at it after dark. We watched a little traffic for some time going either way, but we could not get the ideal size of convoy to attack. We hoped for one large enough to make our efforts worth while, and yet it had to be unescorted by armour, if possible.

It was a frustrating night, and in the end we had to content ourselves with firing at one large petrol-tanker at very close range before stopping a 10-ton lorry with a well-aimed grenade. By the time we had dealt with the opposition and set the truck on fire we counted two officers and seven Italian soldiers dead by the roadside. We cut the telephone lines and beat a hasty retreat to our trucks.

Not only had the night been frustrating but it was also a thoroughly cold one; and it ended rather disastrously by my having to abandon one of our trucks, which just would not start, and we were then pursued by the enemy in the dark. We had a very unpleasant night altogether, and drove through the rest of what remained of the darkness in order to put as much distance as we could between us and the enemy.

Tony Hay, with one of the Guards Patrols, had had nothing to report in the earlier days of the main offensive, and he was as glad as I had been to receive orders to take offensive action. He moved across to the Beda Fomm area, and on the way was spotted by an Italian bomber. This did its best to destroy Tony's Patrol; but the latter fought back with every weapon available, and they had the satisfaction of watching the enemy aircraft fly away while dropping one final bomb a mile away from its target.

Some twenty minutes later he was attacked again, this time by a Junkers 87 bomber. This engaged the Guardsmen in a far more determined fashion, using the classic method of dealing systematically with each vehicle in turn, dropping bombs and machine-gunning from both the front and rear armament. How all the trucks managed to avoid any damage was either a miracle or the result of the great skill with which they turned just when they were about to be attacked. But eventually the enemy flew away to replenish his ammunition, and this respite gave Tony Hay a chance to escape. He grasped it, and sped as fast as he could to the escarpment east of the main road where he concealed his Patrol and their trucks. They rested that night.

Next day Tony Hay moved forward to within three hundred yards of the road where he could see what was moving. However, he noticed that there was a white building, probably a troops' road-house, a few miles away to the south, and through his binoculars he could see men strolling around it and about thirty vehicles parked at the back.

This looked a very inviting kind of target, and Tony Hay decided that it was just what he was looking for. That evening, as the sun went down, Tony led his Patrol along a track which would join the main road about half a mile from the building. He drove fairly slowly towards it, and in doing so passed several vehicles going north along the road. They were mainly Italian, but there was one anti-aircraft gun with a crew of four steel-helmeted Germans sitting to attention!

As they reached the building Tony Hay closed his trucks together, and they turned into the car-park. At this moment they opened up with their guns and hurled grenades into trucks, wasting no time in escaping from the hullaballoo that they had stirred up. It was getting dark, and he took his Patrol off into the desert for the night.

He had an uncomfortable time next day, for the enemy were flying about looking for him, but he was well camouflaged and they were not seen. At dusk he moved once more down towards the main road, but a little way farther to the south. Here he dismounted his guns off their trucks and sited them on a slight rise, behind which they tucked the vehicles. He waited until he had a large and vulnerable tanker in his sight, and they then opened very concentrated fire on it. Tony made sure that this was destroyed, and when he saw that all the other traffic to the north and south of it had halted and turned back from whence it had come he decided to move away while there was still plenty of darkness to give him cover from enemy aircraft. After reporting news of his activities, he was recalled to Siwa.

The actual nuisance that Tony Hay and his men had caused was nothing to the alarming effect that it had on the enemy, who thought that he was the advanced guard of an enemy force striking towards Agedabia. The Italians stopped all traffic on this stretch of the road, and when convoys did start up again they were only allowed along it with an escort of armoured cars.

These were the first of many raids to come, launched from the inner desert against the Axis lines of communication. These raids must have caused the enemy a lot of worry, and the problem of how to deal with them, without pulling too many fighting troops and aircraft from the battle front, was a very difficult one.

Other Patrols were out at the same time, and had similar success. Tony Browne and one of the New Zealand Patrols joined up with John Olivey and his Rhodesians. They got unmolested on to the road between Barce and Benghazi, and took up position about thirty yards apart, with their bonnets facing away from the road, and at about fifty yards from it.

This was the most efficient way to bring all our guns to bear on enemy transport, and at the same time it enabled us to make a really quick getaway if this should be necessary. Several vehicles were dealt with in one place before they moved away six or seven miles nearer Benghazi. This time they destroyed a further two heavy lorries, together with their trailers, and also an oil-tanker. The occupants were killed. Next this enterprising party moved a bit farther away, and were all ready to try to derail a train when they were called back to Siwa to refuel and to get fresh orders. John Olivey was very upset that he had been unable to achieve a lifelong ambition of blowing up a train!

All these raids—pin-pricks as they may have been—were concerted with the operations of a force commanded by Brigadier Reid, which had moved to Giarabub and was to advance along the northern edge of the Great Sand Sea. This would pose a considerable threat to Rommel's flank, and it was hoped that Reid would be able to take Jalo. He had a battalion of 2nd Punjab Regiment, the 6th South African Armoured Car Regiment and some Field and Anti-Aircraft Gunners.

It was a great mark of his leadership that he succeeded, and took Jalo on 27 November, despite the length of his line of communications and the terrain which his force had to cross. He faced a great many problems, especially those of an administrative nature.

Soon after Jalo had fallen to Reid the LRDG moved into the oasis with three Patrols under Don Steele. The rest of us were all being collected at Siwa in preparation for the next phase of operations.

CHAPTER 7

# LRDG and SAS together

The failure of Stirling's first raids and his subsequent safe journey back to Siwa with Jake Easonsmith gave him first-hand knowledge of the possibilities that I had discussed with him; and I remember David Stirling telling me later on how he had been impressed with the nonchalant ease with which Jake's Patrol had moved about behind the lines.

David's conviction that he could operate effectively only with the full support of the LRDG resulted in a brilliant partnership between the two organisations. Providing the separate aims of each were not allowed to clash, there was no reason why they should not co-exist happily. In the event I think that this was achieved pretty well, due in some measure to the tactful handling of all concerned by the Operations Staff at GHQ. It cannot always have been easy for a sensible balance to have been drawn between the requirements of reconnaissance for intelligence purposes and the need to stir up trouble in the enemy's rear areas—particularly when said trouble was in the hands of such an original and determined character as David Stirling. The enemy's reaction to Stirling's operations was bound to make the work of the LRDG a little less simple than it might otherwise have been.

The next major effort by Stirling's men was to destroy as many aircraft as they could on the enemy's airfields to the west of Benghazi. It was intended that Stirling and Paddy Mayne should be taken to the Sirte area; Jock Lewes would go to Agheila, and a week later Bill Fraser would be conducted to Agedabia.

From Jalo to Sirte was about 350 miles, and Holliman was detailed to take the SAS party up to the area, where the latter would destroy all they. could on the two airfields at Sirte and Tamet, which were used as reserve airfields for staging aircraft on their way farther east. The night of 14 December had been selected for these raids. Stirling was to go to Sirte and Mayne to Tamet, with Holliman and his Patrol lurking in the shadows and waiting at a rendezvous to collect everyone and take them back to Jalo when all was done.

On the way to their target the LRDG vehicles had been spotted by an Italian reconnaissance aircraft. After some rather half-hearted machine-gunning the plane flew off, and the inevitable bombers appeared shortly afterwards. Luckily, these never found the Patrol, but shortly after another reconnaissance aircraft saw them. It was thus very probable that the enemy was suspicious and alert, considering the shocks that they had already suffered.

Stirling and his party reached their objective without difficulty, and he got right on to the airfield in the dark without realising that he was quite so close to it. Each of his men had been carrying about seventy pounds of explosives on their backs, and so he decided to rest that night and see the layout the next day.

In the afternoon a great many aircraft took off to fly to the east, and none of them returned. It is possible that the Italians had feared a raid on Sirte, and had consequently evacuated the airfield. Whatever the reason may have been, Stirling was once more thwarted in his attempt to blow up aircraft.

Paddy Mayne meanwhile had been dropped within three miles of his target, and was left at the north end of the Wadi Tamet. When he got into position to watch what was happening in the airfield he could not have hoped for a happier situation. There he was with his gang of raiders, in full view of an airfield with aircraft parked all round the edges; and they had only found it necessary to walk a mile or two, thanks to the courtesy of Gus Holliman with his Patrol of Rhodesians. To date everything had been perfectly stage-managed, and Paddy Mayne was to take full advantage of the setting.

At the western edge of the airfield Mayne had seen some huts where the aircrews were living, and after dark he decided to deal with the occupants of these before turning his attention to the aircraft. Paddy waited till he thought that most of them would be asleep; then he and five others rushed into the huts, and with bursts from tommy-guns fired from the hips they made quite sure that there would be no one left alive to prevent them dealing with the aircraft.

He wasted no time. The whole raid only took about a quarter of an hour, but this was the SAS method of working, and when they were on their way to the rendezvous with Holliman a total of twenty-four aircraft and the fuel dump were either blazing or ready to explode into flames.

The story was often told of how Paddy Mayne—who was an immensely powerful man and had been an Irish rugger international before the war—personally destroyed one aircraft with his own hands. He was always reported to have returned with the instrument panel, which he ripped out for a souvenir!

Lewes had had the same sort of misfortune as befell Stirling, and he found no aircraft at Agheila.

Bill Fraser had much better luck, and with a party of three men he had

71

got to the airfield at Agedabia, only to find it well wired and guarded. Presumably the enemy had learnt a lesson from the success of Mayne's raid a week earlier. But none of this prevented the very resourceful Fraser from getting in among the aircraft, and he destroyed thirty-seven of them. He was picked up after his success by John Olivey and a Rhodesian Patrol, who then returned with them to Jalo.

The bad luck that had come Lewes's way had resulted in an extra bonus for Fraser, for all the aircraft that had been on the airfield at Agheila had in fact been moved to Agedabia.

David Stirling had every reason to feel on top of the world, for his chaps had destroyed sixty-one aircraft and caused a great deal of confusion behind the lines. Much of the success of these and subsequent raids by the SAS was due to the inventiveness of Jock Lewes. He had set his mind to creating a bomb which would not only explode after a given length of time but would also have incendiary properties.

After many experiments he found the answer. He used as a fuse a time-pencil, which worked on the principle of acid eroding a small wire. This when severed released a spring, which resulted in the explosion. Then, by some extraordinary mixture, which I have now forgotten, the bomb burst into flames. This was the ideal instrument for the destruction of aircraft, and the timing device enabled the perpetrators to get clear of the machine before the thing blew up.

The LRDG Patrol which had taken Lewes and his men was commanded by a New Zealander—Bing Morris. They had orders to take Lewes to Agheila, and also to attack Mersa Brega, about twenty-five miles to the north-east. After Lewes's abortive attempt at Agheila, Morris moved on up towards Mersa Brega, and reached the road where it ran along a kind of embankment.

Morris had five of his own trucks, and for disguise the SAS party had a Lancia lorry in which they had travelled from Jalo. They watched the enemy moving along the road for a time, and then Morris decided that the only way to get at Mersa Brega was to drive along this road himself, despite all the enemy trucks that were also on it. He planned to lead with the Lancia without lights, and follow this with his trucks. From these he had removed the dimming masks which were normally fitted to their headlights.

He had ten miles to go, and they passed some fifty or more enemy vehicles coming from the opposite direction. After a nerve-racking journey Morris came across one of the road houses where Axis troops could halt and get some refreshment on their journey to or from the front, and it was after midnight. They drew up near almost twenty vehicles which were full of German and Italian troops. Morris was just waiting for two of his trucks which had got a little behind the rest of the convoy, when a sentry or some alert soldier started to fire at them.

In no time Morris and his men returned fire with every gun that he had, and the range between the protagonists was only about twenty-five yards. It was a miracle that they suffered no casualties. While all this was going on the SAS threw time-bombs into the enemy transport, as well as killing any of the drivers who happened to interfere with them.

Morris knew that his only line of retreat lay along the same route that he had come, and so he drove the ten miles along the embankment till he could get off it and into the open desert. The last truck of his party was instructed to drop mines to inhibit any over-enthusiastic pursuer. By dawn they were well hidden and counting the result of their night's work. Morris estimated that they must have killed at least fifteen of the enemy and wounded a number of others, and had probably destroyed some seven vehicles. They had also taken two prisoners. After lying concealed all day, he moved on the following night to start his return trip to Jalo.

Up on the coast the Allied army was moving forward, and Tobruk had been relieved. I had been ordered to move up to attack enemy transport on the road between Derna and Tobruk, but owing to the changed situation I was told to go farther to the west and join up with Tony Hay and his Guards Patrol to attack enemy transport on the road between Benghazi and Agedabia. Tony had been working around there in November, so his knowledge of the desert in that area was going to be a help to me.

We met as planned and spent some time discussing the best thing to do. In the end we decided that we would both attack the road at places separated by a few miles, and then pull out to meet together in hiding in order to make a new plan for what we would do the next night. We had about sixty miles to go, and left in the late afternoon of 14 December 1941 to cover the distance to the road, which we reached just before dusk.

We arranged our trucks in the normal fashion, with the bonnets pointing away from the road, and we were within thirty yards of it. However, the convoys that came along were all escorted by armoured cars, and I saw no merit in engaging these if I could wait for unescorted convoys.

But we were frustrated for a time as a large fire suddenly lit the sky a few miles away to the south, and shortly after that all movement ceased. I assumed that Tony Hay had struck before I had.

It wasn't long before the traffic started to move again, and I decided to take the next good opportunity that came along. Before very long two trucks appeared, and I could see that the first of these was a large petrol-tanker with a trailer. I decided to open up on it, and we killed the driver in the first burst of fire, and then shot the passenger as he leapt out of the cab.

The other vehicle was full of troops, and when some of them were unwise enough to fire back at us we gave them a lot of discomfort as they jumped out of the back of the lorry. They made their way in a hurry across the desert into the darkness. We set both vehicles on fire before driving along the road to the south, as I realised that the burning vehicles would halt all traffic again. We soon came across two more large tankers and trailers, and these we also set on fire. We had destroyed probably between three and four thousand gallons of petrol and killed a dozen or so of the enemy. I reckoned this was enough for one night; so we cut the telephone wires running along the roadside and withdrew east into the safety of the desert and the darkness. It was always fun to tie the ends of any cables that we had cut to the back of a truck and drag them off into the desert in order to make the task of repair as difficult as we could.

It was perhaps even more exciting, as we did that night, to drive away and watch the fires that Tony Hay's and my own Patrol had started, and see these illuminate the sky for the next two hours. It gave one a great confidence to think how much one had intimidated the enemy, and thus a great sense of power.

We didn't meet up with Tony Hay until the following afternoon, when he had some rather disturbing reports of enemy ground patrols, which had been causing him some concern all day. Although we both felt that things might not be quite so easy for us as they had been the previous night, I don't think either of us had any lack of confidence in our ability to give a repeat performance. We drove off together to the road and got to the escarpment some five miles to the east of it. From here we could see enemy traffic. There also seemed to be patrols protecting this between us and the road. As the light began to fade we drove away to our targets, Tony going about ten miles to the south of us.

Once again Tony was first to deal his blow, and the sky was lit up with the result of it. And once again all traffic ceased. But this time it did not start again as it had done the night before, and nothing came my way. I had decided that if I had not struck by a certain time I would get away to some cover and lie up for three days before coming back again.

So we did not wait, and we ran about seventy-five miles that night to some thickish bushes south of Msus. We had had little sleep for two nights and were glad of the rest. It was not until later that I heard what had happened to Tony, for we never met up as we had hoped until after the war was over. He had got down on to the road that night and had laid into the first thing that came along. This happened to be a truck towing a staff car, which was destroyed. Tony knew that it would be foolish to hang about and wait for more, so he drove off into the desert to lie up for the next three days. He covered almost a hundred miles from the scene of his crimes.

Next morning they moved on at dawn to look for good cover, and in the early light they topped a rise to see below them a whole lot of men and trucks which they took to be part of Reid's force. Leaving the rest of the Patrol to get their breakfast, he drove off to make contact with them. Alas! too late did he realise his error, and before he could get back to warn the Patrol, he had been captured and three others of his trucks were surrounded.

Tony Hay and ten Guardsmen were seized, and only two trucks got away to return safely to Siwa. This was not the sort of mistake the LRDG ever made again, and the loss of Tony Hay was a particularly bad blow as he had done such excellent work until then. And it was a loss of a friend to me personally, for Tony and I had joined at about the same time, and he had a delicious sense of the ridiculous, and one which appealed so much to my own sense of humour.

It was certainly good to hear how well the Eighth Army were doing. A week before Christmas Rommel was driven back from Derna and on Christmas Eve 1941 Benghazi was entered. But eventually Rommel held his ground at Agedabia.

One other LRDG enterprise of interest at this time was the one and only instance when the Royal Artillery Section was tried out in action. Originally this small party, under 2/Lt Eitzen, had a 4·5-inch howitzer which was moved about in a 10-ton lorry. It also had a light tank, which somebody hoped would be useful as an armoured observation post. With all respect to my many friends in the Royal Artillery, I never quite understood why they had to have armour to protect them, when the rest of us were prepared to observe from open thin-skinned trucks! However, these totally unsuitable items of weaponry were soon disposed of, and Paul Eitzen settled for a 25-pounder, which was also carried in a lorry.

They were sent out with an escort of John Olivey and some Rhodesians to attack a fort about twenty-five miles south-west of Agedabia. They made the approach without trouble, and after sizing up the problem they attacked the small fort of El Gtafia on 16 December. Fourteen shells were fired at the place, and the garrison fled. Four of them were captured, and Olivey then entered the fort triumphantly. He destroyed everything that he did not think was worth keeping, and then had a rendezvous with Bill Fraser and his party of SAS after their very successful raid on Agedabia airfield. The whole party then returned to Jalo, but not before they had lost two men killed when they were attacked by two of our own Blenheims.

These early raids by Stirling's men, with the LRDG providing the method of transport, had an immense effect on Rommel's actions at a time when the Eighth Army was forging ahead. Already his Italian allies were none too certain of how much they wanted to be involved in it all, and these quick and unexpected thrusts, with absolutely no warning, were very definitely demoralising to an enemy whose most marked characteristics were hardly those of the finest soldiers! At the best of times they were very unhappy under fire.

It must have been tremendously encouraging and rewarding to David Stirling to have seen his bold daring reap the fruits of his confidence and vision. He himself had suffered the darkest agony of failure, but had never failed to believe that he could do just as well as his men actually did. I know of no words to describe how I would account for these successes other than inspired leadership—for this is where much of David's great strength lay.

Most of us in the LRDG had a feeling that we might be lucky and spend Christmas 1941 in Siwa; but this was a pious hope! However, I got back with the Yeomanry Patrol on 21 December.

The same day Guy Prendergast flew up to Derna—where Eighth Army then had its HQ—and he was given new orders for the future. Basically these were to operate offensively as far to the west as possible where surprise would cause the most consternation; to make particular note of any information on the type of country which could be of value to future operations and to report on whether there were any signs of the enemy preparing a position at Buerat-el-Hsun, which was about fifty miles to the west of Sirte. Prendergast was also told that he would have to continue the job of taking agents to their various destinations. For his part, with his usual clarity, he divided the area for which he had been made responsible into five separate sectors, and these were allotted to various Patrols.

Gus Holliman left Jalo on 24 December with a party of Stirling's SAS, which was to have another crack at the airfields of Sirte and at Wadi Tamet. This little exercise resulted in the destruction of a further twenty-seven aircraft at Tamet by Paddy Mayne, who seemed to lead a charmed life at this time. Stirling, who had led the party to Sirte, ran into his usual bad luck and was seen by a sentry as they approached the airfield. The alarm was raised, and this raid had to be abandoned.

Bing Morris also left Jalo at the same time to take two other batches of Stirling's men to the airfields at 'Marble Arch' (about forty miles to the west of Agheila) and at Nofilia, some sixty miles farther along the coast to the west.

Two days after Christmas Bill Fraser with four men were put down by the New Zealanders about five or six miles from the Marble Arch airfield. The next day they dropped Jock Lewes with six men about the same distance from Nofilia. Bing Morris then found some cover about ten miles to the south where he was to wait for Lewes. On the following day Jock Lewes turned up as planned and warned Morris that he had seen an enemy patrol hovering suspiciously about. However, they moved on back to Marble Arch to collect Fraser and his men.

Soon after they had left they were attacked by a Messerschmitt from a very low level. Morris took the usual evasive action, and scattered his Patrol to the four winds. The fighter used up its ammunition and then flew off, only to send back two Stukas and a third observation aircraft, and these proceeded to attack the New Zealanders with cannons and incendiary ammuntion.

Morris had attempted to hide his trucks during the respite while reinforcements were being called up, but this failed to save his Patrol. His own truck was hit first, and everything caught fire and blew up. A moment or two later another truck was bombed, and a further bomb got yet a third of the trucks. During this attack Jock Lewes was killed; and thus David Stirling lost one of the finest men he was ever likely to have serving with him.

One truck had survived this onslaught, and it picked up Morris and five of Lewes's men; but nine of his own men and one of the SAS were not traced after a considerable search had been organised for them. Morris then decided to return to Jalo with the remaining survivors. It was a journey of about two hundred miles.

I remember well how everyone took it almost as a matter of course that the nine men of Morris's Patrol turned up safely at Augila, on the outskirts of Jalo, eight days later. But it was a remarkable feat of endurance, and I suppose it was only possible because it was the end of December and the weather was cool. The total resources of this gallant band of men for their long walk were three gallons of water, nine biscuits, an emergency ration of chocolate for one man, a compass and a map of the area.

It would have been unthinkable to these men that they should do anything other than attempt, with everything in their power, to get safely back to Jalo. They suffered terribly from the cold at night, and they were quite unable to sleep because of it. They even had to cut up their greatcoats to make something to put on their feet, as their sandals wore out in no time. But they fed on snails which they found, and these helped to keep them going. The chronicler of the party who wrote the story afterwards described how they ran out of tobacco; 'A good job too really, as it only tended to increase our thirst.'

They had started walking at dusk on 31 December 1941, and heralded in 1942 with a mouthful of water each while they watched 'the RAF paying their respects to the Luftwaffe at what we thought was Marble Arch aerodrome as the flares were very bright'. They marched on till sunrise and rested till midday, but it was too cold to sleep. All the rest of 1 January and that night they walked. At dawn the next day they saw some fires 'and we reasoned that where there was fire there was wogs and where there were wogs there was water and perhaps food'.

The Arabs they found were very friendly and they looked after them with water and dates, which gave them enough strength to continue. So they struggled on, getting weaker and more tired because of the lack of sleep. But they made it in the end, and never even began to despair. I particularly enjoyed reading afterwards the comments of one of them under the heading of 'One or Two Points of Interest:

One or Two Points of Interest:
1. Hunger did not unduly worry any of us.
2. It would be OK if each man had a map and a compass. I have omitted to mention that we were lucky enough to have both.
3. Lastly, that grumbling and grousing were not features of our trip. Everyone was helpful to one another.

While Holliman and Morris had been working so successfully from Jalo there were other Patrols leaving Siwa, still the LRDG base. But it was beginning to be too far back, and it was soon to move forward to Jalo.

I left Siwa with the Yeomanry Patrol the day before Christmas. Of the five sectors that Guy had divided the area of operations into, I had been given one which was to the south and either side of Tripoli. When I looked at the map I found that the most westerly edge of my area was nearly nine hundred miles away from Siwa, measured in a straight line. I was told to take as much petrol, food and water as I could possibly carry with me, and to call in on the way at Jalo, where I could top up what I had used.

My task was to attack garrisons in the area I had been given, but I was not to take on anything too formidable and risk losing either men or vehicles, and it was important that we should get back with any information that we collected on the way. I was also to take with me on this trip Captain Sam McCoy, an officer of the 2nd Royal Lancers, who was with the Indian Desert Squadron, which was being trained in Syria.

In order to carry sufficient petrol and stores and the necessary spare tyres for a journey of this distance it became obvious to me that we would have to load the 30-cwt vehicles with at least two tons of stores. This was easy enough provided the cargo could be arranged so that the gunners could still use the machine-guns mounted on a central mounting. We would also have to travel with some care for the early part of our journey.

We had not long returned from our last operation, and there were some very busy days getting everything ready before we could set off. But we left on time and spent Christmas night of 1941 in the wreckage of the ruined hangar at Giarabub. It was not a comfortable or clean billet by any standard; but at least it gave us a little shelter from the bitingly cold wind.

Giarabub at that time had nothing whatsoever to recommend it, and I will never forget the flies and the filthy taste of the salty liquid that passed for water in the well there. It was not a happy place to spend Christmas, but an extra tot or two of rum helped us keep out the cold and did something to stir up memories of happier and more convivial Christmases.

We reached Jalo two days later, and spent only long enough there to draw up sufficient petrol, water and rations to give us a capability of covering fifteen hundred miles and staying out for twenty-five days without further replenishment.

I was not to know that I would be back in two weeks and, for various reasons beyond my control, without enough fuel to go on any further.

We drove on westward, seeing no sign of the enemy until we watched a convoy of twelve heavily loaded lorries moving north on the track from Marada to the coast on 30 December. But this was outside our area, so we had to let this temptingly easy target go unmolested.

I wrote some time later how New Year's Eve

found us cold and rather depressed, for I had discovered that a lot of our petrol was leaking and that two of the forty-gallon drums we were carrying contained diesel and not petrol. It was also drizzling and there was nothing to stir us into heralding the birth of 1942 in traditional fashion. We drank a little rum and toasted each other's health, but more in the desire to stave off the cold than in the joy of revelry.

1. David Lloyd Owen, with Titch Cave on the back of a 30-cwt
truck outside the Farouk Hotel in Siwa, November, 1941.

2. Ralph Bagnold.

3. General Sir Archibald Wavell (*centre*).

4. Bill Kennedy Shaw.

5. A study of men of the Yeomanry Patrol at Siwa by Cecil Beaton.

6. Jake Easonsmith and Guy Prendergast.

7. "The first essential was to get the trucks really well hidden" (p. 85).

8. Marble Arch.

9. Bartering tinned salmon for eggs and vegetables at Kufra.

10. 'A young, incredulous Indian soldier' (p. 101) between Brian Springford and Titch Cave.

11. *Left to right:* Shorty Barrett, Ron Tinker and Nick Wilder.

12. The aftermath of Wilder's rampage round the airfield at Barce (see p. 109).

13. The wounded being loaded into the Bombay at LG125. Popski is talking to David Lloyd Owen in front of the truck. Note the empty four-gallon petrol tins in the foreground after the contents had been poured by hand into the aircraft's tanks to enable it to return to base.

14. David Lloyd Owen *(left)* with Dick Lawson at LG125.

15. Hazards of desert travel.

The next day we had gone farther west than any LRDG Patrol had ever been by that date. But we were delayed by a rash of bad mechanical trouble caused by our heavy loads and the very bad terrain. It rained without stopping for two days, and we saw hardly any sign of the sun. This, of course, threw an extra heavy burden on Alan Denniff—my Patrol's brilliant navigator—who had to steer us by the inaccurate and slow method of using a prismatic compass.

On 3 January we decided to attack a place marked as Scemech on the map but which we knew absolutely nothing about. It poured with rain all that night, but as we were then only about ten miles from our target we sat round a fire to discuss our plans. From what I remember we decided to attack the place, simply because it was marked on the map. It was probable therefore that it might have some sort of garrison. Information about places so far to the west was very scant.

Next morning we moved off towards Scemech, but very soon ran into the most awful series of steep wadis. One could make reasonable progress along the bottom of these, if only they had all run in the right direction. Once out of them we found ourselves in a stone-belt such as I have never encountered again anywhere in the world. The whole desert as far as we could see seemed to be covered by sharp, dark boulders, dripping from the endless rain. Our target all the while lay in full view of us; and we presumably were as obvious to anyone in the small fort that we struggled to reach. We were only able to go a few hundred yards in an hour, and I just could not find a way out of this nightmare country. And it never left off raining the whole day! By dark, when I sat down with Alan Denniff to survey our position, he pointed out to me that we had moved forward no more than four miles, but had probably covered about sixteen in the process.

But what was worrying me most was the appalling rate at which we were consuming petrol. We had not been out of bottom gear all day, and had used sixteen gallons per truck. It was a cheerless night spent in the cold and wet some four hundred miles behind Rommel's front line. We were rather far from help, and our salvation depended only on ourselves.

However, the next day the rain stopped; we got out of the stone-belt and we drove merrily up the track from the west straight at the fort. Sam McCoy and I had decided that this would give us the only chance of surprise if there was any hope left of achieving any at all.

What an anticlimax it was to find the fort empty when we had come so far and with such difficulty! We learnt from the Arabs who came to greet us that a German patrol had been there that morning and that they themselves had been watching our antics for the past two days.

We left just before dark and spent another night under a raining sky. Our morale was low. But there was nothing that a good fine day would not put right, save for the problem of our petrol situation. I decided to spend the next day in sorting ourselves out, and when we rose with the sun I found a wadi where there was some very thick cover, and we tucked in there for the day.

Everything was soaked, and so we unloaded each truck completely to dry things out and to check on the number of petrol tins that had sprung leaks in the awful conditions that we had encountered. It was a depressing situation. We had lost fifteen cases of petrol through leakage, and each case contained two 4-gallon tins, so we were a hundred and twenty gallons short. On top of this there were the two 40-gallon drums which had contained diesel instead of petrol. So we were short of about two hundred gallons of petrol. This worked out at about three hundred miles' worth of petrol for each of our four trucks.

It was clear that I could not go any farther to the west, and there was no guarantee that I could get back as far as Jalo. I had only one option open to me; and that was to return. I hated having to do so after having achieved nothing, and we had suffered a lot of heartbreak. But we had to do it, and nineteen days after we had set out from Siwa, and some fifteen hundred miles later, we got back to Jalo. On the credit side was much information that we could provide about the 'going' in country where no LRDG Patrol had ever been before.

Of course, when the jerrycan type of petrol-container came into use there was never again a problem of leakage on this scale. But at that time we carried our petrol in remarkably flimsy 4-gallon tins, packed in even more flimsy wooden casing. (The latter was of tremendous use for our fires at night or to brew up at midday.)

When I got back to Jalo I found Alastair Timpson, who with his Patrol of Guardsmen had been given the sector to the east of mine. He too had had bad trouble with his trucks and with the 'going', and had had to return after destroying one heavy lorry and taking the driver prisoner.

Jake Easonsmith had been attacked from the air and then followed up by a ground patrol, and he was unable to do anything effective this time. Only Holliman and Morris had been successful. It was always exciting to hear the news of what the other Patrols had been doing, since we were never given information about this while we were out unless it would affect our own activities.

## CHAPTER 8

# The Road Watch

When I got back to Jalo I found that Frank Simms, with the other Yeomanry Patrol, had been sent up to Antelat to work with XIII Corps HQ. He was soon sent off to get information about the enemy garrison at Marada.

Frank was one of the few people I knew who really did not appear to know the meaning of fear. He seemed to regard the foe with complete disdain, and was never in the least concerned when a member of his Patrol reported to him that they were in sight. I think his men found this a little disconcerting; for they were not able to treat the opposition, either in the air or on the ground, with the utter lack of interest that Frank seemed to show.

Frank Simms set off towards Marada, and when he got reasonably near to it he realised that the only way to get the information he wanted was to enter the oasis on foot. So off he went with one of his men as escort. Unfortunately, he chanced to walk straight into an enemy position, and they were both captured. The rest of his Patrol waited for the remainder of the day, but Frank and his escort never rejoined them.

I suppose that mine was the only Patrol available, so I was sent off to take over Frank's role at XIII Corps. We had only got into Jalo three days before and I was pretty fed up, especially as I had a feeling anyhow that I might be misemployed. I arrived to find that there was nothing immediate for me to do. So I had a couple of days to spare, and time to see many old friends. Everyone assured me that they had Rommel on the run, and that he only had a light covering force facing the Eighth Army. It was at last decided that my task was to go and discover exactly where the enemy was, and in what strength to the north-west of Marada, and I was sent to the HQ of 1st Armoured Division to gather the latest news. Here I was informed that we had such an overwhelming force assembled that we would have no difficulty in sweeping through Rommel's lightly held covering screen.

It always struck me that it was incredible how little we knew of

Rommel's intentions at that time. The very next day he swept forward, and was soon scattering the Eighth Army in front of him. In three days he had reached Msus. Meanwhile I was sent off on patrol, and was told nothing until twenty-four hours later, when I was ordered by Guy Prendergast to return to Jalo.

We got there just in time, to find that our own Group HQ was moving out, since Jalo was probably not going to be safe for very much longer. However, rather than move all the way back to Siwa Guy decided to stage at a patch of palm-trees and good water called Ghetmir about twenty-five miles north-east of Jalo. It wasn't a very preposessing spot as it had no buildings of any sort—just soft white sand and great heaps of stunted palms standing desiccated amid the bareness of the place.

Rommel's quite unexpected advance went even farther than anyone foresaw, and we had to move LRDG HQ right back to Siwa again. The confusion was such that when Richard Carr, the Adjutant at that time, went to Msus with seven vehicles to collect stores he could not be warned of Rommel's rapid advance, and he arrived to find the Germans in possession. He and his whole party were taken prisoner, although seven of them did manage to escape later on that day.

It was becoming very clear that our poor old vehicles had had a dreadful hammering over the last few months, since there had been so little time for any attempt at maintenance. Guy Prendergast therefore got agreement for as many Patrols as possible to have a spell in Cairo to refit. The faithful old Fords were exchanged for Chevrolets, and we were given rather better armament with the provision of two ·5 Vickers guns, three ·303 Vickers 'K' machine-guns and one 22-mm Breda dual-purpose gun for each Patrol. This would make a considerable difference.

Alastair Timpson and I were, however, needed for one more task each before we were given a respite.

Rommel's advance had gone right across Cyrenaica and he had taken Benghazi, Barce and Derna until his front line stopped up against our position from Gazala to Bir Hacheim, where the Eighth Army had managed to make some sort of stand. Information of Rommel's further intentions still seemed to be obscure and the Army commander hoped that the LRDG could provide him with news about how much was being brought forward against him.

Alastair Timpson was sent out to report on traffic movement on the roads in the coastal area between Benghazi and Barce. He left Siwa on 9 February 1942 and took with him one of the greatest of all that curious assortment of people who became involved with working with the Arabs in the Gebel Akhdar area of Cyrenaica.

This was John Haselden, who was a cotton merchant living in Egypt before the war; and I seem to remember that his brother also lived in Egypt and was working with Barclay's Bank. John was officially employed as an adviser on Arab affairs to the Eighth Army, and he was certainly very well respected by the Arabs in Cyrenaica. He was in contact with all the local tribesmen, and through them he not only obtained a great amount of information, but he also knew where various escaped British officers and other ranks were being kept in hiding. On this trip he and Timpson between them managed to collect a lot of stragglers, and they returned to Siwa with a total of forty-seven passengers. This was no mean feat when one considers the dangers of being intercepted by enemy patrols; and the fact that the Mudir of Slonta, whom Haselden thought it would be prudent to rescue, had brought with him two of his assortment of wives, as well as one child and a collection of chickens and goats!

I was given a task which wasn't much fun, for it was a reconnaissance job in the thick of the enemy. We knew that we could do what was asked of us, but that it would mean virtually driving round a large number of enemy-occupied places and doing our best to record details of everything we saw. The Intelligence Staff at Eighth Army wanted to know all that I could find out about Msus, Antelat, Solluch, Agedabia, Grara, Saunnu and Sceleidima. Quite a tall order. I was given strict instructions that I was to avoid any form of aggressive action, and told that the way to do the job was to sit for a time across the tracks leading to these places from the coast and just watch what there was to note in the way of movement. I knew the area well enough to know that there was mighty little cover, and that I would probably not have much time or chance to linger anywhere.

Eighth Army flew a staff officer in a Lysander light aircraft, which landed by the track from Siwa to Mersa Matruh, with the latest information that they had to give me, and with one or two more details of what they expected of me.

We then turned west, and in two days we were in our area of operation. We found things just about as difficult as we had imagined, and we were kept pretty constantly on the move owing to the number of enemy vehicles and camps which we continually ran across.

All was well, however, until we were actually recognised as intruders and the enemy made up their minds to investigate us; and, of course, it was only a matter of time before this happened. We got chased by a couple of armoured cars, and it took us about twenty miles to shake off our pursuers. I don't think those poor heavily laden 30-cwt trucks of ours had ever been driven so fast.

We had sent back quite a lot of information for which Guy Prendergast gave us a warm message of thanks. He also said that he understood how tricky our task must be, and that we were not to take unnecessary risks; but he would be grateful if we could just have a look around Sceleidima before we pulled out and came back to Siwa. This we were able to do the next day, and there were so many enemy vehicles driving about all over the place that our greatest difficulty was to avoid bumping into them whichever way we steered. Somehow we got away with it by keeping pretty well on the move all the time so that we were nearly always in a cloud of dust, and we were never still for long enough for anyone to get a good look at us.

One of the things that has always stuck in my memory about that trip, and which upset us all at the time very much, was the number of perfectly fit running vehicles and tanks of our own that had been abandoned when the Eighth Army was driven back by Rommel. We even got into some of the tanks and started them up, and they were in good running order with ammunition and petrol. It appeared to us that they had been left behind by our own troops merely because they were not a fast enough method of getting away to the east. We felt very ashamed, and, of course, we knew to which units these vehicles had belonged.

It was also very galling to find that the enemy were going to make such good use of their captured booty, for we found lots of our transport collected together in small groups with all the tool kits laid out and ready for checking off.

This was altogether rather a frustrating mission, and we were very glad to get back to Siwa and to be told that we were going to Cairo to refit. For the last three months we had been behind the lines almost continuously, and not only was our kit and equipment feeling the strain but we needed to recharge our batteries ourselves. How anxious we were to get there can be gathered from the fact that we left Siwa before dawn one day and drove the whole day, before reaching Cairo at ten o'clock that night—a distance of 550 miles.

Those halcyon days in Cairo were wonderful after the dirt and filth and strain of the previous few months, and we certainly made the best of them. But there was also quite a lot to do, with the fitting out of the new vehicles and the exchange of worn-out equipment, as well as the selection of some new men to replace one or two who had had to leave us, and others whom I felt should have a change. I went to Palestine and Syria to interview the volunteers.

We were all sorry to see the last of our old Fords, as they had done us so well; but they were getting very heavy in their petrol-consumption, giving us no more than about four or five miles to the gallon over all types of country. We hoped to get almost double this amount out of the Chevrolets, and this would give us greatly increased range.

We were based in the barracks at Abbassia, and, antiquated as they probably were, we were at least able to get hot water to bath in, beds to sleep in, electric light to read by and a table at which to eat our food, rather than on our knees as we sat on an upturned petrol can.

And there was a lot of fun to be had in the bright lights of wartime Cairo. There were no shortages of food or other luxuries in the shops and there was plenty of entertainment at night. The bars and night clubs were packed with soldiers of the Commonwealth and Allies and there was no lack of female company. For here also would come the troops on leave, and they had money in their pockets.

But it wasn't quite all play during those happy weeks we spent in Cairo. There were new men to be introduced to some of our ways, and the weapons and other equipment that we had; there were modifications to be made to the new vehicles, and the better armament had to be mastered. We therefore carried out short training trips in the desert around Cairo; it was good to know, though, that we would sleep the night in a bed, and that there was no need just yet awhile to spend it on the sand.

While we were in Cairo those Patrols which had been in for a refit earlier were back again in the desert and at the end of February the LRDG started to maintain an almost continuous vigil on the main road between Tripoli and Benghazi—certainly it did so for four and a half months in the early spring and summer, and again for nearly two weeks in the autumn of 1942. During these periods the Patrols which carried out this duty—which was always known as the Road Watch—noted and reported every vehicle, its contents, every gun and every tank that moved either east up towards the front or west back to Tripoli through every twenty-four hours of every day.

Throughout these months we got away with using the same spot; and it says a lot for the soundness of its original selection by Bill Kennedy Shaw that we were able to do so. He had been to the area of Marble Arch in August 1941, and he had made careful notes of some good cover a little to the south of the coast road about thirty-five miles west of El Agheila. At this particular patch of sand Mussolini had built a triumphal arch astride the road as a permanent memorial to his great achievements as leader of the Fascist Empire. This was a well-known landmark to the men of the Eighth Army, and was always known as Marble Arch. About five miles to the east of this structure, and a few miles to the north of the Wadi Scemmer, the LRDG were able to make use of the low scrub in a wadi bed in order to hide their vehicles about two and a half miles from the road which they were to observe.

Bill Kennedy Shaw recently sent me the original sketch which he drew for the navigator of the first patrol to do this work. It records the position of the spot where the vehicles were concealed as being at Longitude 18°39′53″ E. and Latitude 30° 21′ 10″ N. It also gives details of the best line of approach and the time of day that he recommends—'best to make first approach to coast p.m. when onshore wind should be blowing'.

This sort of detail is typical of the accuracy and care with which all our Patrols were briefed before they were sent off on any task.

The way this work was actually done was as follows. Each Patrol was normally employed on the watch for up to two weeks, which was quite long enough because of the boredom and strain involved. Having taken over from those whom they were to relieve, the first essential was to get the trucks really well hidden in the wadi. This was done with the use of scrub woven into camouflage nets, and we did all we could to brush out any tracks in the sand which might be seen from the air.

About two hours before dawn the sentry on duty would wake up the two men next detailed for the watch, and they would walk down to the road to take over from the pair who were there. About three hundred yards from the road a small, low shelter had been built, and this was just high enough for us to get our heads under it in order to give us some shade from the sun in the summer.

This was on the plain, where there were a few tufts of spinifex, just sufficient to afford us very minimum cover. But it was only the absolute minimum; and it was quite impossible for the men to move at all during the hours of daylight, except to roll off their stomachs on to their backs without risking being seen, either from a vehicle on the road or by a wandering Arab, of whom there were often too many for our peace of mind.

Of the two men on the road, one would be responsible for taking notes of everything going forward to the front, and the other would record all that went the other way. It was an exacting task, for we were expected to give the details of every tank, the calibre of every gun, the classification of every vehicle, the number of troops or tonnage of stores in them and whether the truck was covered or uncovered, German or Italian, as well as the actual number on all the vehicles that went past our hiding-place.

These two men would stay down on the road until they were relieved by another pair just before dawn; and, when the first two had got back to the wadi where the Patrol was based their reports were collated and a signal would be sent to Group HQ giving a summary of all the major movement observed in the previous twenty-four hours.

It was a monotonous job for everyone. Those on the road could not move during daylight, but at night they moved about, not only to keep warm but also to get to within a few yards of the road in order to see better what was using it.

Those who were back in the wadi had very little relief from boredom. They lay under their camouflage nets, and very often under mosquito nets as well to keep the flies at bay, just reading or, perhaps, listening to the wireless. There was little else that we could do, for we could not risk moving about very much because of the constant possibility of being spotted from the air. The wireless kept us in touch with the outside world, with home or with Lord Haw-Haw. The strains of *Lili Marlene* still evoke memories of the dust, and the flies, and the heat and the movement of the traffic on the road even today. I doubt if I am alone in this reaction.

Not only was it very tedious work but it was something we all hated doing. I don't think we disliked it because of the risks involved, because these were probably no greater than on any other task. (Although if one had been caught unawares by a ground patrol in the wadi the chances of survival would have been none too good. However, it was our business not to be caught unawares.) No, I think we hated it so much because we disliked being pinned down on a sedentary job when we knew that other Patrols were doing something far more exciting.

Despite our intense aversion to the Road Watch, we did, however, understand its importance, which was very considerable. When one realises that we saw, noted and reported to our base every single vehicle and every load that passed along the only road from Tripoli to Cyrenaica one probably gains some indication of the value and importance of this information to the Intelligence Staff in Cairo. Because of the great importance of the news we were able to transmit we were very strictly prohibited from taking any action which might in any way compromise the Road Watch, at the time or in the future. This made it all the more frustrating when we had to watch motionless as we saw lorry-loads of our own men being taken away from the battle as prisoners of war.

I remember that I was doing this duty at the end of June, when Rommel had taken some eighty thousand of our men prisoner, and when his front at El Alamein was very nearly seven hundred miles to the east of us, and that I watched a convoy of them being taken back into captivity. I remember too what a lot of self-control it demanded of Titch Cave and myself to do absolutely nothing as we heard them defiant to the last and singing lustily as they were driven away past us. It was a horrible but memorable experience.

I think in retrospect that the Road Watch, as carried out during those anxious months of 1942, was enough to justify the existence of the LRDG, without even taking into consideration any of the other work that it did. I know that much of the information was often in confirmation of that obtained from other sources, but at other times it would not have been available from anywhere else.

How much the Staff at GHQ in Cairo appreciated all that the LRDG was doing is recorded in a letter sent by the Chief of the General Staff to Guy Prendergast on 7 April 1942 in which he wrote that:

> The Commander in Chief directs me to say how impressed he is with the work of the LRDG in carrying out their deep reconnaissance along the Benghazi–Tripoli road and elsewhere.
>
> The information which they are producing is of the utmost value to us at the present time.
>
> The Commander in Chief would like you to convey his appreciation to the Officers and Other Ranks concerned.

This letter was followed up by one from the Director of Military Intelligence in Cairo to Guy Prendergast, telling him that he thought the work of the LRDG was invaluable in providing the information he required for assessing the enemy's strength, and that their reports were proving to be most accurate. And at about the same time the Eighth Army Commander wrote to say how much he held the work of the LRDG in great admiration.

It was certainly good for all of us to know that a job that we so loathed was being so very generously appreciated by the Staff, whom we all thought were utterly remote and out of touch with reality, because they made such seemingly impossible demands of us. The trouble was that more often than not we gave them just what they wanted, and so they were emboldened to ask for ever more detail. I don't blame them!

We took a great deal of trouble over the accuracy of our information. We were provided with all the recognition pamphlets, and also had photographs and diagrams of enemy vehicles and tanks. These were used by the pair actually watching the road. I even remember arranging for visits to parks of captured enemy vehicles so that we should be better able to identify them.

John Olivey, with one of the two Rhodesian Patrols, had been the first to set up the watch in early March, and it was from that date that the first continuous period of surveying the road began. The advantage of keeping it under observation without break was that the experts could deduce certain trends and patterns from the facts they received.

But it was an expensive method of covering the task, as it kept three Patrols tied up at any one time. One was actually on the job; another was returning and a third was either on the way or was getting ready to relieve the party that was out. The distance from Siwa to Marble Arch was about six hundred miles, and, depending on the route taken and enemy activity at the time, this might take anything up to a week.

For the other LRDG Patrols there was to be a good deal of work linked with the Eighth Army attempts to build up sufficient strength to go back once more on the offensive. Eighth Army laid down the priorities between David Stirling's SAS men and others operating in the offensive role, and made it clear that these activities must be closely co-ordinated with those of the LRDG. The latter was told that its main task was one of reconnaissance, and that it would also be used when necessary for guiding and collecting sabotage parties.

There was plenty of variety in the tasks given to the LRDG at that period. One of the New Zealand patrols under Dick Croucher had been sent down to Zouar, in the Tibesti area of Chad Province, to act as a link between General Leclerc's Free French and HQ Eighth Army. The intention was for the French to operate against the enemy line of communication from the Fezzan, but Rommel's advance toward Egypt from Agedabia had changed all this, and these planned operations had to be abandoned. Croucher and his Patrol came back to Siwa at the beginning of March.

Gus Holliman meanwhile was taking Paddy Mayne to two satellite airfields of Benghazi at Berca where, in another lightning raid, he destroyed a further fifteen aircraft. John Olivey took David Stirling with a party of Special Boat Section men under David Sutherland to Benghazi, where they were to raid the airfield at Benina and damage shipping in the harbour. Once again David had no success, and Sutherland was wounded when the car in which he was travelling went over a thermos bomb and he had to be evacuated to Siwa. However, on his way back from Benghazi, David Stirling destroyed five aircraft in their hangars on the airfield at Benina.

The early summer months of 1942 were becoming very frustrating, for the conflicting demands of the many organisations which were operating behind the lines all seemed to react on the LRDG, and its continued ability to carry out its all-important task of reconnaissance. All of these bodies found it necessary to come to Siwa to seek assistance of one sort or another from the LRDG, and Guy Prendergast found this very distracting.

He knew that the LRDG could undertake every reasonable task given to it, and he knew that Stirling's SAS had a mass of targets with which they could cope, provided their operations were tied up with those of the LRDG. But there was a proliferation of other outfits—there were Commandos, Agent organisations, pseudo-Germans in Nazi uniform working for us, people running escape organisations for collection of our own prisoners or shot-down airmen. All these wanted advice and assistance.

So it was decided at the end of April that all activities behind the lines in Cyrenaica and Tripolitania should be co-ordinated by Guy Prendergast, and even the operations of the various clandestine agents would be controlled by him while they were actually behind the lines. This, of course, made eminent sense; and if the arrangement had worked in practice much of the confusion that arose later on would have been avoided. But it did not work, I believe, because of the personalities involved.

Guy, being a shy and retiring personality, did not want any expansion of his responsibilities, for this would inevitably mean his losing actual control of his LRDG at Siwa while he was sorting out the inefficiencies and the requirements of some of the other outfits (which he thought were quite unnecessary anyway). And then David Stirling was not the kind of man who would willingly work under someone without his own thrustful and persuasive powers. He was used to dealing direct with the Army Commander or his Chief of Staff, and he felt that his ideas could only be sold by himself, and had no chance of acceptance if they were passed on at second hand.

David Stirling was young and impetuous, with some wild ideas among his brilliant ones. His extrovert personality was very attractive, and helped to make him so convincing. But Guy was none of these things, and nor did he want to be. All he wanted was to control the LRDG, without any interference, in the careful and planned technique that he knew to be the least liable to chance.

David Stirling gambled that his share of good luck would be greater than that of the enemy because of the surprise he would achieve. He was also naturally impatient with long-term reconnaissance missions, which might inhibit the spectacular results that might be his if only the LRDG's Road Watch wasn't in the way. He always put the killing of Germans before every other consideration, and greatly did we admire him for it. But it did not always make our life easier; and because I had never taken out a party under the dynamic leadership of Stirling, Mayne or Fraser I had not experienced the thrill of being party to one of their magnificent raids.

The atmosphere cannot have been made any easier when it was laid down that the obtaining of information had absolute priority, and that the disruption of the enemy's supplies was on no account to be allowed to interfere with that aim. The object was to preserve the inviolability of the Road Watch areas by avoiding any unnecessary searches in parts where they were concealed. These restrictions, of course, also had an effect on our own aggressive operations, for none of the Patrols could be expected to operate for ever on silent and unobserved tasks without giving them some alleviation from the constant tensions of such action. They must be allowed every so often to have a bit of a 'beat-up'.

I recall how we spent a lot of time in Siwa sitting round a rough wooden table in the Farouk Hotel (the word 'Hotel' being a euphemism in the case of this mud-built apology for a tavern)—Alastair Timpson, Jake Easonsmith, John Olivey and others—trying to work out an effective method of ensuring an enemy vehicle's destruction without giving away the position of those responsible for the deed.

Somehow some form of explosive/incendiary device had to be introduced into a lorry without this being seen, and with a timing mechanism that would cause it to ignite some distance away from where this had been planted.

We sat round like a lot of Guy Fawkes conspirators drawing up dark, improbable plots. How were we to make quite certain that we could get the contrivance on to the truck without it being seen by anyone on the back of it? And how were we ourselves to avoid being seen?

We thought of all sorts of magnetic devices which would be gathered off the road as the lorries passed over them. We even experimented with releasing a bomb, from a string stretched across the road to a telegraph pole, on to the roof of a covered lorry as it went by. Mostly the snag always was to slow the vehicle down sufficiently; and in the end we hit upon an idea which Alastair Timpson and his Guardsmen rehearsed during many nights of practice.

Alastair left Siwa on 8 May to try out the method that he had perfected and which needed the extra equipment of four 44-gallon petrol drums and two long poles, together with notices in German saying, 'BEWARE, ROAD UP!' and some red hurricane lamps. These were to be used to slow the transport down so that the hidden men could appear from the ditch in the dark. One of them would then lob a bomb into the back of the vehicle, provided this was open.

Alastair had had a number of suitable bomb-mixtures made up in Italian haversacks from which a time-pencil stuck out, and this could be set burning before it was popped into a lorry. These were two-pound mixtures of high-explosive and an incendiary substance fixed to small tins of petrol, and had proved thoroughly potent in rehearsal. The hope was that the various different lengths of fuse, set to go off after more than half an hour, would create inexplicable explosions at varying distances from Marble Arch, since Alastair was to operate some twenty miles to the west of it; and he would only interfere with vehicles going towards Tripoli. On no account could the Road Watch be compromised.

The whole idea was thoroughly ingenious, if perhaps a trifle Heath Robinson.

Timpson's Patrol had bad luck from the start, and was soon having trouble with its tyres, which were blowing out at a rate previously never experienced. Soon they realised that if this continued they would never get to their target area. However, they were saved by making a diversion to one of their trucks that had been abandoned four months before and some eighty miles away. From this vehicle they recovered five reasonable tyres.

After they had come to within striking distance of the road, Alastair sent two men down to find a suitable spot for their ploy. They found exactly what was wanted—a place with a heap of road metal for repairs and a bank and a ditch at the side of the road, with a few bushes to give just a little cover. Alastair decided to set an ambush that night, which was the one on which Nick Wilder and a Patrol of New Zealanders also planned to strike similarly about 150 miles to the east.

At dusk Alastair took one truck with six men to a spot about 150 yards from the pile of road material. He left two men with this to man the machine-guns, and two others were concealed in order to give him and the remaining men any close support that might be necessary. When there was a lull in the traffic he put the barrels round the stones, which he had shovelled over the roadway, and then he put the red lamps and signs in position. The first lorries that came along simply would not slow down, so he had to make some adjustments to his road-repair arrangements. He then found that, if there was more than one vehicle he could not avoid the headlights of those following, and so could not move from behind the barrels. If he lay concealed on the bank he found that the drivers would move on so quickly after the obstacle that he could not get out of hiding before the lorry had gone out of his reach.

By two in the morning only one bomb had been satisfactorily planted, and Alastair decided to try another method. He reckoned that he would chase enemy vehicles, and that an intrepid man on his own bonnet would lob bombs into their rears.

The first vehicle that came along was a lorry and trailer which they followed, only to catch it up halted at their own road block. Here they found two very frightened Italians, who explained that they had been on tow, and that this had broken as the towing lorry had swerved round the obstruction. A curious conversation ensued during which Alastair tried in his best Italian to explain that he would willingly have helped if only he had not been in such a tearing hurry.

The night was fading, and Alastair decided that as there were some miles to go to rejoin the rest of his Patrol he would give the whole project up till the next night. On the way they had a flat tyre in their only truck, and having no spare had to drive for three or four miles off the road in low gear and then go off on foot to seek help from the others.

What a frustrating night they had lived through! To add to their discomfiture they were then attacked by a ground patrol at about lunchtime, and one Guardsman was killed while they were getting the camouflage off their vehicles. The enemy had about twenty-four men, and they were reasonably resolute Italians, who caused Alastair some difficulty in extricating his trucks from the wadi where they had been hiding. However, he got them out, and, in broad daylight, found some sort of cover about sixty-five miles away where they buried Guardsman Matthews.

That night Alastair got in touch with Siwa and sought permission to attack the road again farther to the west. This he was given leave to do some hundred miles to the west.

After some mechanical trouble Alastair eventually found a suitable target—a road-house with vehicles parked all around it. This he dealt with in the normal manner, with his gunners opening up with everything they possessed in the fire-power line together with some of his prepared bombs and hand grenades which they threw around. They left a nasty mess, and some hours later the mines and time-bombs they had deposited also began to go off.

Before the attack Alastair had had to leave one of his trucks—which had no brakes—with two men, and there then followed a very tiresome misunderstanding which delayed his return to Siwa for even longer. When these two men heard the rest of their Patrol coming back they somehow mistook them for the enemy, and they ran off rapidly into the desert. In their haste they had only managed to grab a quarter of a water-bottle between them. They were very lucky that Alastair found them two days later, when they had only gone forty-five miles. It was now 25 May, and the weather was very hot.

Already Alastair was on half-rations, and his water-containers had leaked. He now found himself with only one and a half gallons of water per man for the return journey of six hundred miles. This spurred them on, and they even enjoyed the foul water at Giarabub.

Nick Wilder and his New Zealanders had the same plan as Timpson, but Wilder's orders were that if the project with the barrels and road-repair obstruction failed to work he was to attack traffic wherever he could find it in his allocated area. He had a great deal of trouble avoiding suspicious inhabitants on the way, but when he got to the road he had the same sort of problem getting the enemy to slow down so that he could plant his bombs.

He got impatient with this idea, and blasted into one truck with gunfire, before blowing it up with bombs. But he found no other worth-while target, and returned disappointed to Siwa.

The same day that Alastair Timpson and Nick Wilder left Siwa to try out their new way of destroying enemy traffic I was sent off on what looked to me to be a really thrilling job. We were to take a party of agents up to Tarhuna, which is about forty miles to the south-east of Tripoli. When we had dropped them, and given them time to get clear of the place, I was told that I could get stuck in to a big transport depot near there and create as much havoc as I possibly could. We worked out the distance on the map, and found that it was about nine hundred miles out, and that I would thus have to take petrol for a round trip of nearly two thousand miles. This would take us once again farther to the west than any other LRDG Patrol had ever been.

The day before we left the party of agents arrived. They did not look prepossessing, and I took an instant dislike to the leader of the party (as I believe he did to me). He was an Italian civilian prisoner who professed to be an anti-Fascist, and who had been prepared for special work in Tripoli. The other two members of this motley crew were a Sudanese wireless operator, who I always suspected had little idea what he had got himself involved in, and a young well-to-do Libyan, who was to act as the guide for the party from Tarhuna onward to Tripoli.

With the distance we had to cover, we found that we had a very heavy load to take with us. We therefore had six trucks, and there were fifteen spare tyres. We had the same trouble as Alastair Timpson with our tyres, and I can only conclude that the LRDG had come upon a very poor batch of this particular make of tyre. I have told the story in some detail in a previous book on the subject; and it was one of considerable heartbreak and of double dealing by the unpleasant little Italian with whom I had been saddled.

I had to give up the attempt to get to Tripoli, and soon after I had been told by Guy Prendergast to return to Siwa we mislaid our Italian agent for an hour or two while he attempted to reach his compatriots in Marada. We had decided that we must turn back when we had spent the night about twenty miles to the north-east of Marada, where there was an Italian garrison. We eventually caught up with this unattractive character, and I managed to persuade his sponsors that he should be interned again until the end of the war.

Some twenty-six years later, when I was staying with the British Ambassador in Tripoli, he kindly invited a very charming and polished Libyan civil servant to meet me at the British Embassy. This man had said that he had had dealings with the LRDG in 1942. I got this very pleasant man to tell me of his connection, and he recounted the story of how he had been taken from Siwa by a party of Desert Group men under a young captain, whose name he could not remember. He then told me all about how the Italian whom he was to take from Tarhuna to Tripoli had decided to return to his own side near Marada.

I let him go on with his story, pressing him all the while for details; and only when he had got to the end did I tell him who I was. It was a fascinating reunion, and I was very thrilled to meet up once again with that splendid Libyan. I think he told me that he had only been eighteen at the time and I was full of admiration for his willingness to help the Allies in those far-off days.

While we were away on this abortive journey Robin Gurdon—who had taken over one of the two Guards Patrols from Tony Hay after his capture—took David Stirling together with Fitzroy Maclean, Randolph Churchill and Gordon Alston to Benghazi once again. David had with him four other ranks (among them were Cooper and Seekings, who accompanied him on most of his major raids), and his intention was to sink what shipping he could get at in the harbour.

Fitzroy Maclean gives an excellent account of this operation in his book *Eastern Approaches*, and he tells how Robin Gurdon took the SAS party—who had with them a Ford Utility staff car—to within a reasonable distance of the town. On the way they met Nick Wilder and his Patrol. Nick was able to give the others his up-to-date news, having been to the main road in his attempt to disrupt traffic along it.

Fitzroy describes vividly how David Stirling then drove his party into Benghazi in the British staff car, and how they spent a vast amount of time trying to get one of their two collapsible boats to inflate, but after a while found that it had been irreparably damaged on the way from Siwa. David therefore sent Fitzroy back for the second boat, which he had left in the car outside the harbour. This he reached, then decided that it would be quicker to rejoin Stirling if he went through the main entrance, rather than struggle with his boat to get through the barbed wire as they had done on the way in before.

After a quite whimsical encounter with the corporal in charge of the guard—who was sternly reprimanded by Fitzroy for the ineffectiveness of his team of Italian sentries—the latter continued on to join Stirling, but not until he had first directed the guard commander in his best German to be more careful in future when he saw strangers about carrying loads, which might well have been bombs!

It was beginning by then to get light, as all this had taken some time, so Stirling made his way back to the car. He decided that the only thing to do was to find a suitable place to hide the car and themselves for the day. They had just the luck they hoped for, and found an empty garage with an unoccupied flat above it, where they spent a pretty anxious day, since they soon discovered that on the other side of the street there was a German HQ of some sort.

Stirling determined to have another attempt that evening, but by some ill chance, a burning oil-tanker lit up the whole area of the harbour, and this deprived them of the cover of darkness. So he wisely decided not to tempt the gods any longer, and to get out of Benghazi while the going was good. They drove out once again through the road-block near Benina, and at the airfield near by blew up some machinery *en passant*.

While David and his remarkable team had been in Benghazi Robin Gurdon—who had one or two of David's men with him—went off down to the railway between Benghazi and Barce, and they placed a forty-pound charge of explosive under the line. This was given a pressure fuse designed to explode when the next train passed along that way. It was later thought that this charge was discovered and lifted before it could do the hoped-for damage.

I always thought that this was one of David Stirling's more brazenly daring schemes; and the fact that a Member of Parliament (Maclean) and the son of the Prime Minister went along with him in a British staff car to spend the whole of one night and the following day in the capital of Cyrenaica, two hundred miles behind the enemy front line, reads far more like fiction. But I remember so well hearing those three men talk of their extraordinary experience in the HQ Mess of the LRDG at the Guest House in Siwa, the day they returned there on 26 May 1942.

They had obviously enjoyed every moment of the venture, despite the anxieties and the ill luck that dogged them. I think they were most pleased with the way that Fitzroy had teased the unfortunate Italian guard commander responsible for security at Benghazi Harbour. We had such fun laughing over this, and the story Randolph told of how they had very nearly been caught in the flat where they spent the day. Kennedy Shaw, who was in the Mess at the time, records that incident as follows:

> Till evening they were undisturbed. Then at dusk were heard footsteps on the stairs, slow and unsteady. They neared the top and the party gathered themselves for a fight. Churchill, with a week's beard and a week since his last wash, looked out—into the face of a drunken Italian sailor, intent on loot or rape. In a moment the man was at the foot of the steps, running for his life.

Kennedy Shaw finished his account with the words that

> I write this in Tripoli on 21st May 1943, with a wish that I am afraid is never likely to be realised. It is that one day Mussolini may have this chapter read to him and learn that a year ago tonight the son of England's Prime Minister spent thirty hours in his Cyrenaican capital.

The day after I heard these men tell their tale Rommel resumed the offensive against the Gazala line.

# CHAPTER 9

# Siwa becomes Untenable

At the end of May 1942 Guy Prendergast was given instructions for future operations. These included the maintenance of the Marble Arch Road Watch and a second minor one that had been started at the end of April on the track from Mechili to Msus. He was also given details for more raids by the SAS on landing-grounds at Berca, Benina and Barce.

The secondary Road Watch on the track between Mechili and Msus was the next task given to the Yeomanry Patrol which I was commanding. In connection with it I first met a character who later created for himself quite a considerable reputation, based more, I think, on his strange behaviour than on anything that he ever achieved.

This was Vladimir Peniakoff, who because of the difficulty of pronouncing his name very soon became known to all of us as Popski. At this time he was being used as an agent working with the Senussi in the Gebel Akhdar, gathering information of what was going on in the area.

He had lived in Egypt before the war, and knew the language and the customs of the people. He was certainly a colourful character, and his personal courage was beyond question; but I found he had such a muddled mind that I am afraid I became very impatient with him and his procrastination. I suppose that he had become very Arab in his ways, and so he never found it necessary to get a move on or bother about time. Unfortunately, I had a deadline to keep, and I was not best pleased when I was instructed to take him, with fourteen mangy-looking Arabs together with six tons of stores, to Mechili on my way to the Road Watch.

Somehow I got Popski roughly to where he wanted to be left—but he was not even sure of where that was; and I eventually had to leave him in the desert, as I could not go on wasting time driving around looking for someone who either knew him or was willing to lead him to where he thought he wanted to go. In the end all worked out happily, and Popski stayed in the Gebel until August, when another of our Patrols picked him up and took him back to Siwa.

I went on to do my Road Watch duty for ten days, and it was only memorable for one incongruous and unforgettable reason; and that was the teeming abundance of flies. Because of the excellent thick cover among the large bushes where we could completely conceal our trucks it was apparent that this spot had been used by both sides. As a result there was a mass of litter, filth and tins, which the jackals had dug up—assuming that the majority of them had ever been buried at all. Hence the flies!

We were so used to the comparative cleanliness of the inner desert, and had never seen a plague like this. The result was that we just could not eat any food during the hours of daylight, for it was impossible to get a bite without a mouthful of flies as well. We thus had to have breakfast before dawn; and then when the sun went down, and the flies disappeared with it, we would come out from under our mosquito nets where we had been forced to stay all day. We were quite hungry by then, and glad of an opportunity to stretch our legs.

Those ten days were a severe test of our nerves, and the fact that none of us got seriously on anyone else's says quite a lot for everyone's self-control. There was nothing that we could do all day except sleep or read. None of us was sorry when Alastair Timpson came to take over from us. To make the boredom even more acute, we had not had one enemy vehicle to observe during the whole ten days we were there.

While we were having such a tediously uncomfortable time some of the others were really having fun. Nick Wilder, with two Patrols of New Zealanders, was sent to attack transport on the road between Benghazi and Agedabia, for this would not disturb either Road Watch. On the night chosen he reached the road around midnight, and he successfully ambushed an enemy party of trucks. There were twenty-five to thirty of the enemy in the vehicles, and the majority of these must have been killed in the furious bursts of machine-gun fire which Wilder's men poured into them. The trucks were left blazing. He then drove on a short way and found a car-park, from which the drivers had apparently fled when they heard him coming, and he destroyed everything he found there. He then lay concealed for a couple of days before going on down again to the road. Unfortunately, he ran into an enemy patrol, but he had such superior fire-power that he had very quickly killed two Italians and taken five of them prisoner.

A few days later Robin Gurdon was taking Stirling and Mayne to Benghazi again, only twelve days since they had returned from there. What a tireless, restless couple those two were! On the way up David Stirling's Ford staff-car was blown up on a thermos bomb, so he and his crew had to be carried in one of Gurdon's vehicles. A night or two later they got into the hangars at Benina to the east of Benghazi. They left three of these burning, and put time bombs on five aircraft and on a number of crated aircraft engines.

Mayne had rotten luck, for he had got to the landing-ground at Berca and was about to go in to leave his bombs when the RAF appeared and began dropping bombs and lighting the whole place up with flares. This, of course, made his task impossible, and he was only able to destroy one aircraft before he decided that it was just not on for that night. He made his way back to Robin Gurdon, where Stirling had already arrived.

After a short rest Stirling decided to go and have one more crack at the harbour in Benghazi, and so they drove brazenly along the road towards it, passing on the way the still smouldering hangars at Benina. Also near there was the familiar road block which they had had to negotiate previously.

This time there were Germans on duty. I suppose someone had decided that since the Italians had been so careless in the past in letting the British drive in unheeded proper sentries must be posted to guard the outskirts of Benghazi. When they were stopped with the bar across the road it therefore took one of Stirling's German-speaking men quite a time to plead that surely it wasn't necessary to waste time asking for identity cards and passwords when they had been driving all day and night from the front at Gazala?

Stirling later told Kennedy Shaw that he could see the thought processes on the face of the German NCO in the light shining out from the guard-house. Was the man going to press his doubts and demand identification, or would he grasp the situation and know that if he did he would probably only have a few seconds to live? In the event he saw little future in single-handed heroics in the face of the very heavily armed enemy, and decided to lift the barrier for Stirling and his men to drive through.

On the way to the harbour David saw a number of easy targets, and decided that there was no point in chancing his arm any further. He drove around just shooting up everything that he saw, and inflicted a lot of damage before making his way back to rendezvous with Gurdon.

At dawn, after an eventful night, he reached the escarpment, where he halted for some purpose. For some inexplicable reason the rough journey away from Benghazi had activated one of his time pencils, and one of the men on the back of the truck heard the click of this. He had just enough time to give a few seconds' warning of an impending explosion. They only just managed to leap for their lives before the truck with its very explosive load of petrol, ammunition and bombs disintegrated into the air. Some people certainly seemed to lead charmed lives!

David was now without a truck, and so he and his men walked off and found some locals who hid them in a cave while they went to contact Gurdon. The latter meanwhile had not wasted his time, and had planted another heavy load of explosive on the railway. He saw this blow up from a distance on his way to meet Stirling.

These attacks by the SAS on airfields at about this time were designed, among other things, to reduce the pressure on Malta. Malta had been under attack for a long time, but these attacks had been stepped up in the summer, and the supply situation was becoming dangerously stretched. There was a big relief convoy hoping to get through to the island, and anything that could be done to reduce the number and effectiveness of the enemy's aircraft would obviously help, if only in a small way.

A Patrol under Alastair Guild with New Zealanders therefore took out a party of Free French SAS. To help them they also had a team of the Special Interrogation Group under Captain Buck. These were mainly Palestinian Jews of German extraction who were used for certain selected missions. They would wear German uniforms, and were thought to be trustworthy and anti-Nazi. But, of course, with the variety of organisations that had grown up in the Middle East it is not surprising that some mistakes were made.

The targets for this party were the landing-grounds at Derna and at Martuba, to the south of Derna. Somehow the raiding force was betrayed by one of the Palestinian group, and the French party of fourteen were all captured or killed, though not before they had first destroyed twenty aircraft. This was some slight compensation for their loss.

On the coast the main battle was not going too well. The French at Bir Hacheim fought magnificently, but had to be withdrawn before the garrison could be isolated and overrun. There was then some very heavy fighting round 'Knightsbridge'. On 17 June the Army Commander decided to pull back his main forces towards the Egyptian frontier, leaving once more a garrison to hold Tobruk.

Nothing, however, was stopping Rommel, and he swept forward to capture Tobruk on 21 June, and twenty-five thousand of our troops were taken prisoner. Sollum followed, and then Mersa Matruh, before Auchinleck was able to halt this disastrous rout of the Allied army. This was not until the last day of June 1942 when the Eighth Army reached the last-ditch position at El Alamein.

This great withdrawal on the coast had an obvious effect on the LRDG's continued use of Siwa as a base. It became untenable; and I think everyone was sad to leave that lovely oasis, which had been a wonderful forward base for the LRDG since the early part of 1941. It wasn't, perhaps, the most healthy place in Libya, but it had an abundant supply of sweet water and plenty of palm-trees to give some shelter and shade, as well as a few buildings. These we were able to commandeer for essential stores, a medical post and for Group HQ. Without Siwa we would find it very difficult to continue our uninterrupted patrolling deep to the west.

But there was no alternative. Guy Prendergast had to move first towards the coast near Alexandria until finally coming to rest near the Fayoum Oasis south of Cairo. During these moves there was never any break in communication with those Patrols that were still out on various tasks.

John Olivey was at Marble Arch on the Road Watch; and when one remembers that this was nearly eight hundred miles from Cairo it gives some idea of the problems involved at that time. He was to be relieved by myself and the Yeomanry Patrol, which reached Marble Arch on 25 June. And Alastair Guild was to be sent up to take over from me when I had done my stint on the watch.

As I recall those days I remember particularly how absolutely unperturbed John Olivey was. He was one of the finest of the Patrol commanders, and nothing ever seemed to worry him. The more fraught things became the more he chuckled; and he was not in the least concerned by the defeat of the Eighth Army. His words that day when I met him were typical of his carefree approach to life.

'Oh,' he said, 'don't you worry; they'll be back again in time. Does them good to go back for a bit. It encourages them to go forward.'

'Yes, maybe it does. But they have gone a bit far this time, John.'

'They've got all the blasted way to go to Rhodesia yet. Don't you worry. They'll be back.'

And with that he left me, to return to Kufra rather than to Siwa, from whence he had set out.

I had an uneventful time at Marble Arch, and with the changed circumstances I also returned to Kufra, since my original orders for aggressive operations after my time on watch had been cancelled. I was to have been allowed to go on some hundred and fifty miles to the west, but now I was given a free hand to attack transport on the main road as much as I could, and for as long as my supplies lasted.

Those summer months of 1942 were very hot, and on the way to the Road Watch I had my only experience of what the French knew as *cafard*, or desert madness. I have always blamed myself for having driven my chaps to the extent that I did, and I ought to have recognised this earlier. But I failed to do so.

Because of the uncertainty of when we might be able to replenish our water ration, I had cut everyone down to the minimum ration of water—under a gallon a day for all purposes. It was just not enough. When we were lying up in some sparse cover after being attacked from the air I remember how some of us, in a futile and forlorn hope of finding water, dug frantically in some darker-coloured sand. This ought to have been a signal to me.

Next day we ran into some bad dunes and got ourselves a bit stuck, to the extent that we had to dig some trucks out. We were wholly exhausted by this, and as it was midday, and the sun was too high to give a shadow of the needle on the sun compass, we stopped and lay pretty dead-beat under the trucks for shade.

The temperature was 120°F; and the metal on the trucks was burning hot, and the glare of the sun on the light-coloured sand was almost blinding. It was then that one of the men came to me and asked me to go and have a look at one of the others. The speaker thought that his friend was staring vacantly and was obviously not well. But as I looked at the speaker I noticed that he too was staring and had a curiously wild look in his eyes. Soon I found that there were others who had this same strange, glassy look of bewilderment, and I knew then that I had driven the men too far. Thank goodness that I decided to rest for the remainder of that day and to give out just a little extra water. If I had not done so we would have had some very sick men and it would have been quite a problem to evacuate any serious case, with Siwa no longer available as a base.

It was in the third week of July that the Road Watch was at last called off, having been kept up continuously by the LRDG from 2 March 1942. Now that Tobruk was available to Rommel, and Benghazi was safer from air attack, the decreased importance to him of Tripoli and its great distance from El Alamein meant that little of any significance would be passing by Marble Arch until things changed once again.

I have a feeling that no military historian will in the future dissent from the view that the detailed and accurate intelligence wirelessed back from the road at Marble Arch was of a value to GHQ in Cairo quite out of proportion to the very small cost in men, vehicles and material needed to maintain it.

I for one was certainly not sorry when the Road Watch ceased, as I had done two watches running. But the Staff in Cairo missed the information that we had been sending for so long, and they decided that they wanted another watch set up between Tobruk and Bardia. I suppose mine was the only Patrol available, and I was not particularly amused when I was detailed to set off from Kufra to find a suitable site for the watch. As it turned out, I was quite unable to find a spot where the vehicles could remain unseen, and where one Patrol could be relieved by another, all within walking distance of the road; without this it would be impossible to maintain the Watch continuously, which was vital.

I spent a day or two vainly searching the desert, and was just about to try again when I received a signal ordering me to try to find the crew of an RAF Blenheim which was thought to have come down about thirty-five miles south-east of Tobruk. I never found them, but we did pick up and rescue a young, incredulous Indian soldier who had escaped from prison camp in Tobruk, and whom we found wandering in the desert with mighty little food and water. He was a lucky man indeed!

We were then ordered to return to the Fayoum, moving via the Qattara Depression. This was the so-called 'impassable' barrier on which the southern flank of the Eighth Army hinged. I had not been there, but I had never been convinced that this depression was impenetrable. I therefore took the trouble to cross it on as wide a front as it was possible to cover with only four vehicles.

We got very badly stuck in one place; but this was a perfectly obvious salt marsh, which I would have avoided under normal conditions. However, we were in holiday mood; we were nearly back to the Nile, and we had fun having a race across this splendid flat-looking stretch!

Otherwise the going across the Qattara Depression was as good as it was anywhere else that I had driven in the desert, and I felt strongly enough about this to go to the Intelligence Staff in Cairo and guarantee to them that I would be able to lead a Brigade Group of all arms across it, and thus outflank Rommel's position at Alamein. But nobody would believe me. They had many more important things on their mind, I suppose.

Yet on my way across it I had met Tony Browne leading an Eighth Army Patrol with just that idea in mind. However, he was instructed to take a different route to mine, and he found that this was indeed not passable to any large number of tanks and vehicles.

The next few weeks were mainly occupied with the support of some extremely difficult tasks which Stirling had undertaken in order to do as much damage as possible to Rommel's communication behind his front at Alamein and to his forward airfields. The two Guards Patrols under Timpson and Gurdon and the Yeomanry Patrol under Anthony Hunter were allotted to help guide the SAS parties and to provide their communications.

The SAS had by then obtained their own transport in the form of American GP's—the magnificent Jeep, or General Purpose light vehicle. These were wonderfully suitable for the purpose, since they were fast, low in silhouette, remarkably manœuvrable and excellent through the desert. Stirling armed them with pairs of Vickers K Guns, which had originally been designed as an aircraft weapon but which were now obsolete for the RAF, so that there were plenty available.

The operations that David carried out were under particularly adverse conditions as they were so often seen by enemy air and ground patrols. Yet they were constantly cutting water-pipe lines, and destroying planes and parked vehicles whenever they could find them. It was the enemy aircraft that gave our people the greatest trouble and Anthony Hunter had two trucks destroyed on consecutive days.

Then Robin Gurdon, who was escorting a party of the SAS to raid a landing-ground on the coast at Fuka, ran into trouble. On the way there in the late evening his Patrol was caught by three Italian Macchi aircraft. Gurdon tried the trick of waving to the pilots, but they were not taken in and turned to attack. His own truck would not start, and so he ran across to one of the others, and as he did so was mortally wounded by cannon and machine-gun fire. The driver was also wounded, and the truck burst into flames. Robin Gurdon, gallant to the end, ordered his men to continue with their tasks and to attack the airfield as originally planned. But they decided among themselves to do all they could to get him back to the doctor with Stirling at his base. They drove all night with the two wounded men, but Robin died before he could reach help. Guardsman Murray, the driver, made a slow recovery.

Robin Gurdon's death was a severe loss to the LRDG, for he was a wonderful and fearless leader of men and one to whom everyone was immensely attracted. He had great charm, and perfect manners, and always seemed to me to be so confident and self-possessed.

Nick Wilder and his New Zealanders had come up to join Stirling, and while they were involved with him in attacks on landing-grounds near Mersa Matruh, Nick lost a truck in a minefield. Next morning they were attacked by aircraft, and shot one of them down, while four trucks full of enemy infantry joined in the fray. Wisely Nick got out of it, as he only had three trucks left with which to fight. But his losses were unimportant compared to those of the enemy, for between them Wilder and Stirling had destroyed thirty-six aircraft and Nick had collected four German prisoners on the way.

The Germans had with them a light aircraft to direct the ground troops on to our men and this they used to fly around, keeping an eye on Wilder, then landing to pass on the information. Wilder had damned sharp eyes too, and the Fieseler Storch did this just once too often. While it was on the ground, and the crew away from it, Nick quickly cut them off from their aircraft, which he then burnt!

These remarkable operations could not be sustained without replenishment and Kennedy Shaw recalls how David sent back a request in the middle of July for 1,500 gallons of petrol, 5,000 rounds of ammunition, 300 grenades, rations, oil, etc. He needed this urgently if he was to continue his raids. So the LRDG Heavy Section led by Philip Arnold took it in four 3-tonners to where Stirling wanted it.

Soon after this David and his men were withdrawn to get ready for the next series of raids. He had had some spectacular success, but it is my opinion that from the moment he began to get his own transport, and become independent of the LRDG, he began to lose his effectiveness, because he necessarily had to concern himself with the mechanics of administration. David Stirling was a magnificent fighting leader, but the tedious business of worrying where the food, the ammunition, the communications, the fuel and water were to come from was something with which he did not want to concern himself. Up till then the LRDG had done all that for him.

# CHAPTER 10

# Benghazi, Barce and Tobruk: Raids in September 1942

I had been lucky, and after we came back through the Qattara Depression I had been sent with my Patrol on a short period of leave to Cairo, which proved to be a very welcome break before the next adventure.

The situation at El Alamein was static, with both sides building up their strength for further advances, with most of Rommel's supplies coming through the harbours at Tobruk and Benghazi. Tripoli was too far away.

After the recent operations involving the SAS, the LRDG and other organisations behind the lines there had been yet another meeting at GHQ in Cairo to try once more to sort out how best to control and co-ordinate the varying interests, and thus prevent unnecessary clashes of aims.

Although little concrete came out of this conference, it was at about this time that Shan Hackett became the staff officer responsible for all such activities. He was, as his subsequent career testifies, a brilliant regular cavalry officer with a personality strong enough to control David Stirling's wilder ideas and to steer them along profitable lines. He was also a great friend of the LRDG, and he understood how these two units might best be employed.

Shan Hackett was responsible for the detailed execution of a major effort being planned to disrupt Rommel's main supply ports of Benghazi and Tobruk, as well as a raid against the airfield at Barce. To these was also added a plot for the Sudan Defence Force—on garrison duties in Kufra—to be allowed to sally forth and to take Jalo.

It was clear that Rommel was about to make another move, and it was felt that if these four raids could be successfully carried out at the same time it might push him seriously off balance. I know that Haselden always felt that his plans for the Tobruk raid might have had a far better chance of success if so many others had not been involved.

Philip Warner in his book *The Special Air Service* claims that Stirling felt that he was being drawn into an operation which was quite different to his normal role, and which was full of risks which he could not properly calculate. And I know that Guy Prendergast always thought that the size of the operation, as it was ultimately launched, was far too big, and involved too many people, to ensure essential security. As a minor participant, I was horrified how unwieldy the whole thing had become by the time it all took place.

If there were all these misgivings I am not sure why they were not voiced. Or, if anyone did speak up against the overall concept, why the raids eventually went ahead? I am sure that without Shan Hackett they would have been an even bigger fiasco than they unhappily turned out to be.

The plan as finally envisaged was for Stirling's SAS, with two Rhodesian Patrols of the LRDG, to attack the harbour at Benghazi, where he would sink shipping and destroy oil-storage tanks, as well as carry out an attack on the airfield at Benina.

At Tobruk, John Haselden was to lead a force of Commandos, Gunners and Engineers to capture the harbour in order to allow reinforcements to be landed from the sea. The latter would then destroy the big underground fuel-storage tanks, ransack the two airfields and their aircraft and finally release the large number of British prisoners held there before withdrawing by sea, having made the harbour generally unusable. My Patrol of Yeomanry was to guide Haselden's party there, and to carry out various other tasks.

The plan for Barce was a purely LRDG operation under Jake Easonsmith. Nick Wilder and Alastair Timpson's Patrols were to comprise his force, together with Popski and two of his Arabs who were attached to Jake.

The Sudan Defence Force was given the job of taking Jalo from Kufra, and Anthony Hunter with the other Yeomanry Patrol was to go with them. The idea was that Jalo could then be used by David Stirling for further raids into the Gebel area.

The date selected as D-Day for all these actions was 13 September 1942, except for the attack on Jalo, which was to take place four days later. Because of the Royal Navy's involvement in the Tobruk raid it was decided to set up a Combined Staff HQ in Alexandria, where the C.-in-C. Mediterranean and the Air Officer Commanding, together with the Director of Military Operations (Brigadier George Davy) had gathered. Guy Prendergast also moved in to be with these commanders.

Apart from the troops to be taken to Tobruk from Alexandria by the Royal Navy, and those concerned with Jake Easonsmith's raid on Barce, all the others were being assembled in Kufra. And it was very clear to me when I arrived there from the Fayoum at the end of August that far too many of those who were to take part in these raids were talking too much about the chances. I was already worried, for even before I had first been put in the know by John Haselden in Cairo I had heard rumours; and I had heard these through gossip at parties and in the bars of Cairo. I was very suspicious that security had been blown, and I told John Haselden of my fears when he arrived in Kufra the day before we were due to set off on the 800-mile journey to Tobruk.

There was little that John, or indeed myself, could do at that stage except to tell all those involved with us what was planned in order to scotch all the rumours that were current. This John did soon after he arrived on 4 September.

This did not help, however, to allay our fears that we would be walking into a trap.

Briefly, what happened at Benghazi was that David Stirling approached the town from the south-east through Berca, but met very strong opposition and had no alternative but to withdraw. I have no direct evidence that the enemy were expecting him, but this seems the most likely explanation. All the next day his force was heavily attacked from the air, and according to Philip Warner's account they lost eighteen Jeeps and twenty-five other vehicles. Neither did the Sudan Defence Force manage to take Jalo, so that oasis was not available to David on his return from Benghazi.

Everyone's high hopes for success had been rudely shattered so far as Benghazi and Jalo were concerned; and the attack on Tobruk, with which I was so closely associated, was also an abject failure.

What happened that night has never been entirely clear, but in outline John Haselden and his gallant party of Commandos and others got safely into Tobruk. They went in under escort of some of Buck's pseudo-Germans, who were pretending to be guards over some captured British prisoners (the Commando party). This ruse worked perfectly, and a lot of trouble had been taken to ensure correct passes and Afrika Korps insignia for Buck's people.

Once inside Haselden and his force had some early success, and captured most of the guns they were intended to take. But later these were recaptured from them, and in the ensuing very confused fighting John Haselden was killed leading a forlorn counter-attack on the enemy. As a result the seaborne force, consisting of men from the Northumberland Fusiliers and the Argyll and Sutherland Highlanders, who were coming in to complete the wreckage of Tobruk harbour, was unable to land. Four MTB's, two destroyers and one anti-aircraft carrier were lost during the raid.

My own Patrol had spent that uncomfortable night outside the eastern perimeter of Tobruk with instructions to hold it and prevent any reinforcements from entering the town until I could finally withdraw the following evening.

I had various other tasks to perform, but with the total failure of the main plans I had no alternative but to withdraw duly at first light the following morning. I had had no communication with John Haselden the whole night since he had left me to enter Tobruk in the early evening.

After we had put so much effort and planning into the whole venture it was a bitter disappointment for us to have to leave John Haselden and so many friends in Tobruk. We had travelled nearly fifteen hundred miles together since we had left the Fayoum on 24 August.

However, I realised that there was nothing that I could do with my few men where everyone else had failed; and so we went back to the place where he had spent two nights before the raid, about ninety miles south of Tobruk, and where I knew that there was cover. Here I planned to await further instructions.

I soon received the news that nothing had been heard of the Commando force since they left me, and that the Navy had failed to land the troops as intended.

What a costly failure these three raids had been; and there is no doubt that at each place far stiffer opposition was encountered than had ever been expected. As my Patrol drove to the eastern perimeter of Tobruk along the main road we even had to negotiate a steam-roller which had been placed across it; and we ran into an enemy patrol a few miles to the south of Tobruk very soon after Haselden and his force had left us. Certainly at Tobruk the enemy was alert.

Jake Easonsmith's party left the Fayoum and were to approach Barce through the Sand Sea rather than via Kufra. They had some bad luck when one of the Jeeps, in which Alastair Timpson was travelling, had a very unpleasant spill on a razor-back dune. The driver fractured his spine and was paralysed from the waist downward, while Alastair Timpson cracked his skull and knocked some of his teeth out.

Dick Lawson, the LRDG Medical Officer, was with Jake fortunately, and so he was able to do what he could for the injured. After a time an RAF Blenheim succeeded in finding the Patrols, with the help of Tony Browne to guide it, and the two injured men were flown back straight to Cairo. This of course delayed Jake for a day, and he then pushed on. The rest of his approach march was quite uneventful, and he reached the neighbourhood of Barce on the morning of 13 September. Here Jake went on ahead with Peniakoff and two of his Arabs to within a mile or two of Barce. The Arabs were to go off and contact some of their friends, from whom they would learn all the latest news of what was going on inside the garrison. They would then meet Jake that evening, when he was on his way to attack the town. Jake had left the Patrols hidden among some olive-trees, and he rejoined them that afternoon to give out his plan and orders for the night's work. After dark they set off with Sergeant Jack Dennis now commanding the Guards Patrol after Timpson had been evacuated.

Before long they came to a small police post from which a Libyan emerged into the light of Jake's headlights. He was quickly relieved of his rifle by Dennis and bundled on to the back of a truck. He turned out to be an admirable guide, and was employed for a long time in the cookhouse at Siwa before he was ultimately taken back to his own home near Tripoli six months later. A cheerful character, he never seemed to show much surprise at his sudden metamorphosis from policeman to kitchen orderly. Such I suppose, were the vagaries of war!

Dennis threw a grenade or two into the police post just to quieten any possible thought of interference with the Patrols after a careless police officer had come out to investigate when the Libyan captive had called to him.

Soon after this a machine-gun opened up on them, but this was quickly dealt with by vastly superior fire-power. A little later Jake met up with Popski as planned, but his Arabs had not by then returned. At this stage they left Dick Lawson—the doctor—and a wireless truck. The latter was to act as a link with Stirling at Benghazi, and also as a rendezvous for any stragglers. Jake and the others got on to the main road towards Barce, and, turning left an hour before midnight, drove in quite close formation with their headlights on.

A few miles outside Barce, at the top of the escarpment, the enemy had decided to place two light Italian tanks—one on either side of the road.

Although the enemy High Command was suspecting trouble some-where—not necessarily at Barce—the crews of these two tanks were obviously either asleep or unaware that Jake and his very formidable force was behind the headlights of the vehicles throbbing towards them. But they soon realised all was not well as each of Jake's trucks passed by and opened up with every gun they had.

When they got to the fork in the road outside Barce, Jake dismounted and with quiet unconcern directed the Patrols to their appointed tasks. Nick Wilder and his New Zealanders were sent off to the right to the airfield, and Dennis led the Guards Patrol on to the barracks.

Both these objectives were well known to the Patrols, as they had seen aerial photographs of them, and they knew exactly what they had to do. But despite account being taken of every likely contingency things never work out quite as expected, and they were to be no different at Barce. At least the latest photographs showed that the airfield was very much in use.

Nick led his Patrol of four 30-cwt Chevrolets in a Jeep, and they went round the outskirts of the town to the landing-ground, where at the entrance he found the gate shut. Nick calmly got down from his Jeep, opened it and drove on in; but not before they had shot down some Italians who came to see what was happening. A stray bullet or burst of fire set a petrol tanker on fire, and this gave the New Zealanders much welcome light to see their way around.

They passed some buildings and hurled grenades through the windows and then drove on to the landing-ground itself. Nick's tactics for dealing with the aircraft had been worked out to the last detail, and he had decided to lead his vehicles in single file, firing mixed tracer and normal bullets at every aircraft as they passed it. However, it was possible that some aircraft might not necessarily catch fire in this way, so the last of the four trucks carried a whole pile of delayed-action bombs timed to go off very soon after they had been planted.

Nick spent the best part of an hour making sure that he had done a really thorough job, and at the end of it he left twenty-four planes burning and a further twelve damaged by bombs and machine-gun fire.

The Italian garrison was taken by such surprise that they simply did not know how to stop this savage onslaught, and they resorted to their usual practice of just letting off every weapon in the air as fast as they could; this seemed to give Italians some sort of relief from their abject terror on this sort of occasion. The psychological effect of being able to let off a bang, albeit with no apparent retaliatory result, was always a morale-booster to Italians.

Just before Wilder decided to leave the enemy did get a mortar into action, but by that time Nick had also destroyed all the fuel that he could find, once he had dealt with all the planes. He was running short of ammunition, and knew that he might have to retain some, for the only way out of Barce was back by the same route that he had entered the town.

The Italians, realising that they could do little to stop Wilder on his fierce rampage round the airfield, decided that the only thing to do was to block his way out through the town. They knew very well which way he would have to take. This they did with four light tanks, and these were firing up the street at him as Nick came along.

Nick Wilder saw that his retreat was blocked, but he was not going to be defeated by a tiresome obstruction of this nature. He was in one of the Chevrolets at this stage, and he ordered his driver to charge the first tank at full speed in order to clear the way. This they did, and bounced off the first tank and into the second. It left Nick's own vehicle a twisted mass and he had to abandon it, but it cleared the way for the others.

The next vehicle behind him had been the Jeep, and this picked up Nick and his gallant crew. He himself then got behind a machine-gun and was firing so furiously at the next pair of tanks by the railway station that the Jeep-driver's vision was blinded and the vehicle hit the kerb only to overturn. The others were thrown out, and Nick was pinned, by now unconscious, underneath it. Nothing daunted, the others soon righted the Jeep, dragged their leader out and put him on another truck.

Unfortunately, the last truck of the New Zealanders somehow got cut off from the rest of the Patrol, and it was lost with the crew. So they got out with only the Jeep and two trucks left; but they had not had one man hit by enemy action.

Meanwhile Sergeant Dennis had reached his barracks objective only after its occupants had been alerted by the airfield battle and he found that he was expected. But this did not in the last deter the Guardsmen, and they opened up with the twin Vickers K guns, and also with the larger Breda anti-tank gun. They then got down and threw grenades through the windows of any buildings from which there still appeared to be resistance.

The task of the Guardsmen had been to prevent any of the soldiers in the barracks interfering with Wilder's activities at the airfield; and Dennis could see how well this was going by the flames that lit the sky that early morning of 14 September 1942. As he was soon going to be short of ammunition, he therefore sensibly decided to get out while he could.

Once again the Italians had moved two tanks to block the retreat of the Patrol, and these prevented Dennis dealing with the railway station, which he had hoped to take in on his way out of Barce. After some difficulty and slight opposition Dennis managed to elude the tanks and make his way to the rendezvous to the east of Barce.

All this time Jake himself was moving about the town with two Jeeps, and was lucky not to suffer any serious damage when he too ran into tanks in the dark. He finally came upon an MT park with twelve vehicles in it. He and his driver methodically wrecked all these with tommy-gun fire and hand grenades.

By the time Jake had met up with Wilder and Dennis it was getting late, and he realised that the sooner he got out of the area the better; so they moved as fast as they could along the main road to the east before turning south to pick up Lawson and those that had been left with him. It was while they were going along the track, which took them in the right direction and where it runs through a narrow valley, that they were ambushed soon after they had collected Dick Lawson.

The Patrols were, of course, expecting something of the sort to happen, and were only surprised that it had not occurred earlier. But the Italians had gathered a force of nearly two hundred Libyan soldiers, and their fire wounded three men as well as puncturing a tyre in Dick Lawson's vehicle. However, this was changed (as quickly as we used to change tyres when chased by armoured cars—without even wasting time with a jack under the wheel!) and they got through the ambush.

Jake led his exhausted men on for another ten miles before they stopped to do what they could for the wounded, and to the damaged truck. While this was going on the enemy reappeared, but were soon driven off.

It was now quite clear to Jake that he was going to have a thoroughly bad time trying to extract his force from contact before the enemy was able to catch up with him from the air. He therefore decided to unload anything worth salvaging from the damaged vehicles before blowing them up. He moved on, only to have further foul luck when the wireless vehicle of the Guards Patrol stripped a rear axle pinion. There was nothing that he could do in a hurry to repair it, as six enemy fighters appeared overhead. This was at 10.30 in the morning.

All the enemy had to do was to take on each vehicle in turn and destroy Jake's party in detail. He had no chance to disperse and scatter over the desert. They were not in that sort of country. They were in partially cultivated, scrub-covered, rocky terrain where movement was almost restricted to the tracks across it.

16. General Freyberg, General Montgomery and Tony Browne.

17. Travelling in the desert.

18. John Haselden, who was killed in the Tobruk raid (see pp 104-7).

19. Eric Wilson, who won the VC in Somaliland.

20. A New Zealand patrol leaving the desert headquarters of the LRDG at Siwa.

21. Guy Prendergast.

22. Moir Stormonth-Darling.

23. Ken Lazarus.                                         24. John Olivey.

25. Arthur Stokes "was being such a nuisance to the enemy that they put an enormous price on his head" (p. 162).

26. Bill Kennedy Shaw and Jake Easonsmith.

27. Farewell to Bill Kennedy Shaw. Left to right: Jake Easonsmith, Bill Kennedy Shaw, John Olivey, David Lloyd Owen, Shorty Barrett, Tony Browne and Tim Heywood.

29. Jimmy Parch (on the left), with a Yugoslav Partisan and Ron Hill in

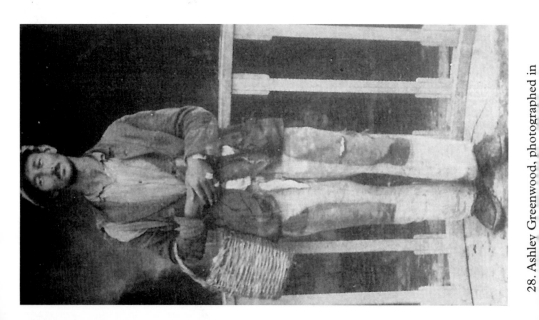

28. Ashley Greenwood, photographed in

30. Alan Denniff gives a dog a lift while on training in the Lebanon.

31. MFV *La Palma* lying in Rodi harbour before her maiden voyage. The tarpaulin covers a jeep.

32. Arrival of the LRDG on Leros, September, 1943.

33. Air attack on Tirana, Albania.

The enemy aircraft remained overhead in varying numbers all day until dusk and just machine-gunned everything that moved. Everything that could be saved in the way of food and water was collected between attacks, but unfortunately Nick Wilder got a bullet through both legs, and another of his men was wounded. Dick Lawson now had a total of six injured men, and he was magnificent during that very unpleasant day, never ceasing to be cheerful and doing everything he could to alleviate the plight of the wounded. One man was shot in the stomach, and it was not easy to move him to cover in a hurry. While Dick Lawson was attempting to do this he sheltered the man with his own body through several machine-gun attacks on his truck, which still had not been destroyed.

When the aircraft finally drew away at dusk Jake took stock. He found that he was left with two Jeeps and two Chevrolets, so he loaded all the rations and water on to one of the latter—just in time for two more fighters to come back again at last light, rake the area with fire and destroy the vehicle with all the salvaged stores. After this he only had two Jeeps and one Chevrolet to take thirty-three men back on the 700-mile journey to Kufra.

But, being the prudent man that he was, Jake had left one more Chevrolet with petrol and rations at some good cover about sixty miles to the south. He had foreseen the possibility of something going wrong, and he had left the truck as an emergency rendezvous—just in case. He resolved that the most important thing for him was to get Dick Lawson and the six wounded men to somewhere where they could be given help as soon as possible, so he decided that the Chevrolet and one Jeep with two drivers, a fitter and a navigator should go with the doctor. The rest of the weary party would set off on foot, with the other Jeep taking food and water for them. They all started that night.

Neither party had much to be cheerful about. Dick Lawson, with six wounded men, little food and water and with no communications, had seven hundred miles to go, and not long after he had started on the way he had to abandon the Jeep, since a bulllet-hole in the radiator was using up more water than he could afford to spare.

Jake's situation must have been daunting, with nothing but a great faith that Guy Prendergast and others at Group HQ would probably make a pretty good estimate of what had happened, and would do everything possible to help. In mid-September in the desert it is very hot indeed by day; both parties were short of water, and since none of the LRDG ever did much walking their feet soon began to suffer.

In both cases the encouragement and cheerfulness shown by their two leaders gave everyone else some confidence in their ability to survive. Both Jake and Dick Lawson had been quite fearless under constant air attack the day before, and neither of them had lost their composure despite the immense problems facing them. The walking party pushed on throughout the 15th of September, and came across a Bedouin camp that evening, where they were able to buy a lamb but could get no water. They did not stop all that night, or the following day or night.

Meanwhile John Olivey and his Rhodesians, who had been with Stirling at Benghazi, had been alerted by Group HQ to find out what they could about what had happened at Barce, since there had been no news at all up to this time.

It was not long after dawn on 17 September when Jake and his party saw the dust of a column of vehicles, and soon recognised the familiar outline of LRDG trucks in the distance. They fired Verey lights, but for some reason these were not seen, and they must have felt very miserable when they saw the trucks disappear.

However, Jake decided to go and investigate in a Jeep, and not too far away he came over a rise to encounter what must have been the most wonderful sight that he could have dreamed about. In a hollow below him was Olivey with his Rhodesians; and I can think of no character more cheerful and more likely to make light of everything, and whom I would rather bump into under similar circumstances, than John Olivey.

Olivey took Jake's party on to find the truck that had been left as an emergency rallying-point, where they found a note from Dick Lawson to the effect that he had taken some food and water and gone on his way.

But Jake was still missing a number of men, and he was not going to leave the area without doing all that he could to find them, so he sent Dennis with everyone else back to Kufra while he and John Olivey scoured the area for the next three days for survivors. They found eight of them, but there were still others not accounted for. Over the months some of these returned safely after having been sheltered by the Bedouin, but ten men were taken prisoner.

When Olivey met up with Jake Easonsmith it enabled the latter to get in touch with Group HQ and tell them the situation. Thus Guy Prendergast learnt that Dick Lawson had left with two vehicles via LG125, with a navigator. Jake's signal went on 'Tell Lloyd Owen hurry LG125 try pick up tracks also RAF if possible. Several serious wounds.'

LG125 was a forward landing-ground on hard desert, with no facilities of any sort, which the RAF had used in the offensive the year before. It was 450 miles from Kufra and about 80 miles south-west of where I was in hiding with the Yeomanry Patrol. We had been kept there for just such a contingency. During the afternoon of 17 September I was given an idea of the situation and told to set off as soon as possible to see if I could see any signs of the tracks of Dick Lawson's two vehicles, and then find them and take them back to Kufra.

We covered those eighty miles to LG125 at breakneck speed, and decided to spend the night there and carry out a thorough search next morning. In fact, Dick Lawson had already arrived there and had seen us come in just before dusk. He sent one of his men over the few miles to where we had camped, and very soon I was able to join Dick and learn his news.

The most important thing to do was to get help for Nick Wilder and the other wounded men. I got a message to Group HQ and passed them the problem. Next day a big old Bombay appeared out of the distant sky and came in to a safe landing some four hundred miles behind our front line at Alamein. The only assistance it had to help it to land was a smoke canister set off by us on the ground, and after landing it had to be refuelled for the return journey. This had to be done by hand from 4-gallon tins which the aircraft had carried with it.

I have never been more relieved than I was to see the wounded loaded into the Bombay, and then to watch it lumber off bumpily across the desert to take off for Kufra. The wounded were in hospital in Cairo the next evening—almost exactly two days after I had found them. 216 Squadron RAF had done a magnificent job for us.

I stayed at LG125 for a bit, as there seemed to be a lot of stragglers from David Stirling's raid on Benghazi, and they were all short of supplies. They were very glad to find me at the landing-ground with plenty of everything and with good communications to Group HQ.

Jake was still looking for survivors, but he sent me a signal to return to Kufra with what I had collected, and he would gather in the tail-enders. How typical this was of him: despite a fairly harrowing and anxious time, he was not leaving the area until he had satisfied himself that there was no more that could be done.

When I finally left LG125 I had with me a total of sixty men and eleven vehicles. Just under three weeks since we had left Kufra, with such high hopes of success and such confidence that we would gain it, we arrived back on 23 September.

For their parts in these actions Jake and Nick Wilder were both awarded the Distinguished Service Order, Dick Lawson a Military Cross and Sergeant Dennis the Military Medal. While we were at LG125 Dick had told me something of the outstanding gallantry of Jake and Nick. The latter could not have been more full of admiration for Dick Lawson's skill, courage and example to everyone. He had no thought for himself, and for the whole time never ceased doing all that he could to help the wounded. All these awards were so well deserved.

Apart from the results of the raid on Barce, the whole concept had been a costly failure. The Royal Navy and Haselden's party had suffered severe losses at Tobruk; and, although the losses at Benghazi, Barce and Jalo were comparatively small, the gains were virtually nil. In no way did they affect the main issue at Alamein except, perhaps, to make the enemy just a little more alert behind the lines than he had been previously.

This was the first time anything on such a scale had been attempted—mercifully, it was also the last. I believed at the time, and all of us in the LRDG who were involved felt the same, that there were far too many people in Cairo who were in the know. Michael Crichton-Stuart goes so far as to write to the effect 'that there was a serious breach of security since the impending raids were the gossip of Cairo. Without the all-important weapon of surpise the attacks were suicidal yet they were not cancelled.'

The final and ironical reminder of these failures came when two days after our arrival back in Kufra, where we were sorting ourselves out, the Germans sent eight Heinkels over to bomb and strafe the place. There were more troops in Kufra on that day than there had ever been, and more machine-guns too. But the enemy first destroyed the Bombays on the landing-ground and then proceeded to sweep the palm-trees with cannon and machine-gun fire.

The venomous reply from the SAS and LRDG on the ground resulted in five of the eight Heinkels failing to return to base, which says quite a lot for the combined fire-power of these two units, considering we had nothing more formidable than 20-mm Bredas. The only casualties on our side were four Arabs killed in the fort at Kufra, while I had a cannon shell through my back and my left arm and one Guardsman was wounded rather less seriously.

I never forgave the idiot who had allowed the BBC to put out a statement about these raids. This had included the fact that they had been mounted from Kufra. Why ask for trouble? I remember how we had specifically requested that no mention should be made of the fact that these raids had been launched from Kufra.

# CHAPTER 11

# Into Tunisia

The 23rd of October 1942 will long be remembered as the night on which the Battle of Alamein began. Almost exactly three months later General Montgomery and the Eighth Army entered Tripoli. The immediate effect of this great advance on the LRDG was that not only did the Road Watch resume its importance but also Kufra became much too far back for the base, and would have to move forward. Moreover, after the losses of men and vehicles during the raids of the previous month there was a good deal to replace.

The Yeomanry Patrol—which had been with me to Tobruk—was intact and ready for operations, and Captain Spicer of the Wiltshire Yeomanry had taken over from me soon after I had been evacuated to hospital in Cairo. They were therefore sent back to Marble Arch on yet another Road Watch on 30 October, and they were there during the early part of Montgomery's advance.

It was not until 10 November that the effect of this became very apparent, when the average number of vehicles reported every day had increased from under a hundred in each direction until some 3,500 poured to the west and virtually nothing went the other way. This confirmed the belief that Rommel was on the way out of Cyrenaica, and it became even more clear when those on watch reported lorries full of Italians with their furniture going hot-foot back towards Tripoli.

The New Zealanders, who had taken over from the Yeomanry Patrol, had a particularly difficult time, for it soon became clear to them that the enemy were about to prepare defences near where their men were on the Watch down at the road. Some thousand vehicles were dispersed near the landing-ground at Marble Arch, and working parties came within two hundred yards of where the men were hiding. They had to be pulled out, and a Patrol of Guardsmen was sent forty miles farther west to re-establish the Watch. This was becoming of more importance as each day went by, and at the same time it became harder to keep it going unseen and without interference.

115

The enemy was well aware by this time of the routes we had been using, and he began to patrol and mine some of these. This had a certain nuisance value, as it increased the distances that Patrols had to cover. It was because of these difficulties Guy Prendergast had to duplicate the Patrols, so that he could be certain of keeping the road under observation.

Typical of the sort of troubles that the Patrols were encountering befell Alastair Timpson—recovered from his injuries—on his way to do duty on the road. One of the New Zealand Patrols was going by another route in case either unit ran into difficulty.

In the gap between Marada and Zella, Timpson met an enemy patrol of eight vehicles, two of which were armoured cars, and since he wished to avoid contact because of the necessity of keeping the Watch going he turned back to take a way round. He then found his path blocked by another patrol, and he had no alternative but to fight it out. He dismounted some of his guns in order to give them a chance of better concealment, but the armoured cars came on and he had to try to get clear.

The enemy were too strong for him, and Timpson only extricated a Jeep and two trucks; the rest of his Patrol was captured. However, he still had his wireless truck, which was some consolation, and when he informed Group HQ of what had taken place he was told that the New Zealand Patrol working in parallel to him had run into a minefield, had casualties and had had to return to Kufra. So he was told to watch the road at all costs. That he managed to do this from a spot only four hundred yards from the road for the next two weeks was a very remarkable effort; particularly as he could not hide his trucks any nearer than twenty miles from the road, and there were only ten men altogether.

They were continually having to move because of enemy activity and the strain on them all resulting from rain, cold and lack of sleep was very unpleasant. But they hung on until they knew that a Rhodesian Patrol had got into position and was firmly established farther to the west.

Then Ron Tinker and his Patrol of New Zealanders came up to take over from the Rhodesians. With the enemy withdrawing—they pulled out of Buerat-el-Hsun on 26 December—Tinker found them all around him a few days later, and he realised that he had to find a new camp site. He was just about to set off to do this when he was discovered by armoured cars. After dodging these some of his men became split up from him, and his rear base was found by more armoured cars. Tinker got all his trucks safely away, but six of his men were missing. About a week later two of these men rejoined the unit, having walked eastward and joined up with forward elements of the Eighth Army.

Not only had the Road Watch become very tricky to maintain but with the Eighth Army advancing so rapidly there was no longer the imperative necessity for it. It was again called off. This was to end it.

An official assessment of its value at that time was recorded at GHQ in Cairo by the Director of Military Intelligence, who wrote:

LRDG Road Watch provides the only trained traffic observers. Not only is the standard of accuracy and observation exceptionally high but the Patrols are familiar with the most recent illustrations of enemy vehicles and weapons.

During periods of withdrawal or reinforcement of the enemy the LRDG has provided an indispensable basis of certain facts on which calculations of enemy strength can be based. Without their reports we should frequently have been in doubt as to the enemy's intentions, when knowledge of them was all important; and our estimate of enemy strength would have been far less accurate and accepted with far less confidence.

The Road Watch immediately in rear of the El Agheila position has been of quite exceptional importance and the information, which it has provided, in spite of interruptions due to a difficult and dangerous situation, has been invaluable. From the point of view of military intelligence the risks and casualties which the Patrols have accepted, and are accepting, have been more than justified.

It would seem a little presumptuous of me to attempt to add to such a well-informed source's view as to the value that was placed upon the Road Watch contemporaneously. It is perhaps of interest for anyone else making an assessment to record that the establishment for the LRDG provided for a total of 25 officers and 278 other ranks. Of the officers one was a 3rd Class Mechanical Engineer in charge of the Light Repair Squadron and one a Royal Signals captain. Of the soldiers 35 were RAOC Armament Artificers and Fitters, and there were 33 Signalmen. It is therefore difficult to argue the case that an excessive number of specialists and technicians were taken from other units.

Many other tasks were pouring in for the LRDG at this time, mostly connected with reconnaissance of terrain for future moves by Eighth Army, while there were many agents to be taken to or collected from their destinations. And once more the LRDG was to join up with General Leclerc and the Free French in Chad, with the object of helping them in their advance towards the Fezzan.

A Rhodesian Patrol went to Zouar at the end of November, and did invaluable work acting as the eyes and ears of the French force. Just after Christmas they were all poised to take Gatrun, and one of the Rhodesian trucks went forward to the oasis to test enemy reactions—if any. This caused an immediate artillery and Breda retaliation, and soon after this the truck was attacked by six fighters and two bombers. The Rhodesians opened up with all their guns, and they were credited with the destruction of one of the aircraft. This sort of thing continued for a week, and one by one the Italian garrisons in the Fezzan lost heart and surrendered to the advancing French.

On the coast the knowledge that the LRDG had gained about the lie of the land ahead of the Eighth Army was in tremendous demand, and the first of these very successful patrols was when Tony Browne led the New Zealand Division and the 4th Light Armoured Brigade to outflank the El Agheila position which Rommel was still holding at the end of December.

As I write this I have in front of me Tony Browne's notebook, which his widow gave me after Tony's early death from cancer, nearly thirty years after he led his New Zealand Patrol to guide General Freyberg's force on this left-hook. He gives his task to navigate 2 NZ Division and 4th Light Armoured Brigade from El Haseiat to Marble Arch, thence west to Nofilia. He adds that they were involved in action with the enemy rearguard, and were heavily shelled before the Division captured four hundred prisoners, five tanks and eighteen guns.

Soon after this Tony was ordered to report on the 'going' in three wadis to the west of Sirte, and it was here that he was injured when his truck was blown up on a mine, and a South African officer with him was killed. Paddy MacLauchlan, who was out with Tony learning the ropes, took over command when the latter had to be evacuated. He was very quick to learn, but found himself in action and very nearly captured by enemy armoured cars within a few days. He had mistaken them for our own! This New Zealand Patrol had left Kufra in early December, and before they returned to base had covered over 2,500 miles. With the general advance the Group HQ of the LRDG had to move forward from Kufra first to Zella and then to Hon in the middle of January 1943.

Ron Tinker with other Patrols was operating in Tunisia to the west of the Matmata Hills, and had gone right through to within twenty-five miles of Gabes with two Jeeps to complete a very full and detailed reconnaissance. He had left the rest of his Patrol at a base camp to the south, and when he returned he found that it had been attacked from the air, and he had lost several trucks and had two men wounded.

He also collected a party of Free French survivors from other attacks, until he had altogether about forty men with him and only five Jeeps. He therefore left with three of these, and moving along the edge of the Shott Djerid found his way to Tozeur. The remaining men were following his tracks on foot with the two other Jeeps carrying food and water for them.

Next day he went on another hundred miles into First Army's area, where he borrowed some transport and informed Eighth Army of his position. He then returned to pick up the walking party whom he found still going six days after he had left them to go in search of help. A very fine performance!

Rommel was moving back fast, and it was becoming clear that his next determined stand would be made on the so-called Mareth Line, which was about 170 miles to the west of Tripoli. Here before the war the French had built a defensive line in order to prevent a possible Italian invasion of Tunisia from Tripoli. Guy Prendergast had been told that Montgomery's plan would be to make a holding frontal attack on the Mareth position, while his main effort would be swung round to the south to outflank it. The LRDG would be asked to report in considerable detail on the country over which this left hook was to move.

Even from Hon it was a long way to the Tunisian frontier—about four hundred miles—and the task of carrying out these reconnaissances could only be done by making forward dumps of petrol and supplies. The first Patrol to cross into Tunisia was led by Nick Wilder, and his work at this time in finding routes for the Eighth Army was to be of inestimable value. He was inside Tunisia when he was instructed to find a route through the hills, running south from Matmata, so that a force could be moved on to the plain to the west.

On 16 January 1943 Nick and his New Zealanders were south of Medenine. This was a week before Tripoli fell on 23 January. He had run into very bad 'going', but continued his task on foot. He found that this was not getting him anywhere, and so he moved farther to the south, where he discovered the pass by which the New Zealand Division was to carry out its magnificent left hook round the Mareth Line two months later. This route came to be known throughout the Army as Wilder's Gap. In the middle of February the Eighth Army had come up to the Mareth Line, and the attack on it was not to get moving until 22 March.

It was at this time that the Indian Patrols of the Indian Long Range Squadron under Sam McCoy really came into their own. They had been working with the LRDG for some months learning the job, and they were a thoroughly useful addition at a time when our Patrols were very stretched and suffering casualties. They were with General Leclerc for much of the time during his great march north from the Fezzan, and carried out some good attacks against enemy transport on the tracks to the south of Tripoli.

February and March were busy months in 1943 for there was so much information wanted. The enemy were getting wiser to the activities of the LRDG and the SAS, and with the use of large sums of money and propaganda they had fostered the Arabs' dislike of the French very effectively, until they had begun to have an equal dislike for France's allies. We therefore found that the Tunisians were by no means as friendly as the Libyans had been. The latter had in many cases done a very great deal and taken dangerous risks to help us.

It was these unfriendly Arabs who were the cause of David Stirling's eventual capture. He had expanded his SAS quite remarkably after the disastrous raids of the previous autumn, and he also had great plans for the future, in which he hoped to create an SAS Brigade to act in conjunction with the 2nd SAS Regiment, which his brother Bill was commanding with First Army. David was hoping to operate in some of the northern parts of Tunisia, and then join up with First Army.

He was moving up through the Gabes Gap—which in itself was a risk that he should not really have taken at that time, since it was swarming with the enemy. But David always was a man in a hurry, and this was the quickest route to where he wanted to go. However, he had realised that they might be seen in daylight, and so he and his party were catching up on some much-needed sleep when they were surprised and surrounded; what is so out of character in many ways was the fact that they were caught unawares, without any look-outs posted. But I suppose David had become over-confident.

What a tragedy it was that he was caught when the end in North Africa was so near! He had done such a lot, and put everything that he had towards achieving this great victory, which before Alamein seemed impossible. His contribution to the final defeat of the Axis in North Africa is not easy to assess, for I believe that after he began to expand the SAS the balance sheet showed too great an excess of expenditure over achievement. But before that time Paddy Mayne, for instance, on his own destroyed far more enemy aircraft than did any of the great fighter aces on either side.

When David was captured much of the inspiration went out of those responsible for the so-called private armies, and the ideas and genius that he injected into so many people had gone. The Axis made probably the most valuable of all their captures the day they took David Stirling.

All was not yet quite over in Africa. There was still work for the LRDG to do, and Bernard Bruce—who had taken over the Guards Patrol when Alastair Timpson departed to return to the Scots Guards—had left Hon on 3 February to report on the going between the Shott Djerid in the north and the Grand Erg Oriental in the south.

He took some time to get to the area he had been given, because of the appalling ground and the greatly increased enemy activity, which all our Patrols were meeting at that time. They found the country very rough, and were continually badly stuck. During one of these really bad moments they were attacked by some Arabs, but their superior fire-power enabled them to get clear without casualties.

They moved on to the west, only to be attacked again that night, with two men wounded. Bernard pressed on towards Tozeur in order to find help, and was quite ignorant of the fact that First Army had been forced to withdraw from the place the day before, when the Americans had been badly mauled by German counter-attacks.

But the French were helpful, and sent Bruce on his way westward, after he had stocked up with abandoned American fuel and rations. He was aiming for El Oued, some 120 miles away. Here there was help, and Bruce got the wounded flown to Touggourt, where he then went to try to get spares for his vehicles. These were not available there, but were flown from Tripoli to First Army, and so Bruce went on to Constantine—250 miles to the north—to collect them.

In order to avoid the trouble he had run into on the way he decided to return south of the Grand Erg via Fort Flatters and Ghadames. He reached Hon on 12 March, having covered altogether 3,500 miles. He had sent his report back by air from Constantine, and his information was just another part of all that was being poured in every day by the LRDG Patrols, operating on a carefully worked-out plan of Guy Prendergast.

There was still one more important task left for the LRDG, and this was given to Ron Tinker and his Patrol of New Zealanders. Bill Kennedy Shaw writes 'that it was only fitting that the Group's last task in Africa should be carried out by the New Zealanders, who had begun its work two and a half years earlier and a thousand miles to the east'. And Ron Tinker, who had joined as a trooper in 1940, been promoted sergeant and then commissioned, had already earned a Military Medal, the Military Cross and been Mentioned in Dispatches.

Tinker's task was to guide the New Zealand Division on its left hook to the Mareth Line. This formation started westward on 19 March along the route which Tinker's men had marked out for them two days before. They remained in the van of their parent division until they reached Gabes after Rommel had been forced to abandon the Mareth Line. Tinker had left Hon on 2 March, and he reported to Group HQ after his task was complete on 3 April 1943.

It had become clear that the very hilly and cultivated country beyond Gabes was not suitable for the employment of LRDG Patrols, as there just was no more desert left between the Eighth and First Armies. Guy Prendergast had foreseen this, and paid several visits to GHQ in Cairo to find out what they had in mind for the future of the LRDG. It had at least been decided that it should not be disbanded, and that there was a future for the LRDG in Europe.

So during the last week of March and early April the LRDG moved back along that coast road to which it had paid so much attention in the past years, until it came to rest in a tented camp by the sea to the west of Alexandria. By the middle of May 1943 the Axis forces in Tunisia had surrendered and the whole of the North African littoral was under Allied control.

Our immediate task was ended; but we were only waiting to be told what was next in store for us. I doubt whether anyone foresaw at that time that the LRDG was going to be reformed and reorganised to operate in Europe, and that it would carry out a hundred more operations behind the lines before the war finally ended just over two years later. What *was* obvious to us all was that we would never again range far and wide over long distances with highly mobile and self-contained car patrols. We would have to adapt our methods to much shorter-range work in the plains and mountains of Europe: from now on we would mostly move about on foot, somehow carrying everything that we needed on our backs.

We also had to be conveyed to the scene of operations, and this would involve perhaps, the use of parachutes, small naval surface craft or submarines, as well as the ability to move on skis in winter. The metamorphosis was to be fairly complicated and very nearly complete.

At the same time we realised that certain of the guiding principles of our form of subversive warfare would still hold good, but that we should have to forget the techniques and experience that had been learnt with bitter tribulation in the sands and open expanses of the Western Desert.

They were happy and carefree days in that camp by the Mediterranean in early 1943. We were able to take leave in Alexandria and catch up with friends whom we seldom saw while we were based in the remoteness of Siwa or of Kufra. And there was a lot to do as well. Guns, equipment and vehicles had to be cleaned and overhauled, clothes to be mended or replaced and time found to enjoy good meals eaten off plates on a table, and beer drunk from a glass. We wanted too to relax jaded nerves, to read and to play games, to write letters home and to look at pretty girls. What fun it all was just to know that for a time at least we were not going to be sent off somewhere behind the lines.

Meanwhile Guy Prendergast was getting a precise definition of our future role so that we would know what to train for and what equipment we would be needing. Soon after we had had our leave and sorted ourselves out he told us what was in the minds of the Staff in Cairo, and how he saw us carrying out our job.

# PART TWO

# THE DODECANESE, ITALY AND THE BALKANS

## MAY 1943 – MAY 1945

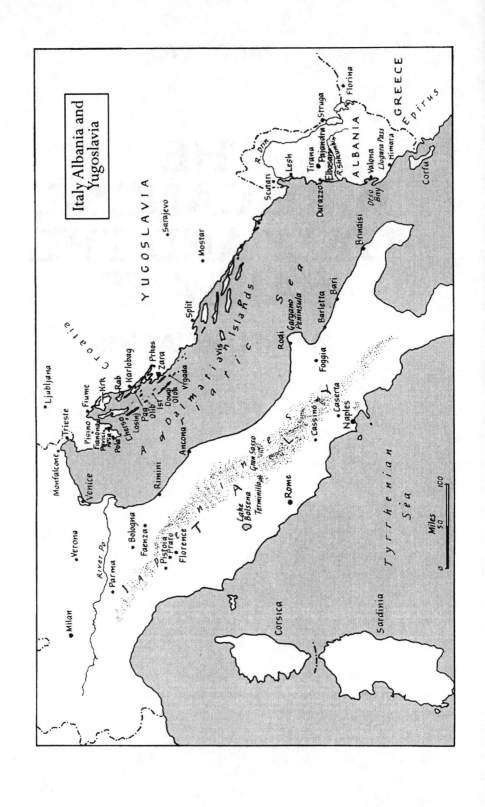

Italy Albania and
Yugoslavia

# CHAPTER 12

# A Change of Role

The new charter for the LRDG specified that we should be organised in small Patrols capable of maintaining communications while operating on foot for a distance of a hundred miles behind the lines. We were to carry on our backs sufficient food for ten days in case it was that long before new supplies could be sent to us. We were to be taught German and Greek, so that some of us would be able to ask the local people to provide us with our simplest needs. We would also retain a proportion of Jeeps, which could be used when penetration through the lines was feasible.

There was such a lot to be done, and we were in a hurry. We all understood that the longer we took to readjust our ideas and to become proficient in our new techniques and equipment, the longer we would be out of active operations. And we believed passionately that we still had something well worth while to contribute towards the successful outcome of the war.

Readjustment was going to have all sorts of repercussions, and not the least were those directly affecting the officers and men. Men who, for instance, were superb gunners on vehicles would not necessarily be such staunch walkers. It was with sad hearts that we had to say goodbye to some of those who had served us well, and who did not quite fit into the new design.

The structure of the unit remained essentially the same, with Guy Prendergast at the helm, but Jake Easonsmith became his deputy. Major Alastair Guild was given command of the New Zealand Squadron of six Patrols, and I was given command of the Squadron of similar size formed from United Kingdom and Rhodesian troops.

I had not until then had a close association with the Rhodesians, but from then on I got to know them well, and to appreciate their real worth. They were wonderfully suited to the LRDG role. They had an inherent sense of initiative, and an ability to look after themselves in the most adverse conditions. They were born to the open air, and thrived on it. They were thus immensely fit, and they had a keen sense of perception. But it was their quiet, though penetrating, charm which endeared them especially to me, and to the Balkan peoples with whom they were later to work.

In many ways those days were difficult ones, with so little suitable equipment available to us, yet Guy Prendergast's great knowledge and Jake's ever-inventive genius somehow overcame most of our problems. Between them they scoured the stores depots and the captured enemy equipment dumps for ideas. For the rest of us the thought of carrying everything we were likely to need on our backs, in the lightest possible form, was very strange, and the most urgent task was to get ourselves as fit as possible. The hot and listless air of Alexandria was hardly the ideal training-ground.

In early May I took the Squadron I was then commanding to The Cedars in the mountains of Lebanon. Here Jimmy Riddell, of Olympic ski fame, was running a school to train men in mountain craft. With him also was Griffith Pugh, who was ostensibly the Medical Officer. To be fair to Griffith, he was an admirable MO, but his chief interest lay in teaching rock-climbing and ski-ing, and he was an inspired instructor. Few of us who knew him then were in the least surprised to learn ten years later that he had gone with Sir John Hunt to climb Everest.

We were wonderfully lucky to have men such as these, who could impart their knowledge and their skills, and whose brains we were so eager to pick. Every day we learnt something useful while making the very best of the snow, which was plentiful there when we first arrived.

We were billeted in a hotel six thousand feet above sea-level, set amid mountains towering another four thousand feet above us. These formed a huge white bowl, in the centre of which stood the survivors of the historic cedars which lent an air of finality to the summit of the road by which one approached this enchanting place.

Those cedars stood outside our very door, and I still recall how they held their greatest attraction for me when a string of skiers would come weaving in and out among them as they were playing down the slopes; and those majestic trees endured through the evening shadows as they had done for hundreds of years. I can hear still the rustle of the skis cutting through the surface of the snow; and perhaps the disorderly clatter of a pair of sticks knocking together as someone fell; perhaps the happy laughter of one who had for the first time negotiated that venerable clump; and then all would be silent as the men reached the bottom and sat down to take off their skis before going off weary and content to their evening meal.

Then there were those crisp, sharp nights when the silence was so acute and frozen that I seemed to hear it as I stood on the hotel balcony to watch the sparkling snow with casual shadows dancing across it as a high cloud drifted idly past the brilliant Syrian moon. How supremely beautiful those nights could be!

But it wasn't all so delightful! We made long and arduous marches carrying sixty- and seventy-pound packs; we passed nights out in the hard and cheerless snow; we struggled with teams of bucking, obstinate, hateful mules and sat daily trying to master the intricacies of the Greek or German languages. And all the time we were getting fitter, and we became daily more able to traverse the mountains in fog, in cloud, in blizzard or under the fierce sun.

We learnt again to strip and fire our guns, to load our Jeeps systematically, to cook our lightweight rations, to operate our new wireless sets; and above all to find our way about. No man must ever lose his way or fail to know where he was. This had always been a cardinal rule in the desert, and there was no reason now to disregard it. While we were training so hard, new patterns of sleeping bags, rucksacks, wireless sets, weapons, boots or rations were being sent to us for trial. Some we accepted; others we had to reject.

Back in Egypt both Guy and Jake were working tirelessly to persuade the authorities to release the necessary stores to us. We were given new vehicles and guns, new clothing and new equipment; and it was all a great and satisfying adventure for us, as we longed to test everything on active operations. I am sure we were often impatient that our extraordinary requests for items such as crampons, or self-heating soups, or boots with screw-on replaceable soles, or whatever it might be, were not met with the dispatch we felt necessary, or in sufficient quantities. We were often critical of the authorities for not having these things; and it was probably a very good thing that we were, for our insistence doubtless spurred everyone on to even greater efforts to meet our needs. Our wants were seldom orthodox; we had no fixed establishment on which to base our demands, and I can so well understand that our suppliers were probably suspicious of us. So it is all the more credit to the staffs who looked after our interests in Cairo that we eventually got most things that we wanted and in good time too.

Most of these items were of a good quality and sensible design. This has always been an important factor in the morale of soldiers, for if they know that their equipment and weapons are as good or better than those of their adversaries they are never likely to doubt that they can match them in individual skills.

As the summer months of 1943 passed for us in Lebanon we began to feel that we were at last retrained and ready to set forth. Already rumours of landings in Sicily and Italy were reaching us, and we felt that we might become involved.

Then there were tales of a landing on Rhodes, and we were all agog to take part in that invasion. Jake went off to Libya to discuss possible employment for us in seaborne landings in conjunction with HQ 7th Armoured Division, while Guy and I flew to Cairo to talk over the plans for taking Rhodes. Both these projects came to naught. So we settled down again to more training.

Several of us had realised that unless we were trained to parachute we would never be able to cover the sort of distances that we had envisaged, and we reasoned that if we were to be thus limited we could do little except against coastal targets. Something was lacking; and that was the range and freedom that parachuting would automatically give us.

Guy Prendergast therefore arranged for us to be trained to jump, and we called for volunteers. Everyone was most thoroughly examined by the doctor, and a few were pronounced unfit. I was among the latter, for I had not quite recovered from being wounded in Kufra after the Tobruk raid. Dick Lawson was still our Medical Officer, and I could not persuade him to let me jump. So I tried appealing to Guy Prendergast, whose only reply was:

'I don't mind what you do so long as Dick agrees.'

That was as far as I could get. However, I am afraid that I had my way six months later. But by that time I was more nearly recovered, Prendergast was in London and Dick Lawson was a prisoner in Germany.

The response for volunteers was magnificent. I put the situation to the Squadron when I collected them together and said, 'I'm not out to persuade anyone to do this crazy thing. And I don't want any of you to feel that I, or anyone else, will think any the worse of you if you don't want to do it. Don't be led into it by the extra two shillings a day that you will get as trained parachutists. But once you have said you will do it, then there's no going back. Now is the time for those who want to stand aside to do so.'

Only six out of a hundred and thirty asked to be excused. And four of these changed their minds and did their jumps in the end. In early September Jake Easonsmith took a party from the Squadron to Ramat David in Palestine for the course.

As I was not going to be allowed to jump I thought a few days' leave would fit in well, and so I asked Guy Prendergast if I could go off to Palestine with Dick Lawson. On the evening of 9 September Tim Heywood, who was still the Signal Officer, rang through from Cairo and said that he had been to GHQ that afternoon. There he had been told that there would be no employment for the unit for at least a month. So Guy agreed to my going on leave. Dick and I left The Cedars the next morning.

We went to Ramat David with the intention of watching the men do their first jump early the next morning. I was met by Jake, who told me that the whole of the Squadron was to be ready to embark from Haifa for an unknown destination the following midday.

I had no orders other than what Jake had told me. Half my men were at Ramat David in Palestine with no operational equipment; half were eight hours' drive away at The Cedars; some of our Signal personnel were in Cairo; and I was on leave with nothing. These difficulties were nothing to the disappointment of the men, who had completed their ground training and were due to do their first jump at dawn the next morning. However,

Jake was firm, and very wisely would not listen to their appeals that he should allow them to do just one jump.

We worked all that night, and we planned and telephoned against a background of convival enjoyment. There was no time for anyone to sleep, so the men decided to relieve their chagrin with alcohol. By the morning much had been done, and some order was resulting from the chaos. Guy Prendergast had arrived, and I went with him to Haifa to attend a conference with a staff officer who had flown up from Cairo.

It transpired that as a result of the recent Italian armistice it had been decided to send token garrisons to the Dodecanese Islands in order to encourage the Italians to resist any German attempts to seize them. For this purpose a small base was just being established on Castellorosso. My Squadron was to be sent up to that island, where we were to hold ourselves in readiness to move at six hours' notice, under the control of GHQ in Cairo.

A few months ago somebody sent me the original 'Most Secret and Officer Only' Operation Instruction concerning this move. It is addressed to me as the commander of B Squadron, LRDG, is signed by Lt-General Anderson and dated 11 September 1943. It says that my 'most likely role will be to move into Cos and Samos, if the situation permits, to stiffen resistance of the Italian garrisons and local guerillas to German control of the Islands. You may however be ordered to operate in Rhodes.'

Thus began, in a tragically vague way, the Aegean Campaign of September, October and November 1943. It was tragically vague throughout, and many fine lives were lost in a cause which few of us ever fully understood.

I remember leaving that conference in Haifa to return to my Squadron, which had been temporarily quartered in a disused monastery in Haifa. On the way I tried to conceive for what possible purpose the LRDG's special training and equipment might come in useful. I could imagine none. But there was little time for idle speculation. There was far too much to be done, for we were to embark at 6.30 that evening. Vehicles were coming either from Cairo or from Syria loaded with the men and the equipment we needed. All these had to be checked, sorted and packed for shipment. We worked like maniacs all that day, and somehow got everything in some sort of order.

That evening we embarked in a Greek sloop. We knew no more than we had been told, and the lack of reliable information was disgraceful. While we were at least happy to be employed again after so long away from it all, I was very concerned that our new task was to begin on such an ill-prepared note, after all the weeks of training and careful preparation that we had put into the future. The chaotic way in which we were being rushed off did not fill us with much confidence.

Protest would have been futile, and maybe, I thought, it will all work out well in the end. I was perhaps allowing myself to be disturbed by the fact that this well-ordered machine of mine was being driven so badly by rough drivers who did not care for it with the same jealous passion as I did. So on we went!

The crew of that Greek sloop were wonderfully kind and hospitable; and they were consummately proud to be sailing under the Greek flag towards Greek territory. We could not help catching some of their enthusiasm, and I tried to pass it on to my men when they assembled on the after-deck under the stars for me to tell them where we were going. The captain very generously gave up his cabin to me. I was confused and tired after the happenings of the past thirty-six hours, and I slid quickly into a sleep of deep oblivion.

Our ship was in company with a French and a British sloop, and these sailed ahead of us throughout the next day. In the evening of 13 September we slipped into the narrow inlet amid whose steep and green slopes nestled the tiny, attractive village of Castellorosso. The narrow quayside was lined with cheering, rapturous Greeks waving little flags. Their genuine and spontaneous welcome did not make the task of unloading any the easier.

I had over a hundred men with all their stores and provisions for three weeks. These had to be transhipped from the sloop into caïques and rowing-boats. It all took a lot of shouting, pleading, cajoling and endeavour to get everything ashore. But the hungry owners of the small boats found great temptation in the plenty that we had.

Very soon we were settled into a few empty houses near the quay, and those who were not busy were bathing in that lovely harbour. We made wireless contact with Cairo, and I informed them of our safe arrival before enjoying an evening meal, a glass or two of local wine and sleep on the wooden floor of our little white houses, with their painted shutters.

We woke at dawn next morning and bathed before breakfast. It was a glorious morning and we felt contented and expectant. We wandered round the little town talking to the Greeks, accepting their generous hospitality and frowning at the Italians of the garrison. Italy had only recently surrendered, and we found it difficult to walk side by side and be pleasant with those who had so recently killed our friends, and of whom the Greeks told us so many tales of terror and bestiality.

Of course, we had not been told the terms of the Italian surrender, and did not know how lightly or otherwise they had been let down. However, if I had it might have been easier to relay the order (which I later received) that Italian officers were to be saluted. I am glad I never passed on that order.

Those Aegean Islands are very beautiful, and it was hard to remember that there was a war on, as not even a German high-reconnaissance plane disturbed our peace. But a signal from Cairo was to do this soon after lunch as I lay on my bedding-roll on the floor, swishing away the swarms of flies which thrived in those Greek homes. This signal read:

'Long Range Desert Group Squadron will move at once to Leros to assist the Italian Garrison.'

Leros was some way to the north beyond German-held Rhodes, and the latest intelligence reported the imminent arrival of a German emissary to discuss the occupation of the island. Leros was important to whoever was going to control the Aegean, for it had a wonderful natural harbour and a good, sheltered seaplane base.

With only such scant information, and with none at all about how the Italian garrison would receive us, I was also faced with the problem of how to get there. I politely pointed out to Cairo that the sloops hd returned to Haifa and that it was impossible to get to Leros with any dispatch, as the only craft available were small caïques.

However, there was one Italian fast motor launch and a seaplane. This latter had been brought from Rhodes by Major The Earl Jellicoe after his gallant but unsupported attempt to persuade the large Italian garrison to overcome the comparatively small German force on the island. George Jellicoe had been dropped in by parachute, and he had sent many signals to Cairo asking for only a few troops to help him, but all his entreaties had fallen on unhearing ears.

I believe we made our first of many blunders in so impotently failing to assume control over Rhodes—the largest and most important of the Dodecanese Islands. This failure to get the airfields on it should have been the signal that those Aegean operations were doomed to disaster unless Turkey could be persuaded at once to come in on the side of the Allies.

We had to get to Leros somehow, so I arranged to send Captain Alan Redfern, with a wireless set, straight there in the seaplane. He would then inform me of the situation as he found it, and I would somehow follow on with the Squadron to join him. Unfortunately, the seaplane—crewed by Italians who were not very keen to make the trip anyhow—taxied into an RAF Sunderland which had just arrived from Cairo. The seaplane was no longer serviceable.

So I decided to go on in the Italian motor launch with as many men as she would carry. We left at dusk with a coxswain from the Royal Navy to keep an eye on our course, an engineer in the engine-room and myself with a pistol in my pocket beside the skipper. We did not trust our new co-belligerents, and neither did we fancy being taken for a ride to Rhodes.

It was a clear, moonlit night as we sped past Rhodes. We could see fires burning. These were the result of a visit by the Royal Air Force an hour or two earlier; and later coming in behind us out of the moon we saw the big RAF transport planes which were to drop a company of our parachutists on the airfield at Cos.

We steamed on between the knots of small islands and slowly drew up along the west coast of Leros. The deep, throaty roar of the high-powered engines were suddenly throttled back to a more respectable marine sound and our senses slowed to a more even tempo. It was exciting. We didn't

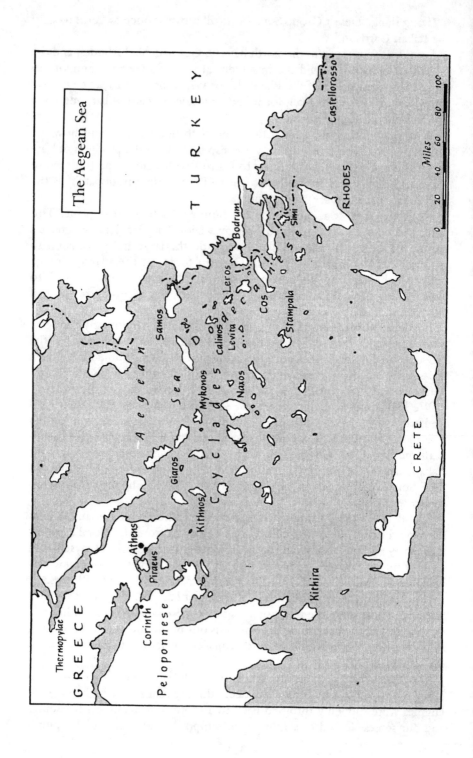

The Aegean Sea

have much idea what to expect. I don't think anyone minded much. We were tired and wet and very cold.

I can remember standing on the deck with Moir Stormonth-Darling. We were sometimes silent and sometimes making that rather artificial kind of conversation that one resorts to when minds are preoccupied with a little fear in the chilly loneliness of the hours before dawn. Our Italian crew were utterly scared as we nosed our way towards the boom which covered the entrance to the harbour.

Suddenly a shot rang out and torches flashed from the rocky coast. There then ensued a bedlam of loud-hailing between most of the members of our terror-stricken crew and an equally terrified boom operator. After nearly half an hour some agreement must have been reached, for the boom swung open and we swept powerfully into the long harbour. We drew in alongside the quay, to be met by Admiral Mascarpa and his entire staff. He had been warned of the arrival of British reinforcements. But I can only describe his reception in the early light of dawn as frigid. The Admiral apparently expected at least two divisions, and was patently somewhat put out by the appearance only of myself and twenty very heavily laden, tired and soaking-wet soldiers.

I hastily explained that I was the forerunner of more to come. I did not add that as far as I knew the only others on their way were my remaining Patrols, and that these could possibly arrive in two days—if they had been able to impress sufficient craft to move them. My explanation seemed to satisfy the Admiral, who politely asked me to attend at his house for luncheon that day.

I duly arrived at the time appointed and felt a tinge of embarrassment in my dirty clothes among so many gold-bespattered Italians who exuded perfume. But my embarrassment soon turned to resentment when I saw how those Fascist officers were living. We sat down to a five-course meal. There were hams, chickens and other delicacies. We ate off beautiful china and drank finest wines and liqueurs from Italy out of golden goblets.

All this was horribly distasteful to me when outside the very door were starving Greeks who begged you for your leavings; and how inappropriate was all the pomp and ceremony of those Italians at a time when, in their own admission, the Germans were liable to arrive at any moment. I did not enjoy myself, and I was ill-mannered enough to let this be apparent.

Next day I called on the Admiral to discuss the island's defences with him. I was shown the fire-plan for his guns and the locations of the wire and the few mines that there were. Even with my limited knowledge of military tactics I could see that the whole defence scheme was futile. There was no depth in the defence, and no provision had been made for a reserve to counter-attack any enemy that might land. All communications were by telephone above the ground, and the transport available was quite inadequate to maintain the five large coastal gun batteries. I pointed all this out and explained that some sort of line must be built across the island to seal off any landing in either the north or the south of its figure-of-eight shape.

The Italians were rudely shocked, and at first they resented my criticisms. They had probably satisfied many visiting generals easily susceptible to being wined and dined even half as well as I had been. But after a bit they seemed to appreciate my arguments, and they agreed to dig weapon-pits from which they could cover the centre of the island. Here was the obvious, and in fact the actual, place where the enemy would choose to land.

Agreement to a plan and its execution are two different things with Italians. First they said that they had not enough men to do the work, and then that the ground was too hard. However, I had seen lots of picks and shovels belonging to the locals, and these were commandeered. I next asked for a strength state, and found that the garrison totalled five thousand. In the end the men were produced, and we gave them explosives to blow holes in rocky places. I think the Italians thought I was mad, for I even made the officers remove their beautifully laundered white tunics and their polished leather belts in order to lend a hand with their men. This was something they had never done before!

This went on feverishly for some days, and still there was no sign of the Germans. Then one morning I was woken with a message to say that three British destroyers were lying in the harbour. I went down to see what was going on, and on the quay I found a British brigadier with his entire brigade. GHQ in Cairo must have forgotten to tell me about them! However, this brigade had spent many months in Malta, and it knew what siege was like, so I was glad to hand over the whole problem of the defence of Leros to them.

Not long after this Jake Easonsmith arrived with the New Zealand Squadron and a small Headquarters. He had left Guy Prendergast in Cairo to watch our needs back there, but Guy did not enjoy being left out of it all, and he soon joined us at Leros.

It was quite clear that there was no policy for the employment of the Long Range Desert Group or of George Jellicoe's Special Boat Service, which had also been ordered to Leros. Eventually it was agreed that it would be better if these units could move to the neighbouring island of Calinos with the Levant Schooner Flotilla of five armed caïques under Lt-Commander Adrian Seligman RN.

These vessels had been especially fitted for transporting agents and raiding parties among the islands. On 25 September the LRDG sailed from Leros to Calinos, where we hoped to be free from interference in order to give our full attention to sending out Patrols to gain information.

From Calinos we could watch the increasingly heavy raids on Cos a few miles to the south and on Leros a similar distance to the north of us. By the end of September these raids had neutralised the efforts of the Allied fighters on the airfield at Cos. I believe the pilots were South Africans, and they did their best to maintain a fairly constant patrol against the swarms of enemy aircraft which came over. I never saw more than two of our fighters in the air at once, yet these tackled any number the Germans chose to send over. We picked up a few pilots out of the sea, and watched others go down in flames.

One incident sticks in my memory. We had sent a boat to pick up a German pilot. We saw him rescued, and watched the boat row back towards us. A few moments later an enemy flying-boat which had been hovering around to rescue any of their airmen shot down into the sea landed by our small boat. Our crew were so flabbergasted that they could do little to avoid handing over their prisoner. A very short period of captivity!

We wondered if others appreciated the efforts of our gallant airmen as much as we did. We wondered also whether the authorities in Cairo realised where all this was leading when we were informed that there was little likelihood of an enemy seaborne invasion of Cos, but that we might expect a few small airborne attempts at sabotage. This was on the evening before Cos was invaded from the sea!

On the morning of 3 October Jake and I—who shared a room in a house by the harbour—awoke at dawn. We had slept on the balcony under mosquito nets, and we watched a fleet of all types of craft moving in towards the east coast of Cos.

'Good morning', I heard Jake say in his easy, confident manner, 'it's a funny thing but I don't think all those ships were there last night.'

'No', I replied, 'and I don't much like the look of them.'

After the reassurances from Cairo the night before, the stark truth had not immediately dawned on us. Any doubts that we had were soon dispelled by the smoke and flashes of the guns and the squadrons of aircraft, which were methodically destroying what little opposition there was.

All day we waited for news, knowing that our own position was precarious. Leros too was being heavily bombed, and our only line of withdrawal lay out towards the enemy, for our little harbour of Calinos lay in full view of Cos. We heard nothing until the evening, when we received orders that the LRDG was to counter-attack on Cos, getting ourselves there by local boats. I always thought that this was one of the most brainless and preposterous orders that I ever heard.

It was very hard to see how about three hundred men, neither trained nor equipped for infantry fighting, could make much material difference where two thousand British infantry had already failed. Nor could we see how a small fleet of caïques sailing at about five knots could get to Cos, disgorge its men and return unseen to Calinos. I quite understood the strategic value of Cos, with the only airfield from which our fighters could operate; and without air cover we could never hope to hold Leros for any length of time. But the island was about thirty miles long, and I could not see how the LRDG could take it.

GHQ in Cairo had been told by the Prime Minister that this was 'the time to play high. Improvise and dare.' This was certainly the improvisation he demanded, and we were to be sent to dare! But we did as we were told, and had everything ready for this futile venture when the orders were cancelled. A short while later it was decided that only my Squadron would undertake this desperate mission, and that a motor launch was to be sent from Leros for the purpose.

Mercifully this did not arrive in time; and we next received news that Cos had fallen.

A little later the same day a further signal arrived telling us all to evacuate to Leros. Once again we assembled a strange fleet of caïques and any available craft capable of making the trip. At nightfall on 4 October a fleet of curious little craft put out into the darkness and we sailed across to Leros. Here we unloaded all our stores on to the quay as quickly as we could in order to disperse the craft as soon after dawn as possible.

The constant change of plan and indecision resulted in a mass of broken ration boxes, smashed up against piles of ammunition, clothing and wireless equipment. We worked hard to try to sort out this litter, and then gave breakfast to the tired and uncomplaining men who had had no sleep all night.

We had no idea why we had returned to Leros, and Guy had gone off to try to find out some news. No one from the Staff had come to the harbour to greet us, and our arrival was almost as unhappy as mine had been the previous month. But at least then the Italians had been on the quayside to welcome us.

Soon afterwards we heard the distant drone of aircraft, followed by the deep roar of anti-aircraft guns. Next came the clattering of machine-gun fire, whipped up into a fury and intensified by the sound of rifle-shots, until the whole reached a shattering crescendo. It culminated in that high-pitched whine when seconds are counted before the ear-splitting crack of bursting bombs. We fell on our faces, counted those seconds and suffered the din in our strange surprise to find ourselves still alive; and then there was silence—a silence accentuated by the stench of cordite and the rising smell of dust from the rubble of buildings.

These bombs had fallen close. We saw them drop. A stick of four from each of the twelve Stukas, which screamed down on us at a height of only five hundred feet.

This raid was only a taste of more to come. We just had time to disperse a little and get a few machine-guns into play before the next ones came. This time a ship was hit and clouds of oily black smoke swirled up into the sky as anti-aircraft gunners sped the parting raiders on their way.

I really do not know how long this went on. Our machine-gunners stood their ground splendidly as the Stukas dived almost, it seemed, into the barrels of their guns. Each time just after the bombs had fallen there was that frightening silence, and a choking, dusty fog permeated the air.

At last we were able to get away from the harbour and up into the hills with as much of our equipment as we could move. Somehow our casualties had been remarkably few; but I remember seeing David Sutherland of the Special Boat Service covered in blood, and one or two others were wounded. On the whole, though, we had had incredible luck.

In the centre of the island the Royal Irish Fusiliers were the main defensive force, and we were placed under their command. We were ordered to send Patrols to each of the five heavy coastal gun batteries, which dominated the island's heights. This was not only a fillip to the Italians manning them but it also meant that if the enemy should attempt a landing we would be able to discourage those Italians from letting their guns fall intact into German hands.

We settled in to a dismal life of waiting. All and every day we waited to dodge the sporadic, maddening air raids, and at night we waited for the supply-dropping aircraft to come from bases in Palestine. And all the while we kept an everlasting watch round the coast.

We lived in miserable caves or just lay among the rocks. I seldom heard a complaint, but it wasn't much fun for anyone. Aircraft in twos and threes were overhead most of the time by day, and a little less frequently by night. Casualties were remarkably light, and damage negligible. A few of the big guns were damaged, and most of the shipping in and around the main harbour was sunk.

The Royal Navy was wonderfully active each night bombarding enemy shipping in the harbours of Cos and Calinos. They did our morale a lot of good. In our ignorance we despised the efforts of the RAF—not the pilots, whose courage we never questioned, but those who seemed to contrive to keep them away from us.

We never saw them and it was hard to believe that they were in fact busily engaged in bombing enemy airfields in Crete, Greece and Rhodes. It was even less consoling to be told that we were keeping a large part of the German's Mediterranean Air Force away from the main front in Italy. All this stuff was less convincing when we knew how glad the Germans were to find somewhere where their obsolete Stukas could operate unmolested against no opposition.

We sent our Patrols out on to various islands, and they were reporting enemy air and shipping movement all the time. Ken Lazarus was on Stampalia, Dudley Folland on Giaros, Saxton on Kithnos and Redfern on Simi. All had their adventures but on Simi the Germans attempted to overcome the garrison of about one hundred and fifty Italians. They landed about eighty men from a schooner and maintained a precarious foothold on the island for about ten hours. They then withdrew, leaving sixteen wounded and six killed, to lick their wounds and send over streams of Stukas to bomb the island on the day following.

We were getting reports at this time of a strong enemy garrison on Calinos. It was so close to Leros that these had to be verified. So Lt

Pavlides, a Greek commissioned in the British Army, volunteered to row across one night to find out all that he could. This he did safely, and brought back useful information. Three nights later Stan Eastwood and two of his Rhodesians were landed on Calinos to try to get more information. But when the pick-up craft went to collect them they were not contacted. It was only later that we heard that the night after they had been landed Eastwood and his men ran into some Germans whom they could not avoid. Eastwood and one other were captured; but L/Cpl Whitehead ran for it and swam out to sea. He then came back in to another part of the island, where he met a friendly shepherd who fed, clothed and hid him.

About ten days later a Greek swam across to Leros with news that Whitehead was safe. He also brought a message from him asking us to acknowledge its receipt by firing off a given number of shells from one of the guns at a given time on a certain day. In this way we were also able to agree a plan that he had suggested for his collection. He was safely rescued five days later. Eastwood and the other man also escaped and made their way back to the unit through Turkey.

It was becoming clear to the authorities in Cairo that the various raiding organisations in the Aegean would best function under one co-ordinating headquarters. George Jellicoe had worked hard for this, and they created an outfit known as 'Raiding Forces' with a Colonel Turnbull in charge. He was a total stranger to the business, and he asked for Guy Prendergast as his second-in-command.

Guy was never consulted about any of this, and suddenly found himself called away from the LRDG, which he had commanded so well for two and a half years. It was a tragic blow to us, and we all missed him dreadfully. It was such a waste of talent, and if only Guy had been given command of the new organisation it might have achieved more than in fact it ever did.

Guy was succeeded in command by Jake Easonsmith, who asked me to become his second-in-command. This was on 18 October 1943. I hated leaving the Squadron which I had trained, but I could not refuse Jake's appeal. He was one of my closest friends, and I admired and respected him tremendously.

Jake had been a wine salesman before the war, and he was certainly the best of the 'civilian soldiers' that the LRDG ever had. Although he was no professional, I never knew his equal. He had a guile which was almost uncanny in his ability to foresee how the enemy would react. He was always thinking ahead and asking himself what he would do if the enemy adopted a certain line of action. Thus he was always prepared, and I never knew him to be caught on the wrong foot.

Jake did so much for me, and I often sought the wisdom of his good counsel. Maybe it was over some operational problem and, after a minute or two of quiet thought, he would say, 'Well, if I were you, I'd have a go. The risk is worth taking.' Or maybe it was over some question of discipline, and Jake would then say, 'David, there is only one fair thing to do, and that is to give him the benefit of the doubt.' Jake was always fair.

What we lost in Guy's departure we gained in Jake's promotion. Fundamentally the change made little difference. Alan Redfern took over my Squadron and led it very well, until his death only a month later.

Jake's first task as Commanding Officer was to order a raid in which he did not believe. We knew that it was pointless and violated all the principles by which our small hit-and-run attacks were guided, and I am afraid we had no confidence in our immediate superiors. We sat up most of one night discussing the problem, and Jake agreed to protest to the brigadier, but was overruled by him. Jake had to send a force of fifty men to recapture an island called Levita which had fallen into enemy hands. In early October the Royal Navy had intercepted a German convoy bound for Cos, and sank all ten ships. Only about a hundred of the thousand troops in the convoy survived, and these were taken to Stampalia as prisoners.

Later on a small caïque called HMS *Hedgehog* sailed from Stampalia with forty of these prisoners. The vessel had engine trouble, and put into Levita, which was only occupied by a few Italians. The next day the prisoners overcame the little crew of HMS *Hedgehog*, who were outnumbered by five to one, and they then took complete control of the island.

CHAPTER 13

# The Battle for Leros

The LRDG was told to retake Levita because anyway it would be easy (we were informed), and it would be a good idea to stop the Germans getting away with such a thing. There was no further information, and when Jake asked for a postponement to find out a bit more this was refused.

On 23 October John Olivey was put in charge of this operation. He was given forty-five men, and Dick Lawson, the doctor, went with them. At 7.30 p.m. that evening Jake and I saw them off. Our hearts were heavy. We disliked the whole foolish enterprise, which we saw as a wicked and misplaced attempt at a spectacular success to regain the confidence that Cairo had lost in the direction of the Aegean campaign.

The two motor launches which had taken Olivey and his men returned to Leros at 3.00 a.m. the next morning. They reported safe, unopposed and successful landings. One party under Lt Kay was landed on the south-west extremity of the island, and a party of New Zealanders under Lt Sutherland was landed on the north-west end. All this went according to plan until Sutherland ran into opposition, and Olivey reported that he was out of contact with him but could hear heavy fighting.

All afternoon Jake and I watched heavy and continuous air attack by Stukas and JU 88s, which we could see from Leros. That evening Jake left in an ML to go to the prearranged rendezvous on Levita to collect the force which we assumed by then would have completed its task. He had a good deal of difficulty, but eventually contacted John Olivey, Dick Lawson, one wounded man and five other ranks.

There was absolutely no sign of the rest of the party, despite every attempt to contact them. The next night another party was sent off to attempt the pick-up, but they failed to find anyone. John Olivey could only tell us how he had been heavily attacked both from the air and on the ground until his small party was nearly surrounded. He managed to break out, and he assumed that the others were taken prisoner, but he had no news of Sutherland's party.

This was a bitter blow to the LRDG. We had lost more men in a few hours than we had lost in all the previous years. But no recriminations would bring them back, and we suffered this loss with as much grace as we could summon. It was only later that we learnt how heavily Olivey's men had been outnumbered, even before German reinforcements came in during the day. At one time Jack Sutherland's New Zealanders had captured thirty-five prisoners, but in the end he was forced to hand himself and his men over to them.

Soon after this costly and fruitless débâcle Brigadier George Davy, then Director of Military Operations in Cairo, paid us a visit. He arrived very wet and rather oily after having had his destroyer sunk beneath him on the way. He at least was alive to the problems we were up against, and he saw how we were being wastefully employed. The then GOC Aegean was replaced as a result of this visit, and a little sanity returned to the garrison on Leros.

But we had lost mobility through overwhelming German air superiority, and it seemed to me that we should have cut our losses and got out of the Aegean before it was too late. Turkey would not come in openly on our side, and without her bases we could only flounder. All this was very obvious to us on the ground.

We could not train properly because the island was too small. We could not operate on other islands, for the GOC was not willing to spare a single man from the defence of Leros when the inevitable showdown came. The days dragged on under constant air attack. Each morning we 'stood to' to greet the expected invasion in the cold October dawn. Everyone was getting tired and irritable among the three Regular regiments on the island and on the Staff. Only the inherent discipline of these regiments kept morale at a reasonable level, for there was little encouragement from above.

In all there were about three thousand British troops, with the Royal Irish Fusiliers holding the central feature of Meriviglia, the Buffs in the north and the King's Own in the south of the island. There was a battery of 25-pounders, twelve Bofors guns which had been brought in strapped to the hulls of submarines, and the five coastal-defence batteries, each of four 6-inch naval guns taken off British ships.

All was set for what one war correspondent called at the time 'a highly improbable film'. But I personally was not to see it shown. A few days before the battle began Jake asked me to return to Cairo. Ostensibly this was to collect more recruits and to start a training organisation for them, but secretly Jake had decided to get me out of Leros for other reasons. One was that we knew that disaster lay ahead, and he wanted me to do all that I could to alleviate it as much as possible. The second was that the authorities in Cairo had to be made more aware of the true state of affairs in Leros, and it was thought that I might be able to bring them up to date.

One evening on the Meriviglia feature I said farewell to Jake. Somehow

I sensed that it would be the last time that I would see him. We talked about home and about his family, to whom he was devoted; we talked about what we would do when it was all over. We talked about the LRDG, which meant such a lot to both of us; and we had so many ideas for the future. Jake and I had been through quite a lot together in the desert, and I hated leaving at this stage. But there was no alternative. I knew that one of us had to go, and he certainly never would.

I went aboard an Italian submarine, and after five fairly daunting days we arrived in Haifa. I went on to Cairo, and arrived there as the battle for Leros began on 12 November 1943. I was lucky to have a wireless set directly in touch with the LRDG in Leros, so my news was both interesting and up to date.

Soon after dawn that day fifteen landing craft each carrying about fifty men landed troops in the north-east and centre of the island, and although some were sunk, the enemy gained a foothold. At about 2.30 that afternoon forty JU 52 transport planes began dropping parachutists, and they were able to fly in at five hundred feet. That evening Jake sent me a signal to say that 'the lack of RAF support was absolutely pitiful. Ships sat around all day and Stukas just laughed at us.'

As soon as the parachutists landed our Patrols were sent off to deal with them. In one of these sorties Alan Redfern was killed, and his loss was a great blow as he was a much liked and respected officer. He had done invaluable work with us, and also in the early days of the war when he trained Commandos at Gwelo in Rhodesia.

That night the situation was under some control. The enemy were confined to small areas on the beaches where they had landed. But off the island there lay three separate convoys escorted by destroyers, waiting to come in to disgorge their cargoes. This they did during the night.

All next day the situation was confused. Jake sent another signal to say that 'everything [was] difficult but we are all confident of outcome if no more Germans landed. Parachutists pretty to watch but suffered many casualties.'

John Olivey with the 6-inch-gun battery on Clidi in the north of the island was driven off his position, but only after he had fired those great guns over open sights at the advancing enemy infantry. The Italian crew had deserted him, save for one officer who fought gallantly throughout the battle. Before leaving the position Olivey destroyed one of the guns when the Germans were but a few yards from the heights. However, the next day with a party of the Buffs he retook the position, although he was slightly wounded in the action.

On 15 November the tempo of the battle increased. The enemy threw in 450 aircraft during the day. All our troops were terribly tired, and exhaustion was probably their worst enemy. The total lack of RAF support was a disappointment.

The next day the situation grew worse, and urgent appeals for reinforcements were sent by the garrison. The Germans launched a heavy attack on Meriviglia, and to quote one historian, 'all types of aircraft including Stukas and outmoded seaplanes, flew more than six hundred sorties against the British positions and strafed everything that moved, without a shot being fired in return except by small arms'.

But the worst news of all that day came when Tim Heywood rang me. 'I've got bad news for you, David.'

'It's all right, I know what it is. You needn't tell me.'

And somehow I did know. I had a horrible premonition that Jake would be killed, and I was profoundly shaken by the news. I was in Rufus Montagu's flat when Tim had rung me, and it was my good fortune that Rufus was there to talk to. I needed help very badly. The loss to us all was incalculable. Yet, somehow Jake's memory and his example remained with many of us as an inspiration throughout the years ahead.

Jake was thirty-four when he was killed leading some men into the little village of Leros. The Germans had occupied some of the houses and they were obviously a threat to the headquarters in the massive caves and tunnels on Meriviglia. The GOC wanted to know how many of the enemy were in the village, and Jake was ordered to send a patrol to find out. He felt that this might be a difficult task, and as he knew the area so well he decided to go himself. Jake fell to a sniper's bullet as he approached the houses where the Germans were.

Meriviglia was overrun, and Fortress HQ had to destroy much of their wireless equipment and documents before withdrawing to the harbour at Portolago. At dawn on 17 November the position was critical after the Germans had made further landings. An attempt was made to rally the troops in the south of the island 'but morale by this time was very low and the result was a dismal failure'.

Organised resistance collapsed, and silence descended on the island. All communication with the garrison ceased, except for one wireless set of ours which was being operated by Sergeant Hughes, who was still on the Meriviglia feature. He told us at 6.35 p.m. in clear that the Fortress had surrendered, and then reported next morning that isolated fighting still continued but he did not know what was going on. That was the last message we received from Leros.

John Olivey refused to surrender, and he fought on with his redoubtable Rhodesians until he was captured having fallen asleep through sheer exhaustion. He had been ordered to hold the Clidi height until 'his casualties became heavier than the enemy's'. John was certainly not going to accept the fact that the rest of the garrison had surrendered. I suppose it was lucky that slumber solved the dilemma for him.

But before this had happened John decided that he was not going to let the enemy capture the magazines of the position from which he had been obliged to withdraw. He entered one of the concrete emplacements and found two Germans.

'They were surprised to see me,' he told me later, 'but they didn't have long to think about things because I had to shoot them. What else could I do?'

For his courage on Leros John was awarded a bar to the Military Cross that he had won in the desert. The citation for this ended with the words:

> Captain Olivey was himself still firing a Bren gun and throwing grenades thirteen hours after the island surrendered. Throughout the battle he showed no thought for his own safety and at times fired heavy coastal guns over open sights against the advancing enemy. This was despite persistent bombing attacks on a very large scale.

Sergeant Coventry, who was with him, was awarded the Distinguished Conduct Medal.

Thus ended the ill-starred battle of Leros. It was never a worth-while risk, and when it was clear that it could not be given adequate air support I do not (and never did) understand why we did not cut our losses and withdraw with as much decorum as was possible. But we did not do this, and we suffered an unnecessary and humiliating defeat.

When the island surrendered the LRDG had 123 men on it. Of these about seventy escaped in the ensuing weeks. But we lost many of our old desert hands, and they and their experience were irreplaceable. We were lucky to recover as many men as we did. But we could have got more.

GHQ in Cairo was never willing to admit the possibility that Leros might be overrun, but I was convinced that this was not only likely but a virtual certainty. For this reason I felt that it was only prudent to make contingency plans to rescue those who were not immediately taken prisoner. I felt too that with my intimate and up-to-date knowledge of the island, and the poor state of morale of its garrison, I had a duty to press the authorities to make provision for saving the survivors of an invasion.

The battle for Leros began on 12 November. That evening I drafted a 'Most Secret and Officer Only' signal to go from GHQ to the Fortress Commander, and I took it to the Director of Military Operations for approval before dispatch. The wording of that signal was as follows:

> in unlikely event of Leros being overrun and evacuation of survivors being necessary what are your plans. If you require assistance signal RV's and other details. If communications are cut caïques will visit PEGA, SAN DOMENICA, SCROFE nightly from night 14/15 if situation appears to us to warrant it.

The word 'unlikely' was inserted into my draft; and the three place-names are islands a short distance from Leros.

I kept a copy of that signal, and at the bottom of it I wrote:

> despite all my efforts this signal was never sent until just before the end of the battle when all ciphers had been burnt and then in plain language in a disguised code. As a result many valuable lives were lost.

I was very bitter about this, for although we got just over a thousand men away from Leros, I know that we could have recovered a great many more if I had not been ordered to stop making rescue plans. Suffice it to say that I did everything possible within the limits imposed on me, and so the LRDG got quite a respectable proportion of its men to safety.

Ashley Greenwood, who had been on the island throughout the battle, escaped to Turkey and then volunteered the very day he got there to go back again to help others. This he did dressed as a Greek civilian, and he saved a number of lives. What courage that man had! Peter Mold, one of our Signal officers, spent until 2 December on the island, and eventually managed to reach Turkey with the help of some Greeks. He was one of those contacted and given directions by Ashley Greenwood. Guy Prendergast, who had resumed command of the LRDG after Jake was killed, managed to collect a few men together after the Fortress had surrendered, and they were eventually contacted by an RAF Air Sea Rescue launch.

In an account of the battle and of his subsequent escape which he wrote at the time he told of the disorganisation of the troops before the final capitulation; and of how he did his best to collect together the LRDG from amongst the large crowd of demoralised troops. He tried to persuade officers of other units to reorganise their men and to make for the various escape points, but 'everybody, however, appeared too tired to want to do anything but sleep'.

Guy and his party got away to Bodrum in Turkey, from whence they made their way back to Palestine.

Others had some remarkable escapes. John Olivey eventually got back to us. I had a letter from him written in Athens after his escape, and dated 30 January 1944, in which he asked me to try and hurry up his recovery from there. This was effected, and I also forwarded to his wife in Rhodesia a letter for her which he had enclosed.

But I think one of the better stories was of two men of the Yeomanry Patrol, who had been captured on 24 October 1943 at Levita, and who returned to the LRDG in early February 1945, which was fifteen months after they had been lost. They were Gunner Patch and Trooper Hill.

They somehow kept a diary, and they later gave me a copy of it. The following are extracts from it:

26 Oct.    Our two Officers and the wounded evacuated by flying boat to Piraeus in Greece . . . We followed later and saw JU 52's being mounted on floats, in preparation, our guards said, for the attack on Leros.

2 Nov.     We were marched through Athens and entrained horse-box fashion for Germany . . . Food provided for the four day journey was one kilogram of sour black bread and two small tins of Italian bully beef.

| | |
|---|---|
| 3 Nov. | Reached Thermopylae ... Are now about fifty to a wagon. |
| 4 Nov. | Reached Salonika. German commander threatened to shoot prisoners in any carriage from which men escaped. |
| 5 Nov. | Reached Yugoslav-Greek border. |
| 6 Nov. | Spent day loosening staples and cutting through barbed wire on windows. Shortly after leaving Veles, escaped through window followed by two New Zealanders. |
| 7 Nov. | Took stock of supplies. Had very little. Awfully cold, huddled together for warmth. |
| 8 Nov. | Too cold to sleep. Some snow. |
| 9 Nov. | Violent snowstorm. Food situation critical. |
| 13 Nov. | Joined Guerilla HQ and found they were followers of Mikhailovic's Chetniks. |
| 14 Nov. | Shaved first time since October 23rd. Legs covered with sores, hands and face festering. Chetniks quite incapable of looking after themselves. We became their doctors, handymen and advisers. |
| 26 Nov. | Spent last few days moving from barn to barn. Everything very sordid. Snow. |
| 27 Nov. | Ill in bed with, I think, Malaria, Jim (Patch) sick with lumbago so he can't lie down. |
| 17 Dec. | Very hard frost and bitterly cold ... My boots now worn out. |
| 22 Dec. | No food again today. |
| 23 Dec. | Brush with Bulgar patrol. No casualties. No food again. |
| 25 Dec. | Very dark and raining hard. No food again but opened small tin of syrup and biscuits which we had kept to celebrate with. Given a bottle of Raki as Christmas present. Listened on wireless to King's speech. Tried hard *not* to think of home. |
| 27, 28 Dec. | No food. |

On 7 January 1944, the day that the Serbs recognised as Christmas, they even had eggs, cheese, meat and milk.

Nothing very exciting happened for the next few weeks. Patch and Hill were living in the most primitive conditions in caves and barns. They suffered appalling hardships from cold and hunger. Yet these two young men remained cheerful. On 5 February a party of Serbs arrived with a wireless set from a British liaison officer in Serbia. On 10 February they were able to contact him.

Patch gave a very good description of the kind of men with whom they were living. He says that

the Officers of the gang were a useless crowd. A & B thought of nothing save their own comfort and went to great lengths to achieve it. They

146

even went so far as to oppose strongly any proposal to take an active part in the war because they feared they might have to endure some sort of hardship.

Colonel C had no mind of his own and was easily overruled by A & B.

D, E, and F were all drunkards always at loggerheads and sometimes coming to blows.

G was the only active Officer among them. He sometimes did lead raids against the Bulgars but even he was out for his own ends.

On 10 March they were very nearly caught by a Bulgar patrol. In the chaos that followed they had to leave their wireless and batteries, as these were too heavy to carry at speed.

| | |
|---|---|
| 11, 12 Mar. | No food. |
| 13 Mar. | Much snow. Too cold to sleep. |
| 14 Mar. | No food. |
| 16 Mar. | Still no food. |
| 17 Mar. | Patrol brought in twenty-four kilos of bread for forty men. . . . We have now decided to leave this gang. The larder is often bare and this is tiresome. |
| 23 Mar. | No food for last three days. Gang commander will not allow us to go to Albania. Eight of our men captured. |
| 5 April. | Two informers shot and mutilated. |

At the end of April they received another wireless and some batteries. At first they could not get it to work, but after rewinding the transformer they made contact again with the Serbian headquarters on 3 May.

They then felt that their duty was to remain with their Chetniks, since they had re-established communications. They had gathered nearly three hundred around them, and they estimated the potential manpower at about four thousand. They also realised that Tito was the true resistance leader, and they hoped to wean the Chetniks away from Mikhailovic. On 19 May they heard on the News from London that the latter had been deposed as War Minister and a new government had been formed. During June they did all they could to contact some British mission but they had no luck, and they were constantly harassed by enemy patrols. Eventually on 19 August they were allowed to leave their Chetniks and go off in search of some Tito supporters. On 1 September they joined forces with a British mission, and the worst of their troubles were over.

I still have a letter that Ron Hill wrote to me from Yugoslavia on 17 October 1944. He said that he had heard that the LRDG was still operating and, he was told, successfully. He continued, 'We hope very much that we'll be able to find a job with you again when we get out of here . . . it should be fairly soon.' In fact, it was not until February 1945.

These two had been through a very great deal, and they were not only determined to stay out of captivity but were also keen to come back to the

LRDG and to do yet more work behind the lines. They had certainly lived up to the high standards that they had set themselves from the time they had joined the Yeomanry Patrol in the desert.

Six years after their escape I was working in the War Office. The war in Korea had begun, and I received a number of letters from officers and men who had served with me in the last war. All of them were ready to offer their services once more. The first letter I received was from Ron Hill, who wrote on behalf of himself and Jimmy Patch to say that they were both available should they be required. I hoped most sincerely that they never would be.

My own personal feelings after the fall of Leros were pretty desperate. Jake had gone. Guy Prendergast was missing, and so also was Dick Lawson. All three of them had not only been great friends of mine for over two years, but were also older than myself, and I appreciated their advice. I was young, and I had had comparatively little experience. I began to wonder how on earth I could—or even whether I should—attempt to rebuild what had been destroyed. Was I going to try to revive the LRDG, or was I going to agree to any suggestion that the unit should be disbanded?

Temporarily I was very dispirited by the whole rotten business. I did not, of course, know how nearly the gamble of Leros had succeeded, and nor did I know what efforts the Prime Minister had put into trying to make it so. If only we had all been told more than we were! But this was a failure of leadership, and it was the lack of it that contributed so greatly to the disaster of Leros.

We did not know until after it was all over that Winston Churchill had cabled to say:

> If there is no hope and nothing can be done you should consider . . . whether the garrison of Leros should not be evacuated to Turkey or perhaps wangled along the coast after blowing up the batteries. Efforts must be made to withdraw the Long Range Desert Groups who are on the other islands. This would be much better than their being taken prisoners of war.

That signal was sent in October, and the Prime Minister was considering the possibility of defeat at that stage. I was not permitted to do so on the 12th of November.

A sad episode altogether.

# CHAPTER 14

# Recovering from Leros

I very soon snapped out of my feeling of being defeated and at a loss, and my mind was made up. There was no doubt that I should try and hold together that spirit and sympathy that was the strength of the LRDG. There was an indefinable but immensely strong bond which linked us all together, and it had been forged in hardship, privation and the sharing of mutual fears, hopes and joys.

Nevertheless, we had lost many of our oldest hands: men who had been out time and again on hazardous operations were now missing or prisoners of war. The benefit of their advice and experience was lost to us. It would take some time to replace them.

Although I was quite clear that the LRDG should be reformed, and everyone else seemed to think the same, there was one man whose advice I felt I must first seek. This was Brigadier Ralph Bagnold, who was the Deputy Chief Signal Officer in Cairo. Although he had been away from us for some time, we all looked upon him as the father of the unit.

So I made an appointment to see him. He received me, as always, shyly but with great charm. I told him why I had come. It was, I said, not only a pity but a sin to break up the association of so many volunteer and chosen men. They had conclusively proved their worth in battle. They were prepared to go anywhere and to do anything.

He remarked that it would need a great deal of new blood to fill in the gap left by those we had lost on Leros. I pointed out that if we were given a free hand in selecting volunteers we would find men as good as those who had gone before, but told him that I had only one reservation. This was that unless I could obtain and train the new members within a reasonable period of time—say six months—then we might find that we had missed the boat.

I told him that I foresaw great opportunities for us in the Balkans and in Italy. Partisans everywhere were just beginning to become organised, and their value to be understood. It was also clear to me that they not only needed supplies and some co-ordination, but most of all they needed leadership and communications.

I felt that with a few trained soldiers to support each band, a few men who could teach them to use their weapons properly and a few to provide the cohesion, the potentialities were unlimited. There was the most magnificent material. They were guerrillas, whose souls were fired with hatred for an enemy whom they loathed and despised; they were fighting on ground which they could choose themselves, and it was ground which they knew intimately and loved as their birthright.

These were the new castles in the air around which my thoughts were floating and taking shape. I saw clearly what we might do. I began to see how we could do it. I soon started to believe that we could do it. And then I convinced myself that we must do it, and that we would be wanted to do it.

I wish I knew what went through Bagnold's mind. He didn't keep me long. He listened to all I had to say, thought for a moment and then said 'I think you should try to keep the unit in being.' Maybe he was mindful of the past and still believed in us; maybe he saw a real use for us or maybe he was struck by my enthusiasm. I shall never know what influenced him; but that moment was the turning-point in the life of the LRDG.

Brigadier Turnbull was commanding Raiding Forces, and he was my immediate master. I had a long talk with him that evening, and he was sympathetic. He gave me every encouragement, and also told me officially that I had been selected to command the LRDG.

I was more than fortunate to be given command of such a unit, after only five years' service in the Army, and I was very aware of what a great chance I had been given. The course which lay ahead was not going to be an easy one. But my target was clear, and I had some ideas as to how I was going to reach it.

There were all sorts of ups and downs to be faced. (Mercifully, I was young and resilient!) On the credit side was the return of Guy Prendergast, whom I was very glad to have around again with advice and ideas. I tried very hard to persuade him to come back and take over command from me, but he would not do this. He felt that he could be of more assistance to us in his appointment as second-in-command to Brigadier Turnbull.

On the debit side was the decision of the New Zealand Government to withdraw its Squadron from us—that Squadron which had been the cadre around which the unit had been formed, and whose early exploits made the name of the Long Range Desert Group. It was as though half the cylinders were taken from a car and it was then expected to win a race.

We had been fearful for some time that we would lose the New Zealanders. Jake had written to me from Leros on 4 November (a few days before his death), saying that if the New Zealand Government did exercise its prerogative and withdrew the Squadron it would be an extremely bad day for the LRDG. He added that 'they supply us with such good, intelligent Officers and men that it will be an extremely difficult task to maintain the standard'. He then suggested forming a Rhodesian Squadron, as being the best of four alternative solutions to the problem.

I wrote back on 6 November saying that I had seen the NZ liaison officer, who said that it was the fears of their Government at home about keeping the Division up to strength that had prompted them to consider removing our Squadron. I also said that, unless we could get a guarantee of continued maintenance of the NZ Squadron up to establishment, we would be far wiser to let them go. In that case we should try to get a Rhodesian Squadron if we could.

Nothing I could do was to reverse the decision. I sent Alastair Guild by air to Italy to plead with General Freyberg; beseeching telegrams were sent home by General Sir Henry Maitland Wilson, and HM Government reinforced these appeals. All were to no avail.

It was a bitter blow, but I understood the reasons for it. Firstly, the New Zealand Government was concerned about the large number of casualties which its Squadron had suffered in the Aegean—and it had not been consulted about their employment there. Secondly, the New Zealand Division in Italy doubted its ability to keep its own units up to strength with the heavy fighting which lay ahead.

The casualties on Leros were the result of the unit playing a role forced on it by circumstances. Guy Prendergast had done all that he could to extricate us from Leros; but there came a time when continued pleas would have given the impression that we were not prepared to stay and face the music.

It was understandable that the New Zealanders felt that they could not continue to maintain a Squadron of about eight officers and over a hundred men with us when their own units urgently needed reinforcement. It was typically generous of General Freyberg that he later allowed me to have back some of the officers I had to lose.

It was a stroke of good luck which brought Sir Ernest Lucas Guest, the Rhodesian Air Minister, on a visit to the Middle East at that time. During his tour he came to see our Rhodesian contingent. He was full of understanding, and I took to him. I did all I could to persuade him that in future the LRDG ought to have a Squadron of Rhodesians. I could think of no better substitute for the men from New Zealand. I wrote to Sir Ernest after his visit, saying that 'I hope that you will be able to take back to Rhodesia a true picture of the spirit and keenness of those Rhodesians who are serving in the LRDG and that you will successfully arrange the provision of further Rhodesian personnel to complete the Rhodesian Squadron.'

His visit bore fruit, for we got our Rhodesians, and Sir Ernest took a kindly interest in us until the end of the war.

By mid-December 1943 the unit was reorganised into two Squadrons, each of eight Patrols of one officer and ten men. The UK Squadron was commanded by Moir Stormonth-Darling, who had got back safely from the

Aegean. He had been left out in the cold on the island of Mykonos when Leros fell, and it had been difficult to collect him. He and his Patrol became very short of food, and they had an uncomfortable time with a lot of Germans about on a rather small island. Eventually an RAF Rescue Launch reached him on 25 November. He was taken to Turkey, and he made his way back to us from there. Moir was to remain with me as a loyal and stalwart friend throughout the war—and, indeed, for all the years since it ended. I knew from the day he joined us that I had found a winner. He was a regular officer in the Cameronians, with the laird's natural understanding of his men. He and I had both been at Winchester, although he was five years my senior. This was all the more reason why I should, and did, respect him so much for the unqualified support he always gave me.

Command of the Rhodesian Squadron I gave to Ken Lazarus. Ken had made his living as a surveyor in East Africa until 1939. He then joined up and came to the LRDG in 1941 as a professional surveyor for mapping the Libyan sands. He had earned great credit over many months of lone and often dangerous desert survey behind the lines, and indeed many of the maps used by the Eighth Army were based solely on the work of his Survey Section.

On 18 September 1943 he had been sent to the island of Stampalia to bolster the Italian garrison, and to report on such enemy air and shipping movements as he saw. On 22 October the Germans dropped sixty parachutists after a four-hour air bombardment, and the garrison quickly submitted. Ken decided that the best thing to do was to get off the island, but this was extremely difficult. However, after Ken had heard about the fall of Leros on 19 November he eventually got a boat to row himself and four of his Patrol to Turkey, which they reached on the 27th. After sailing in a caïque via Cyprus they reached Haifa on 8 December and returned to us that day. Ken reported that the Germans had behaved with much brutality towards the civilian population on Stampalia, and he had been very lucky to escape.

It was a very thrilling and also an inspiring time. Not only were there many tales of considerable courage and hardship by our own Patrols and individuals, but the way in which the Greek civilians were so often willing to take extraordinary risks was quite remarkable. They knew only too well the dangers of reprisals, but they helped the Allies with open eyes and fearless hearts.

I was extremely lucky with my two Squadron Commanders. Ken was a quiet, rather dour man who took a bit of time to get to know well, but he had great courage, a fine heart and a true love of his fellow-men. Moir was much more of an extrovert, with an infectious laugh, a splendid sense of duty and a slow, deliberate and thorough mind. He was worshipped by his men, for they trusted him implicitly, and they always knew that he would support them.

Our base at this time was in Palestine. A few miles from the Syrian border and not far north of Haifa was a place called Azzib. It was an Arab village of no outstanding note, smelling as strongly as most Arab villages, and its houses were just as squalid. Near this village to the east of the coast road from Haifa to Beirut was a camp built on sandy, barren soil amid the olive groves. This camp had a few Nissen huts which housed the essential stores, dining rooms and wash-houses. The rest was tented.

We were not comfortable but we were glad of shelter over our heads, and we were very happy in many ways, because we had so much to do. I was personally very busy. There were the new officers and men to interview; new equipment to obtain; the training to be organised and watched; the painful letters to be written to the parents of those we had lost on Leros; and there was all the tidying up of accounts, personal property and casualty lists which followed the loss of a high proportion of our strength. My Adjutant, Quartermaster and Squadron Commanders helped beyond measure and we worked far into the night to keep our heads above water.

Christmas of 1943 was protracted, for the New Zealand Squadron was to leave us on the 29 December. I cannot remember there being any time by day or by night when there was not a party until they went. They did not take their departure from us lightly.

They were fun, those enchanting days, yet they were tinged with sadness, for we were saying farewell to many friends among the New Zealanders. A few were to rejoin us later, but most of them I have never seen again.

In early January 1944 we got down to training as hard as we could. All of us had to learn to parachute, and this we did at Ramat David, where the school was run by Wing Commander Murphy, who had been at Ringway in the early days of parachuting at home. His team of instructors were a good lot. Clowns and philosophers rolled into one—a winning combination.

We also had to learn the art of small-boat handling, and George Jellicoe's men of the Special Boat Service were our knowledgeable and willing teachers, while the Mountain Warfare School at the Cedars once more opened its doors to us to teach us how to operate in snow conditions.

There was a lot more to be taught. The recognition and description of ships and aircraft; handling explosives; map-reading and navigation; driving and maintenance; handling of animal transport; movement over all sorts of country by day and by night. Besides these there were lectures on Balkan topography, conditions and politics; security and the care of arms and equipment; the art of packing loads for Jeeps, mules or aircraft; reports and message-writing; field sketching. There was so much to be done.

We had to train signallers and medical orderlies in order to augment the limited number of technicians which we were able to have. Tim Heywood was still with us, and he was a hard taskmaster who turned out trained signallers at a very remarkable rate. Michael Parsons had replaced Dick Lawson as the Medical Officer, and his sterling qualities helped to reduce the loss we all felt when Dick had been captured. Michael was very able, but he also had a relaxed way with men, which quickly endeared him to them. He trained all of us in first aid, and perfected the light medical kits which we carried with our Patrols.

Then, when the elements of training had been adequately mastered, Patrols would go off into the countryside. These expeditions were designed to give them the feel of living off what they could carry, moving over all types of country and sleeping where they came to rest. They taught us how to make our loads and boots comfortable; how to find our way about; how to protect ourselves against the rain and the cold. Above all, they made us fit and wiry.

Towards the end of January I sent both Squadrons to Syria, where we found a reasonable barracks at Abla, a few miles from the historic ruins of Baalbek. This was a good move, because there was quite a lot of snow and it gave Patrols a chance to move and exist in it.

Luckily I still had the Wacos, and was able to fly up to Syria or down to Cairo, where some of the Signal Squadron were being trained. In these little single-engined aircraft we flew across the bleak Syrian mountains, we flew to unused landing-grounds on the Dead Sea, we knew the route across the Sinai Desert from Cairo to Beirut like the back of our hands and we flew in all kinds of weather. It was exhilarating, for the single engines had a horrid habit of expiring at the most irresponsible moments. However, they always seemed to fire again—just in time!

In the middle of February Guy Prendergast flew off to Algiers to discuss the employment of Raiding Forces with Allied Force Headquarters. As a result of this I received an order on 28 February to send someone at once to Italy, and so I flew the next day to Cairo and on by Dakota the next day. Before I left I was told that the object of my visit was to discuss future operations with Field-Marshal Alexander's Headquarters, and also to contact the SAS, which was about to be sent to England.

I arrived one evening at Bari to find myself without transport and with nobody knowing of my arrival. I eventually found a friend, who gave me food and lent me a car, and I drove the fifty miles to see the SAS. When I got there I found that practically the whole unit had left. There were four men still packing what was remaining, and they had certainly never heard of me. So, rather angry, I drove the fifty miles back to Bari.

I then tried to get a seat on an aircraft to fly me across Italy to the Headquarters at Caserta. I was rudely told that I had to give two days' notice when applying for an air passage. I was not enchanted by my first impressions of Italy nor of our American allies.

That night I borrowed a car and drove 170 miles across Italy to Caserta, where I arrived at 5.00 a.m. very tired, very cold and very fed up. After a shave and breakfast I had recovered and reported to the Operations Staff, and there found a friend in Brigadier Hugh Mainwaring. He had known the LRDG well in the desert, and was kindness itself. I then saw General

Harding, who was Alexander's Chief of Staff. I had known him also in the desert, and as always he gave me a courteous and friendly welcome. I was particularly glad to get his agreement that we should come to Italy as soon as our training was finished, and that we would operate directly under his headquarters.

Before I returned to Palestine I wanted to have a look at the country over which the Eighth Army was then fighting. I wanted to see the possibilities of infiltrating the lines. Everyone told me this was impossible. I therefore went to Tactical Headquarters of Eighth Army, where I found Bernard Bruce, who had commanded the Guards Patrol in the desert. I got every possible help from then on, and had a long talk with General Sir Oliver Leese about our plans before travelling across the entire Eighth Army front.

As a result I wrote to Guy;

> I visited the 2nd Parachute Brigade and also the Poles. From talking to these people it seems very definitely possible for us to get through the lines at several places. Everyone was inclined to tell me that the mountains were dangerous and difficult to move over but I hope that fact will be an ally to our Patrols, who are trained for it. On the whole I think the country is ideal for our kind of work.

After exactly a week away I returned and arranged for the unit to sail on the next convoy. I sent Tim Heywood at once to find a suitable place for a base on the east coast of Italy. He and Bob Maxwell, who went with him, were able to get everything ready. They chose a site for our base from which we never moved until the war was over. This was at a place called Rodi on the Gargano Peninsula. It was a lovely situation, but very isolated. The isolation had its advantages, however, for in spite of the good communications to the Balkans and the proximity to the big Foggia airfields, we were some miles off the main routes and unlikely to be disturbed by inquisitive people. In many ways it was ideal, and we spent many happy months there.

There were drawbacks, of course, and one was the appalling road to it from Foggia. There were also very few houses which we could requisition, and in which we could live. Rodi itself was a pretty little Italian town with narrow, cobbled winding streets, and it was a little cleaner than many similar places.

The people were typical of the rather indolent and backward southern Italian. They did not like the British much, but then I doubt if they would have liked anyone who disturbed the peace of their existence. Yet some of them were very kind to us, and friendships were made over glasses of raw and cheap wine.

The next few weeks were frustrating ones, and I spent much time at Caserta. Many projects were mooted. Some were accepted, and wild plans were made. Some ideas were totally impracticable and others were good.

But we were new to our task and still had to prove our worth, so I did not want to launch Patrols into anything that did not seem to have a reasonable chance of success.

But I had some splendid friends at the lower levels. Ralph Snagge and Peter Marsham gave me a great deal of help, advice and encouragement, particularly in the support they gave me to withstand some of the utterly foolish proposals that were thrown at me.

There was a fundamental rule which always guided me in the selection of any operation. I would never commit any man behind the lines unless I could see a reasonable chance of getting him back at a later date. Only once did I accept a task which did not fulfil this condition, and I was surprised at the response I had to my call for volunteers.

Early in 1945 I was asked to find a party to blow up the railway tunnel through the Brenner Pass. It was very heavily defended, and it was pretty certain that there would be little one could do to extricate any survivors. Anyway, I called for volunteers who might be prepared to undertake an operation which was not only hazardous but in an area whence there was small prospect of withdrawal.

The list was completely over-subscribed.

In the event the operation never took place, and I can remember only that a Rhodesian officer—Captain Bill Armstrong—was the first to volunteer, and that I chose him to lead the party.

Eventually we were at last earmarked for a task which would involve the use of twelve of our Patrols, together with various other American and British organisations. Railways were to be the primary target, and when these were sufficiently disorganised we were to strike at road convoys. This disruption of supplies was obviously timed to coincide with an advance by our armies in Italy.

We were given three main railways to attack: the line from Parma to Spezia, the lines from Bologna to Pistoia and to Prato and the track between Faenza and Florence. There were already Allied agents in those areas, and the idea was that we should drop in to their reception arrangements.

Planning began in earnest and I sent Moir Stormonth-Darling and Dick Croucher—my Intelligence Officer—over to Caserta to co-ordinate with the other organisations involved. They spent two or three weeks putting in a great deal of detailed work, and they overcame many seemingly insuperable difficulties. My two chief worries over this operation were the ones which so often troubled me, but Moir was more than alive to them. Firstly, I wanted to be sure that there was a reasonable chance of getting the Patrols back when the party was all over. After all, I was going to commit three-quarters of my operational strength, and I could not afford a major disaster. Secondly, I was anxious that the arrangements for receiving the Patrols were satisfactory.

I began to sense some uneasiness about this operation when Moir and

Dick asked me to go back at once to Caserta no sooner than I had returned from there to Rodi. So I went back, and they came up with a plan to put three Patrols in before the main operation because they were not at all happy about the reception arrangements. I agreed at once with this view, and did what I could to get this idea accepted.

Soon after this I was called over again and was met by Moir, who told me that the operation had been cancelled because there were not sufficient aircraft available to drop and maintain all the forces involved. It seemed to me a little odd that this had not been discovered in the early stages of the planning.

I was fed up with this sort of treatment, so I went over to Caserta again to ask bluntly whether all or any part of the unit would be required, either in the near future or at a later date. Nobody knew the answer. I therefore suggested that one Squadron should be offered to Force 266. This was an organisation responsible for co-ordinating the activities of the missions and agents supporting the Partisans in the Balkan countries. This was readily agreed, and I set off at once to Bari, where it had its HQ.

I found that the GSO1 was an old friend—Tom Pearson of the Rifle Brigade. We had known each other in Cairo and the desert, and I found in him an enthusiast with definite, clear and practical ideas. They were keen to have us. I obtained permission from Caserta for the Rhodesian Squadron under Ken Lazarus to be lent to Force 266. This loan was conditional on it being released again at once if operations should develop favourably in Italy and the Squadron might be needed.

Ken Lazarus moved himself to Bari on 7 May and set up a headquarters with Pavlides, his Intelligence Officer. From then until the end of the war we maintained an operational headquarters in Bari where the majority of our operations were planned and directed. No time was lost. On 16 May 1944, almost exactly six months after the battle on Leros, our first Patrol set out again—the first of a long line of successful jobs in enemy-occupied territory.

This was the moment for which we had all lived and worked. We had pinned our faith on it. I know that it was because of this faith that many of us did not chuck it all, rejoin our units and go back to the war. Those officers and men of mine hadn't joined the LRDG to avoid the battle—far from it.

# CHAPTER 15

# In Yugoslavia and the Dalmatian Islands

On the main front the battle for Cassino was at its height, and the town fell to British troops on 18 May. The same day the Poles took Monastery Hill. The end of the war still seemed a very long way off.

Ken Lazarus chose Stan Eastwood with a Patrol of four Rhodesians for the first task to be carried out. Stan was a young, dark, curly-haired man, who had been with us in desert days. He was thin and wiry, always cheerful and loved the rough, happy days on patrol.

His mission was to go by sea from Brindisi across the Adriatic to a small island off the north-west coast of Corfu. Here a Greek agent would meet them and they would then go on together. They were to obtain details of a suspected enemy radar station in the north of the island, so that a larger raiding party could land and destroy this target at a later stage.

Corfu—even then a holiday resort—lay off the coast of Albania, and was about thirty-five miles long and fifteen miles wide at its broadest point. It was thought to be occupied by about 2,500 German troops.

A Royal Navy motor launch took them to their rendezvous with the Greek agent and they rowed the two miles to Corfu in the early hours. Next day the agent went off to spy out the land, and came back with the news that he had found the target. That evening one of Eastwood's men—Pte Marc—went off with him to see what he could discover. When they reached the radar station he decided that the only way to learn much about it and its defences was to get inside the surrounding compound. He borrowed some old clothes and spent much of the next day gathering information. His ingenuity and daring were rewarded by a good deal of rough treatment at the hands of the Germans. The soldiers of the garrison were fed up at being pestered by the locals hawking their fish; nor could they appreciate the irony of a disguised British soldier selling it to them!

Marc sold no fish, but he received a number of ignominious kicks in the pants for his troubles. In between these discourteous outbursts he was able to draw some very useful sketches from no more than 150 yards away from our target. He then wandered off to the shore to have a look at the possible landing-places. This little stroll was uneventful apart from his meeting five Germans bathing. They ignored him. Stan Eastwood was meanwhile gathering a lot of other information about enemy dispositions, wire, mines and such things as the searchlights on the island. By the following day he had all he wanted, and he asked us to send a boat to pick him up.

We collected Eastwood and his men safely, and Stan also brought out with him a young Greek fisherman who had given his Patrol a lot of help. This young man—named Spiro—became so attached to the Rhodesians that he asked to stay with them. Somehow this was regularised and he was put on the payroll and became a loyal member of the LRDG. He went with Stan Eastwood on all his subsequent sorties, and even parachuted into Albania with him later on.

A few days after this successful effort another Rhodesian Patrol under Jacko Jackson was detailed for our first parachute operation. Jacko, like Stan Eastwood, had also been commissioned to us from the ranks. He was a fair-haired, stolid, thickset little man with a strong round face and great strength, both of body and of character. He was dropped with nine men not far from Himara in Albania to report on enemy dispositions in the area so that a larger raiding force could be landed later to liquidate them. After four days Jackson was picked up, but left Sergeant Ryan and the rest of his Patrol behind in order to receive the raiding party.

In the event the raid did not take place until much later, and we got Ryan and the others out after two weeks. The day he was due to be collected he sent us a typically cheerful signal which read, 'If no boat, don't worry as we will endeavour to swim the Adriatic.'

Things had begun well for us in the Balkans, and I was suddenly reminded of our obligations in Italy when I was called to Eighth Army HQ on 4 June to discuss a plot for an operation in Jeeps. Moir Stormonth-Darling was still at GHQ patiently planning all kinds of tasks, which never came off. Somehow he never lost his enthusiasm, and after each cancellation he would begin again, with just as much devotion, to work out the details of the latest proposals.

This time we were ordered to provide seven Patrols of four Jeeps each carrying fourteen days' food and water and five hundred miles worth of petrol. No sooner was all this ready than the plan was cancelled yet again. The rapid advance of the Army towards Rome had overrun the areas where we were to operate.

It was next decided that we should send four Patrols by air on the nights of 11 and 12 June to get information about enemy traffic on certain roads north of Rome.

I left Moir at Main HQ to plan the details and went forward to Tactical HQ of Eighth Army to see General Leese. At breakfast with him on 6 June 1944 we listened to the news of the landings in Normandy the previous night.

I then drove back to join Moir, and I remember so well the mass of Allied transport which was moving rapidly and relentlessly towards Rome. There were all kinds of lorries, cars, tanks, guns and caravans; there were lorry-loads of troops, their morale very high, pouring on and straining to be the first to enter Rome. It took me three and a half hours to do thirty miles.

Moir had everything in hand, and so I took an Auster and flew back to see Brigadier Mainwaring to arrange for the necessary aircraft to drop Moir's Patrols. In the dusk of a lovely evening I flew forward again to rejoin Moir, and we listened that night to the King broadcasting to the nation. They were very emotional days.

All was ready on 11 June for the first two parties to be dropped, but they did not go that night because of bad weather and heavy enemy A.A. activity. The next night Patrols under Simon Fleming and John Bramley were dropped. It was not for some time that we learnt of Simon Fleming's death. He was never seen alive again after Bob Maxwell had dispatched him from the plane. His parachute failed to open. Simon had joined us soon after the fiasco of Leros. I was very fond of him, because he had great charm and a glorious sense of humour. He was essentially straight and open. He also had an impertinent disregard for authority, but was wise enough to know that it was important to keep just on the right side of it. Outwardly he had a light-hearted and carefree attitude to life, but this façade hid a wisdom and intelligence unusual in one so young. We could ill afford to lose such a fine officer.

The following day I went to Foggia to see the other two parties under Ashley Greenwood and Gordon Rowbottom. They were to jump that night, and I found them in high spirits.

But these operations also had bad luck. Ashley Greenwood's party was landed twelve miles from where they were meant to be, and on top of a village occupied by Germans.

Ashley himself came to rest on the roof of a church and, after extricating himself from this, spent the early hours of the morning dodging round the graveyard to avoid the searching Hun! He never found the rest of his Patrol, and returned safely to our lines two weeks later. All but one of his men—Fusilier Ford—were captured.

Gordon Rowbottom's party all landed safely. By 4.00 a.m. on 14 June they were all gathered together. However, late that evening they bumped into a German post and were forced to split up. Next morning Rowbottom was captured. He had a remarkably short period of captivity.

After about half an hour's drive in the back of a truck guarded by one German the incredible happened. The truck ran into a ditch and turned over. Gordon's guard was stunned, so he gathered back his arms and equipment and made off as fast as he could. He somehow became reunited with Corporals Buss and Matthews of his own Patrol, and they enlisted with a Partisan band of about sixty strong. He then led them in a consistent policy of wrecking and mining wherever he could until he reached a company of Grenadier Guards on 26 July and finally reported back to the LRDG.

One other member of Gordon's patrol carried on an enterprising little war of his own. This was Sergeant Morley, who after collecting a great deal of useful information rejoined our lines at the third attempt. He reported to the HQ of 4th Indian Division, who immediately asked him to go back as a guide to 1st/9th Gurkha Rifles. He at once volunteered to lead them to their objective over country which he knew. The Commanding Officer wrote to me of his gallantry, and Morley was awarded a well-deserved Military Medal. Gordon Rowbottom received the Military Cross.

Of Simon Fleming's party one or two were captured, one other was killed in the drop and the remaining men eventually trickled back to our lines.

John Bramley was the only one who had any success. For a week he sent back most useful reports, but then his wireless gave out. However, he kept a written record of all that he saw, and this information proved to be of considerable value to our advancing troops.

Thus ended this unfortunate operation. We had failed to do what we intended, although much of the information we gained was certainly of use. It turned out to be the last task that we were to attempt in Italy south of the river Po.

Just before the start of these operations in Italy we began to turn our attention to the Dalmatian islands. The Allies had started to build up a base on Vis, where Tito had set up his HQ after the Germans had very nearly succeeded in capturing him. I flew across in a seaplane to look into the possibilities of operating to the north from Vis, and was encouraged by all I saw and heard.

I realised, though, that if we were to be free to act independently of the Royal Navy we had to have some craft of our own. The Navy had so many calls on their time and would always help, but they could not be expected to meet every demand at short notice. So from somewhere we obtained a motor fishing vessel, and were assured of our mobility. This was a splendid little craft—M.F.V. *La Palma*. We stripped it of all its superfluous superstructure, and mounted a motley collection of guns on its decks. We made accommodation for the crew, and there was space where Jeeps could be lashed on deck.

Captain Alan Denniff became the skipper, and he did great work with his military crew. Alan had been the navigator of my Patrol in the desert, and he chose Titch Cave as the bosun. *La Palma* sailed on her first voyage to Vis in June, and she took seven and a half hours to do the seventy miles. On that trip she carried a crew of nine, twelve passengers, 11,000 pounds of stores, a Jeep and a great deal of other equipment.

The object of these Dalmatian sorties was twofold: firstly, to report on enemy shipping so that the Royal Navy and Royal Air Force could strike against them, while secondly, we planned small-scale raids against enemy shipping in harbour and against the garrisons in the islands.

I set up an advanced base on Dugi Otok, and at the end of June Captain Arthur Stokes with four men left to establish a shipping watch on the mainland. They stayed for nearly five months, and sent back a mass of excellent information. We kept them supplied by air, but only with great difficulty, for bad weather often delayed the arrival of supplies, and they were under frequent German pressure. Arthur was being such a nuisance to the enemy that they put an enormous price on his head. He was not allowed to rest with any safety, and at one stage he was kept on the move for three successive days and nights. He reached the stage where he had only a few biscuits left and these they ate 'boiled for breakfast, straight for lunch and fried for dinner'.

Every day during those weeks Arthur sent back most cheerful signals. He in fact sent us over two hundred messages, and many of these contained valuable information on which the RAF was able to act. Many ships were sunk as a result. Great credit went to his wireless operator—Signalman Hansell—who managed to keep his set going despite various technical tribulations.

For his part in this operation Arthur was awarded a Military Cross to add to the Military Medal he had already earned.

A party under Lt Gatchell was on the island of Ist for two months doing similar work. They had the satisfaction of rescuing the crew of an American Flying Fortress which had come down on a near-by island. But perhaps the highlight of their time was when they helped the Partisans to attack and capture an enemy schooner. It turned out to be the German equivalent of a NAAFI boat, and apart from the supplies of good cheer which they captured, there were also two female members of a German concert party.

We then heard of an isolated coast-watching station near Valona in Albania, and this had been reporting the movement of our shipping off that coast. We decided that it ought to be liquidated, and so Stan Eastwood was sent off to find out about it. An officer of Force 266 had recently been in that part of Albania, and so I contacted him to learn what I could about it. He turned out to be Antony Quayle, the well-known actor-producer and later Director of the Shakespeare Memorial Theatre. He gave us a wealth of valuable intelligence.

Stan spent a week wandering round this post at Orso Bay, and it seemed that it might be quite a tough proposition. It was a rectangular concrete building with pill-boxes at the north-west and south-east corners, and the whole surrounded by wire. Stan also said that there was little cover from which to approach it.

As luck would have it, the Royal Navy was very keen to get some target practice, and they offered me three destroyers to assist with a preliminary bombardment. This was just what we wanted.

I decided to send two other Patrols to join Stan on the night before the raid. Captain Tony Browne, who had just got back to us from the New Zealand Division, was put in overall charge. At the last moment I went along too, as I had not been on active operations for so long, and I was beginning to feel stale and tired. I wanted a breath of fresh air again. Stan sent a message at dawn on 28 June to say that all was ready to receive us. A short while later he sent another to say that the RAF had just flown over and strafed the post. This was a pity, as it would draw attention to it.

Tony Browne, Mike Reynolds, Jacko Jackson, Michael Parsons and I all had a merry dinner in the Officers Club at Brindisi before sailing with thirty-five men at 8.15 a.m. in an Italian MAS Boat. There was a second of these small, fast torpedo-boats as our escort.

It was a lovely night, calm and with a bright moon. It was very exciting as we sped across the Adriatic until we sighted the Albanian coast and then reduced speed. The sea was too calm to stifle the telltale wash of our craft, so we hung about until the moon went lower. I didn't like the Italian skipper, and wasted some time trying to cajole him into acting with slightly less trepidation. It was 2.30 a.m. before we finally reached the shore, guided by flashes from a torch held by Stan Eastwood, who was waiting to receive us. It took an hour to get everything ashore, and dawn broke at 4.15 a.m.

We had to get away from the beach, and it took us nearly five hours to move a few miles over rough and rocky country to where there was thick cover under some trees near a well of clear, cool water. After a while Tony Browne, Stan and I went forward to observe the target from a point about a thousand yards away. Between it and us was a steep, scrub-covered ravine and we could clearly see the concrete pill-boxes, a sentry on the roof and other Germans sitting around in the sun. I climbed a bit higher, to the top of a rocky ridge about 1,200 feet above sea-level. From there I could see the township of Valona nestling quietly in the morning light.

We rejoined the others and then made, and ran through, our final plans. They were simple. We would move up to within seven hundred yards of the target at dusk and then await the blitz of the three destroyers. When these had done their best the final assault would be led by Stan. We were to be in touch with the destroyers by wireless, and had brought a trained Gunnery Officer with us to control their fire.

By 11.00 p.m. all was ready. Stan was in position for the final assault, although he had gone rather too near the target for comfort. We could see the destroyers in the moonlight, and we flashed a torch to give them our position. There they lay off shore—dark and sinister forms on the gentle ripple of the water.

There wasn't a sound save for the hushed whisper of the wind in the trees. And this would soon be dismissed by the deadly bark and whine of shells.

The silence was a little weird, but fascinating at the same time. I would have been insensate if I had not felt the thrill of that moment. We lay there stealthily and with evil intent, a few hundred yards from an enemy who individually had done us no wrong. It seemed almost unkind that there was so much on our side and so little danger to ourselves. But such romantic thoughts were foolish!

At 11.25 p.m. we signalled to the ships that all was ready—we had planned back in Italy for their bombardment to begin exactly five minutes later. With typical naval punctiliousness a blinding flash lit the sky at the precise second of 11.30 p.m.; a star-shell illuminated the whole mountain-side on which we were. A few seconds later the first ranging shot tore through the air and struck the mountain-side a little below the target. Then other guns opened up with ranging shots while star-shells lit the target. After a bit the three destroyers fired majestic 12-gun salvoes of screaming red tracer shells. These flew madly toward the hill, which crumpled into torrents of rock, debris and dust to hurtle down the thousand-foot cliff before crashing noisily into the sea below.

Some shells went over the top of the target and sailed on to burst somewhere far off in Valona Bay. At midnight the target was so obscured in dust that we called off the high explosive and asked for more star-shells to light it up. These came, and we could see the building still standing intact.

Stan on his walkie-talkie to us demanded that we should 'give them another dose', as he could see a few Germans running around still. This was translated into naval parlance, and all hell was let loose again at the hillside. We soon saw the red tracer shells smacking into the target. After a few moments of this Stan called off the fire and went in to complete the wreckage. Soon we heard the tiny, odd little patter of machine and tommy guns and a few small explosions.

It wasn't long before we saw three long bursts of tracer fired straight into the air, followed by three short flashes on a torch. This was the signal for success. It was then a quarter to one in the morning.

We all began to make our way down to the beach. It was a rough descent, made worse by the darkness, for the moon had gone to earth. I got there after an hour, very hot, tired and bruised, for I had fallen a lot of the way. A few others had arrived, and with them were three miserable, weeping Germans.

But to my surprise no boats came in for us, and we stood frantically signalling to them. No answer came in reply. I decided to wait till 3.15 a.m., and if nobody came then we would have to move away into cover for the day and hope that they would pick us up the next night. The destroyers could not hang about and risk being spotted so near the Albanian seaboard at dawn. Maybe they had already sailed away.

With five minutes still to go a whaler and a pinnace arrived, and by 3.30 a.m. we were all off the beach. An off-shore breeze was blowing, and we had to wade out to be picked up. We drew alongside the destroyers and scrambled up nets to the deck. By 4.00 a.m. we were heading across the Adriatic. I found Brigadier George Davy on board—he had just taken command of Land Forces Adriatic, and we were now under his control. I also found a rather sour destroyer captain, who was angry that we had kept him waiting until just before dawn. However, when I congratulated him on his shooting, and told him the result of his bombardment, all was forgiven.

We sailed into Brindisi at 7.15 a.m. at the head of the Flotilla after an extremely good breakfast with the captain (Commander Behaig of HMS *Terpsichore*).

I was pleased with the results of the raid, although they were limited. We captured a few worthless individuals, and were lucky to have only one man slightly wounded—by our own shell-fire, because in his enthusiasm Stan had moved in a little too near the target a little too early. The main result of this first raid across the sea from Italy lay in the uneasiness which the enemy was to feel along the whole of their Adriatic coast.

It was also valuable experience for us, while I was assured by the Flotilla leader in a letter of thanks that it had been good for the crews of the destroyers—HMS *Terpsichore*, *Tumult* and *Tenacious*. He wrote thanking me for 'a good evening's entertainment and for providing the live exhibits in the form of the first Germans many of my sailors have seen'.

Two days after I got back from Albania I turned my attention once again to operation in Italy, and flew off to Field-Marshal Alexander's HQ on the shores of Lake Bolsena. I met Moir Stormonth-Darling and discussed the latest plans for us to give support to Italian Partisan bands in the north of Italy. There was a lot of scope for us, and Moir had made plans for sending seven Patrols into the area east of the road from Verona to the Brenner Pass. All was eventually agreed, in spite of petty objections from other vested interests. But in the end the operation was cancelled in early August.

This was a severe disappointment to Moir and his Squadron, and it was only due to his careful handling of a lot of frustrated soldiers that there was no trouble with them. Nevertheless, we were both fed up with all this shilly-shallying and waste of time, so I asked the Staff once more whether they held out any prospects for using us in the near future. I reckoned that there was plenty to do in the Balkans, where we had started well.

After a day or two it was agreed that the LRDG would cease to be under the direct command of the Allied Armies in Italy, and we came under George Davy's Land Forces Adriatic, the military component of the Balkan Air Force.

I was sorry not to have been able to contribute more to the main fighting in Italy, but it was not to be. However, my life would be easier, for we would be working on only one front and to one headquarters. George Davy established himself in Bari, and I reinforced Ken Lazarus there with Tony Browne. We kept our base at Rodi, which was a long way from Bari but was a good site for our base communications and a quiet place for the Patrols to rest when they returned from their travels.

We wasted no time, since the Balkan Air Force, under Air Vice-Marshal Elliot, had been set up especially to control and co-ordinate all Partisan and other operations; and they had plenty for us to do.

Mike Reynolds went back to Albania to have a look at the enemy's reactions after Orso Bay, and found that he had reinforced the position and begun to repair the blockhouse. However, for some strange reason they then changed their minds and blew it sky-high. Mike was then told to find out about a near-by coastal battery. This he did admirably, and got back with some excellent photographs.

On 14 August the first of Moir's Squadron was sent out. Archie Gibson left Vis with instructions to keep Mostar aerodrome on the mainland of Yugoslavia under constant observation during daylight for a period of not less than seven days. By means of a special code and a one-to-one wireless link he was to report all information relating to movement of enemy aircraft to and from Mostar. It was hoped that our own fighters would then be able to intercept the enemy in the air soon after take-off, and Tim Heywood devised a system to meet the stipulation that the time taken by a signal from origination to decipherment should be limited to five minutes.

Archie set off and had to return to Vis after one day on the mainland as for some reason the Partisans did not want him around. Nine days later he set off again. By the end of the month it was clear that reaching Mostar was going to be far more difficult than had been anticipated. The Germans were trying to locate them, and put in quite a strong attack against the Partisan band they were with. Archie used up nearly all his ammunition in this action.

He was therefore ordered to stay where he was, and to send back all the information that he could about the enemy in his area. The local Partisans had now become very friendly, and forgetting their former animosity, Archie records that on 10 September 'I became a god-father to the child of one of the Partisan Lieutenants. This ceremony was followed by a feast.'

Archie stayed on where he was until early October, and had many lucky escapes. He was supplied by air when possible, but his men suffered greatly through lack of food. He managed to harass the enemy continually, and sent us back a lot of good information. His senior NCO was Sergeant Jetley, and Gibson spoke afterwards of how well Jetley had supported him throughout. He also recorded that the Partisans unfortunately had orders from above that no British personnel were to participate offensively against the enemy. A curious state of affairs!

Two other Patrols of Moir's Squadron left Italy in August for Yugoslavia. David Skipwith and John Shute were sent to the Dubrovnik area to reconnoitre suitable targets for George Jellicoe's Special Boat Service. The latter had come to Italy to reinforce us because there was more than we could compete with. In theory they were primarily trained for fighting, while we were intended for intelligence missions, but both units had similar characteristics, aims and organisation. We worked together in harmony until the end of the war.

David Skipwith, with four men, landed safely from the sea at 2.00 a.m. on 19 August. This was the one and only time we tried using carrier pigeons as a second string to the wireless. David took six with him. None of them ever got back to their loft at Brindisi.

After a week David had obtained all the necessary details about a fairly large railway bridge, so on the night of 27 August a party of SBS under Captain Andy Lassen was landed. Andy was a Dane, then aged twenty-four, who had already won three Military Crosses and was later killed in an action for which he was posthumously awarded the Victoria Cross. I saw a lot of him in those days, and he was never without a little mongrel dog called Pepo. Pepo went everywhere with him, and he even did a parachute jump. Andy was such fun. Why is it that such blithe cavaliers are killed? There was less gaiety and laughter when he went.

During the night of 29 August Skipwith and Lassen blew two 40-foot spans of this bridge. This little act of sabotage resulted in the enemy hunting them mercilessly for three days and nights. Finally they came face to face with a force of about three hundred Ustachi—a collection of pro-German Yugoslavs. For most of one morning there was a spirited battle until Skipwith with Sergeant Leach and one of Lassen's men held out a bit too long in covering the retreat of the others with hand-grenades. These three were forced to surrender, but Andy and the others were picked up from the coast three nights later.

John Shute's Patrol also had some excitement. Soon after midnight they were put over the side of a RN motor launch by Moir Stormonth-Darling, who had gone along to see them safely landed. Their assault boat was overloaded, and the sea was not very calm. About four hundred yards from the shore John and his party were spilt into the sea, and he became separated from the others. By some good chance he found his wireless operator—Signalman Thurgood—that night, who had managed to salvage his set from the chaos. He obtained a car battery and was able to transmit, but he could not get his receiver to function. Two days later Shute found the rest of his Patrol, but they had very little kit with them, as the Germans had collected it from the beach, but they could at least look for a suitable target. After a bit they came across a railway tunnel.

On 28 August a party of the SBS were landed, and spent a day or two making a plan to attack the tunnel, which John Shute had already found was lined with stone blocks, and pretty solid. They therefore asked us for more explosives to be dropped to them, but as we could not get the stuff to them in time, they decided to do their best with only 100 lb of ammonal. As they feared, this small amount of explosive had little effect, and they had to be content with destroying the telephone system and three railway points before leaving the target.

By mid-September they were fairly short of supplies, and their boots were in threads. We had difficulty in getting a supply drop to them, and when we did manage it the Germans got most of the stores. On 7 October we got them out of Yugoslavia in a Dakota which had landed on a Partisan-held airstrip.

Tony Browne, who had been working with Ken Lazarus in Bari, wanted to try out an idea that they had cooked up between them. The Navy had been very appreciative of our information on shipping, and we had been successful in directing our striking forces on to enemy convoys. We felt there was scope for developing this technique.

The idea was for Tony Browne to be landed with a wireless operator on the west coast of Istria so that he could find a suitable place to establish a permanent shipping watch. The Royal Navy would then send a flotilla of fast motor torpedo-boats up at night to lie some ten miles or so off-shore and with the leading ship would be one of our wireless operators to communicate to our Patrol on shore. The latter would then report details of the enemy convoy's speed, direction, numbers and attendant escort.

Tony went off from Ancona in an MTB. As they approached the Istrian coast they spotted two schooners in the dark. One of these they sank, and the other was boarded by the Navy, who took sixteen prisoners. Tony was able to paddle quietly ashore in the confusion. He found a splendid place in thick scrub where there was good cover and a clear view of the sea. His choice proved perfectly secure, for he was not seen, either by two woodmen—who spent the whole of one day clearing the scrub a hundred yards from him—or by a party of schoolchildren who played hide and seek all around him one morning.

We landed Jack Aitken to establish this watch. Jack was another of the New Zealanders, who had been with us before and who moved heaven and earth to rejoin us. I was very grateful to General Freyberg when he agreed to let us have him back, for Jack was a first-class type of officer and one who knew little fear.

As it turned out Jack had little success, for the four weeks he was there in September and October were miserably wet, cold and often very rough. The Navy was thus unable to hang about waiting for targets at night, but the RAF did manage to act promptly and effectively on some of Jack's information. As a result very little shipping was able to move by day.

The Partisan movement in Yugoslavia was gaining more and more successes, and its members needed more arms, more ammunition, more supplies of every sort. We could provide the vital wireless link with Italy, whence these supplies came. We could show them how to use the guns and other equipment, besides calling upon the Balkan Air Force to support them. The mission under Brigadier Fitzroy Maclean, M.P. was doing all this to the limit of its resources, and doing it very well, but we could augment those resources.

In August I sent off four more Patrols under four Rhodesian

lieutenants—Jacko Jackson, Joe Savage, Mike Reynolds and George Pitt. The first three went by air, and George Pitt went by sea and on foot.

Jacko's party spent seven successful weeks doing exactly what was wanted of them in giving the Partisans every support. They were flown out from a Partisan-held airstrip in mid-October.

Joe Savage with eight Rhodesians and two Americans—who were going to lend a hand at one of the Partisan HQs—took off from Brindisi and dropped on 2 September. This was a few minutes after we had heard that the place selected for their drop was quite unsuitable for landing men. However, we could not stop them, and all went well in the event.

On arrival they were asked to join 19 Partisan Division, and were assured in the usual Balkan fashion that this was nine hours' walk away. After a total of twenty-seven hours' extremely hard going they were greeted by the divisional commander, whom Joe described as 'a big silent type; really an exasperating fellow who is obsessed by the need for air bombardment'.

It was at this time that difficulties with those infuriating, gallant, devious Partisans began to develop. They were only too anxious to take all that we could give, but they offered little in return. They began to hinder our free movement, and even to withhold information from us. In the early stages it was non-co-operation, but it grew to open hostility later on. Joe Savage had his activities seriously curtailed, but he too did all that was asked of him and we got him out by sea to reach Italy on 19 October 1944.

Mike Reynolds took only three Rhodesians with him when he was flown to a Partisan-held airstrip to the east of Fiume on 27 August. They had made an unsuccessful attempt to parachute two nights before, but bad weather had prevented them from landing when they were only a few miles from their dropping zone.

His orders were to establish a shipping watch in Istria between Fiume and Pola, and he spent some time trying to get through German formations near Fiume. They knew of his presence, and were hunting him. Some idea of the difficulties he was facing can be gathered from the following signal he sent us in mid-September:

Advanced twenty miles night before last. Huns did the dirty, attacked us yesterday afternoon. We had to retreat fifteen miles this morning.

When they eventually got into Istria they were ordered out again by the Partisans.

Somehow Mike overcame this problem, and he set up watch on the east coast on 29 September—one month after he had landed in Yugoslavia. But the Germans were after him and chased him with a portable direction-finding station, hoping to pick up his wireless transmissions. One day a patrol got so near them that Mike had to fight. He laid a successful ambush, and killed three of the enemy. But Mike and his men were never found, and he continued to send us the most admirable information.

When he already had these difficulties to cope with it was odious to think that the Partisans saw fit to add to them. They always resented our presence in Istria, for it was too near to the Trieste that they coveted. Their technique was to make things impossible for us, but they found Mike a very determined character who was not going to be put off easily. We were therefore not surprised, but heartily sick, when Mike was ordered out of Istria by our allies—the Partisans of Tito. He asked to be picked up by sea rather than to have to retrace his steps over difficult and enemy-ridden country. We got them back to Italy on 17 October, after having done a very good job.

George Pitt was given the task of finding out all he could about shipping in Trieste and Monfalcone harbours. He was also asked to report on airfields, troop concentrations and movements, strengths and identifications, enemy dumps and installations in the area. It was a difficult area, and George decided to take only one man and a wireless set. He took Signalman Wigens.

Pitt was a good choice, for he was a big, strong, friendly character whom no amount of toil deterred. This time he was to have what would have been too much for most men. He travelled by devious means to Dugi Island on 9 September. An American fast torpedo-boat took him to the small island of Kria together with a Partisan guide. From there they rowed to the mainland of Yugoslavia about due east of Krk Island. He walked northward for a week towards Fiume, meeting Jacko and Mike Reynolds on the way. The weather was vile, and there was ceaseless rain. On 22 September he reached the main road from Trieste to Ljubljana and decided to rest for a bit, so he lay up in some hills to sleep. No sooner had that blissful state arrived when some Germans came too. They were on a field firing exercise, and George found himself at the centre of the target area. He 'thought it provident to move because the exercise became rather too realistic. Our departure was a hurried one entirely unhampered by the fact that Wigens and I were in the nude. We had taken off our clothes to try and dry them.'

The artillery practice went on for three hours, and they were then able to go back and recover their clothes. They then walked for nineteen hours without stop.

Soon there was Partisan trouble. George was marched before the Commissar at 9 Corps HQ and asked for his pass into the area. This sort of futility went on for days, and he was eventually shown a signal which read 'English Lieutenant Pitt not granted permission to remain in 9 Corps area. Request him to return at once to Dugi and that he does this amicably.'

George somehow did not hurry to comply, but hoped for official permission to remain. While waiting he contacted two escaped British prisoners and five of the crew of an American aircraft which had crashed. Eventually he reached his target area, only to be forced to withdraw because of an enemy swoop which he estimated at a division strong. He was then on the run for some days, and getting short of food. For two and a half days he had nothing to eat until he feasted on a meal of boiled potatoes. All the while he kept us fully informed of every scrap of news he could gather. But he could not get to where he wanted to go and after he had covered several hundred miles we extracted him from Yugoslavia on 20 October.

One other small party of interest was a Patrol led by Gordon Rowbottom. He was sent to the island of Vrgada to watch shipping, and while there he went one night with three of his men—Sergeant Morley, Corporal Buss and Rifleman McConnell—to a neighbouring island.

They went in a rowing-boat at dusk. Soon after they set out they saw three E-Boats, which turned towards them and came up to Rowbottom's little craft. There was little he could do; the game was up, and they were ordered aboard one of the E-Boats. They then joined a convoy of ships escorted by seven other similar craft and were taken to Split, where they were flung into the local prison. Rowbottom gave his rank as Private, and his name and number. The others gave no more extensive information, and after being interrogated they were incarcerated in separate cells. Gordon Rowbottom learnt that he had as his neighbour a Slav who was to be shot for spying. This was not encouraging news.

Sergeant Morley was taken as being the senior member of the party, since the Germans were presumably not interested in 'Private' Rowbottom. He later wrote an amusing account of his interrogations. It was a creditable story, which was later substantiated by documents that were captured.

The following are extracts from his narrative:

12th September 1944. First I was asked my number, rank and name. Answered correctly. They were very interested in the town where I was born . . . then they wanted to know my unit and what I was doing. To all these questions I answered: 'I am sorry, Sir, but I cannot give more than my number, rank and name. I may be your prisoner but I still serve in my Majesty's Army.'

This annoyed them very much . . . they said unless I gave the information they desired they would not hesitate to put us up against the wall and shoot us along with the Partisans. I told them the answer was as before.

The last half hour of this interview was practically all of politics. My interrogator called it a chat. Why do you fools of English fight for Russia and America when you are losing the war to them? What do you think of the dirty trick of America sending you those old warships? I said I had no desire to discuss politics and that he spoke like Goebbels anyway.

. . . he then said that he supposed I knew when the war would end . . . I said by Christmas. He said I had it all mixed up. To this I told him that he hadn't a hope in hell.

In Morley's pay-book his trade in civilian life was given as a gardener.

. . . he then annoyed me rather by saying that he supposed I grew roses for Joe. I told him Germany was the only country frightened of Russia.

At this stage he got very bad tempered and took to threatening me. He said, 'you will be placed in solitary confinement and if neither you nor your comrades speak you will be shot tomorrow.' I told him to save himself the trouble of waiting and shoot us that afternoon because tomorrow or any day my answer to him would be the same.

Morley was interrogated again on each of the four following days. But still he gave nothing away, and eventually the Germans decided to try no more. They had attempted all the usual tricks of persuasion and temptation, but Morley was alive to them all. The Germans sometimes knew when they were beaten, and this time they were utterly defeated.

For six days Morley and the others planned escape, but on the seventh they were marched into Split. They were quite glad because they had been continually threatened with being shot because the Germans said they were not dressed properly as soldiers. I think I would have been very surprised if they were! However, despite all the threats made to them they divulged nothing.

At Split the party was loaded into the back of a 3-ton lorry, which also carried five guards. This was in a convoy of about a hundred vehicles. Plans were very soon made for an escape during one of the frequent halts.

The convoy eventually moved off, and shortly after dark shooting started. All lights were extinguished, and a shower of bullets flew in all directions. The five guards joined in and fired their rifles into the hills wildly, knowing only that somewhere out there lurked the Partisans whom they feared so much.

This was Rowbottom's opportunity, and he saw that he could undo the tarpaulin at the side of the truck. At that moment their guards decided to take cover, and they leapt into a ditch. At the same time Rowbottom and Corporal Buss got out on to the roof of the truck. Sergeant Morley and McConnell hopped out of the back.

About an hour after the shooting began the convoy moved off again, and so did Rowbottom and Buss in the opposite direction. Two days later they met up with Morley and McConnell, and we were able to evacuate them safely from Yugoslavia.

Thus for the second time in a few months Gordon Rowbottom had been taken prisoner but endured a remarkably short period of captivity. This was not entirely due to his good fortune; it was also because he was not the kind of man to suffer a prisoner's status lightly. He grasped every opportunity to escape in both his big hands, and he succeeded where others, less determined, might have failed.

# CHAPTER 16

# Control of Operations

I have described some of the operations which were going on in Yugoslavia and the Dalmatian islands. There were other Patrols active in Albania, and even one on Greek territory. The Albanian operations I shall describe later on. They were going excellently, and the whole picture at that time was a satisfactory one.

However, the organisation and control of it all was complex. In the middle of September 1944 there were a total of eighteen different parties on various tasks stretching from the north-east corner of Italy through Yugoslavia and Albania to Greece. Between them there was a maximum distance of 850 miles. Such a front was an unusually large one for the activities of one unit; nor was it easy to control so many operations in such diverse types of country.

These were sufficient problems, but on top of them was the changing political scene in each country. In Yugoslavia we had started our operations with the greatest co-operation from the Partisans. Nothing was too much for them, and many of them became our friends.

However, the atmosphere became more cold as it grew apparent that the Yugoslav Army of National Liberation wanted the whole credit for the clearance of Germans from their soil. They forgot the aid that we as allies had given to them. We were treated as suspect aliens and thwarted at every turn. They shot those who remained friendly to us and they imprisoned others.

The effect on our Patrols was far-reaching. We had to withdraw them all—not because of German pressure but because our 'allies' didn't want us. By October only Arthur Stokes was still in Yugoslavia, with one party in the islands. All the effort and the energy expended in establishing and maintaining these Patrols was to be wasted. When we could sort the whole thing out and return to Yugoslavia we would have to go through all the preliminaries again. Patrols would have to be put in once more, contacts made, supplies built up. This in itself was enough. The irony of it all was so much worse. Little did I know at this time that these tiresome restrictions were only a foretaste of greater insults yet to come. We were at least given a safe passage out of the country. Later we were to have our men arrested and made to suffer far greater indignities.

In Albania similar problems were just starting. Every time we wanted to send more men in to fight and to kill Germans we had to obtain permission. We had to outline in detail what we planned to do, how long we intended to stay and how we would come. If they didn't like our reasons we were forbidden to come. Yet they would accept every single item of equipment and every golden sovereign they could lay their hands on.

This was no way to fight a war. It was terribly galling. We often wondered why the Allies stood it, and came to the reluctant conclusion that there was no reasonable alternative.

In Greece it was a very different story. We asked and it was given. We fought and the Greeks fought with us. They wanted to kill Germans, and didn't really care who did it so long as there were plenty of dead Germans at the end of it.

The first party we sent into Greek territory was under Lt Michael Barker. It was also the first formed party of British troops to re-enter Greek soil before the final liberation. Michael was sent by parachute to the island of Kithira off the southern coast of the Peloponnese. We suspected that the Germans might have evacuated the island. If so the Allies would be able to send a force to occupy it in order to safeguard the passage of further troops beyond it into Greece.

We had little information about Kithira, and had to select a dropping ground from air photographs. Moir went with the aircraft and dispatched Barker and his party of seven men. It was a long flight from Brindisi, and a great credit to the RAF, who found the selected field with no difficulty. Moir waited over the area long enough to see Barker flash a satisfactory signal from the ground.

As it turned out Kithira was unoccupied. The Germans had left a few days before Barker's party arrived.

It may be of interest to outline some of the thought and inter-Service co-operation which went towards the planning and execution of these operations.

There were the four phases. First, the planning of the operation. Secondly, putting the Patrol into place. Thirdly, maintaining it; and fourthly, its final evacuation.

The planning was all done by Ken Lazarus and his team at Bari. There he was in touch with the Navy and RAF elements of the Balkan Air Force, as well as with the representatives of Fitzroy Maclean's mission to Yugoslavia and Alan Palmer's mission to Albania. Once a suitable task had been agreed Ken would have many things to decide. How was the party to be infiltrated, how large was it to be, how long would it have to stay, what other organisations were already in the area, how did he want the communications to work, how could he resupply the Patrol, how did he propose to pull them out in the end?

Many other details as well had to be carefully considered—the intelligence available, the equipment necessary, the phase of the moon, the state of the weather, and the orders to be given.

Then when he had decided on the method by which the Patrol would go in he had to find out whether the Royal Navy or the RAF could do the job. Often aircraft were not available and plans had to be altered for a party to go by sea. We often preferred Patrols to be put in by sea because the risk of damage and loss of their equipment was less. It was normally only when the target was far inland or there was some necessity for speed that we sent Patrols by air.

The communications were not always easy. Tim Heywood had to ensure that his base organisation could fit the extra stations on to his networks. The cipher staff had to work out arrangements for dealing with incoming traffic. The equipment sent into the field had to be prepared for air dropping, or alternatively to be waterproofed if the Patrol was going by sea. Batteries and charging sets had to be designed into manageable loads, and sufficient spare parts provided.

It is no exaggeration to say that good and reliable communications were often the most vital factor in the success of every Patrol which went into the field. It was therefore essential to have good operators, suitable sets and a simple system. That we had so few failures was due to communications which reached the heights of wizardry; that we achieved such success was very largely due to Tim Heywood and his Signal Squadron. In Stuart Hamer as his number two he had the most excellent support. There were also Peter Mold and Harry Tame, two other officers of the Royal Corps of Signals, who together formed a team of the highest standard.

To say Tim was a genius would perhaps be an overstatement, but it is the nearest description I can find for his incredible ability as a Signals officer. I don't think he will mind my saying that not everyone liked him; they couldn't, for Tim was hard and ruthless. But I am sure there was no one who did not respect him. I personally was always only too aware of the soundness of Tim's perception, and of his voracious desire to make certain that our communications could not be better.

To those who have the knowledge it may convey something when I say that during the heaviest time of our operations—in August 1944—our Signal Squadron was handling up to six thousand 'groups' in a day. When one remembers that every signal had to be condensed to the minimum, this is a fairly large volume of signal traffic with which to cope. Every message was sent in cipher, and the load on a very small cipher staff was often heavy.

So much for the planning. I think I have said enough to give some idea of what was involved. When many such parties were running simultaneously all these details were multiplied.

If the Patrol went by sea the difficulties were not so great. There were available special craft and crews who had great experience at the job. Mostly fast torpedo-boats were used; some of them were Italian, but we obviously preferred to travel with the Royal Navy. These ships were splendid, for they were fast enough to cross the Adriatic in a few hours and to keep clear of enemy forces. They were also low in the water, and it was easy to disembark men over the side from them. We would provide our own small boats for putting the Patrol the last mile or so ashore, and otherwise we were in safe and cheerful hands. The Royal Navy always did us well, and we felt secure with them.

If the Patrol had to go by air there were other details to be decided. We had to arrange the packing of the loads. We had to weigh them up; and we had to get them to the right place at the right time. There were dropping-zones to be thought about, and recognition signals to any reception party there might have been waiting on the ground.

Then there was always the weather with which to contend, and the moonlight to consider. It was never easy to drop men unless there was some moonlight, because they cannot be dropped from as great a height as stores can be dispatched. There was also the eternal question of the availability of aircraft for the task, and aircrews trained for it.

Once the Patrol was on the ground there was then the problem of resupply. This often began from the moment they arrived—perhaps a wireless set had broken or a man been injured, or their stores been lost in the drop. If they could be resupplied by sea then all was relatively easy. But if it had to be by air we were again up against the limitations of availability, moonlight and weather. Sometimes it was weeks before we could deliver supplies. Either the weather was bad or the Patrol on the ground was unable to secure a suitable place. The enemy was wary and did everything possible to stop these aircraft at night. Once again the stores had to be properly packed and loaded on to the aircraft. On the whole these sorties worked beautifully and without delay, but there were times of endless postponement. We even sent in mail and other comforts when the risk was reasonably small.

Lastly there was the evacuation. Sometimes it was by sea and sometimes by air. I remember well trying to collect Mike Reynolds from Albania when he went back to observe the damage at Orso Bay.

It was in the middle of July and the weather was surprisingly bad when I left Brindisi at 6.30 in the evening aboard an Italian torpedo-boat. There was a cracking thunderstorm raging. As we left the harbour the skipper wanted to go back, but I would stand none of it. Crossing the Adriatic the weather was very bad, and we shipped a lot of water. At length we saw the coast and picked up Mike's flashed signals. Every few seconds lightning lit the universe and our craft heaved massively beneath us. For two hours we lay off trying to launch a boat as the waves swept over us. For two hours I clung to the rails, trying to encourage the Italians to encourage themselves.

But it was no good, and we gave up after very nearly losing a man overboard.

There was a really heavy sea that night, and we set our bows right into it as we turned to go back to Italy. Only the skipper and I remained on deck, and we were both wet through. The rest of the crew were sick or they were below invoking the aid of the Almighty.

At dawn we reached the shelter of Brindisi. No one was more glad than I, for we had passed a miserable night. We had very nearly foundered, and there was much damage to the craft. Iron doors had been ripped off, their rivets torn out and we had lost two depth-charges over the side.

Such were the limitations of weather at sea as they affected us. On this particular occasion it was serious, as I had heard from Mike before we left that the Germans were all round him. I was desperate to get him out—and failed.

It was usually much easier. Sometimes even our own small schooner *La Palma* did the job. She certainly made a number of useful supply runs. As time went on she had added considerably to her armament, and later boasted a 20-mm Oerlikon and a 2-pounder gun. Alan Denniff was continually crossing the Adriatic in this quaint little craft, and had his adventures.

On one occasion in September he was sailing *La Palma* from Dugi to Vis in particularly bad weather. She carried a heavy load of men and supplies. Somehow she sprang a leak, and plaintive signals of distress were received by us in Italy. However, Alan jettisoned most of his cargo and made for shelter. When the weather abated the inadequate pumps gained the upper hand and the good ship sailed safely back for caulking and overhaul.

As already related, some Patrols were taken out by air from Partisan-held airfields. This presented no problem, save that of the reaction of the individual. There was no more complete and swift mental and physical metamorphosis. From having been for some weeks in enemy-held territory the men suddenly found themselves transported back to security and a certain degree of comfort. From nights out in the rain, and drenched already from the day's downpour, they found themselves no longer numbed with the cold. They might be again in a feather bed in a centrally heated hotel in Bari. Or they had come from days of strain and filth and activity to days of normal, clean and peaceful living. There was no wonder that men sometimes drank more than was good for them or played harmless practical jokes on the well-meaning but sometimes unbending Military Police. Neither could quite understand the other.

It was this side of the men's lives to which I had to pay a good deal of attention. There was always the danger and tendency to use the best Patrols for the most tricky job. I had continually to resist this urge, and I did not always succeed.

Some men were so willing to risk their lives; they were never happy unless they were on patrol. Unless you watched them their vigilance grew less keen and their nerves more frayed. It was only fair to these to rest them and to see that they had the leave and change they needed. One or two officers were brave enough to tell me that they couldn't go on without a rest. It takes some courage to admit that you have had enough, and I admired them for it. Others could never bring themselves to do so, and they had to be coaxed carefully into inactivity.

I have outlined some of the thoughts which were behind these operations. The difficulties were often very great, but never as severe as those with which the men in the field had to compete. Often these could not discover who was friend and who was foe. They suffered hunger, cold and exhaustion. They put up with considerable provocation, and they met many disappointments. It is primarily of them that I think when reliving some of the anguish we went through in controlling their efforts. It is to them that I hope the credit for any success we had really went. It is they whom I remember most vividly now.

I can recapture impressions—sometimes sombre, sometimes gay—on those many occasions on which I saw Patrols go off. Sometimes they departed furtively by air from Brindisi, and sometimes rather more joyously as they drank with the sailors aboard some naval craft. Always the men were longing to get back over the 'other side'; always they were supremely confident in their ability to achieve the target they had been set. Never did I see them frightened. Never.

Then I used whenever possible to see them when they came back. They would relate their experiences with enthusiasm and reserve. How much they had enjoyed themselves; how keen they were to get back again.

They were inspiring days in which I really felt we were doing a worthwhile job. Also we all knew that we were contributing something towards the defeat of Germany. Our days of waiting were past, and we were in the full flood and surge of success and the confidence that it brings.

It was my job to keep a general control over it all. I could do little more. The details were worked out by Ken, Moir and their staff at Bari. When I could offer advice or help to oil the wheels I did so, but I could not exercise complete control, nor would it have been right for me to have done so. No Commanding Officer could have been served better.

At the time I never properly appreciated the size of the task which Ken and Moir had to undertake. I knew they worked long hours, for I could always speak on the telephone to them in their office in Bari at any time up to midnight. It was not only the long hours they had to bear but it was the strain of waiting and hoping and the realisation of those two conditions. Night after night they might be thwarted by the weather, and day after day they sometimes waited for the expected call from one of the Patrols. Then there would be the frenzied rush to obtain what was wanted, to pack and to dispatch it. That this strain never told on them says much for their worth. It does not reveal how much they did and worked for a cause they loved.

The few occasions on which we failed were either due to ill-luck or to a gamble which did not come off. I cannot remember one which was caused by bad planning or through any fault of those involved in the operation. As a factor in this success I also willingly admit the natural proportion of good luck which accompanies any risk. We certainly had our share of it, for the gods were often unaccountably on our side.

That we had so very few casualties proves nothing conclusively. It does seem to suggest an inordinate slice of good luck which I freely recognise. Surely it must also reflect some credit on the work and thought and care which Ken and Moir lavished on their preparation of our operations? We were extremely fortunate to have lost a very small proportion of those who took part in them.

# CHAPTER 17

# Operations in Albania

Our operations in Albania in 1944 and early 1945 were superimposed on those already being carried out there by Lt-Colonel Alan Palmer's mission to that country. We had come in at his behest, and at a time when his men had thoroughly prepared the ground for us. Alan and the members of his mission had been in the country for many months, living under dreadful and often primitive conditions. It was largely because of their help and advice and the result of their experience that we were able to gain the few successes that we did achieve.

Albania at that time was of less importance than Yugoslavia. It is much smaller, and its resistance movement was neither so well organised nor so large. It was therefore never accorded the same priority for the provision of equipment, and the aircraft to drop it, as was given to Yugoslavia. But this detracts nothing from the effort of Alan Palmer and the few officers who had struggled for so long to foster a spirit of resistance against the enemy.

One of my officers wrote the following notes about the Albanians after he had spent some time in their country of strange paradoxes:

1. The Partisans are unreliable and have little organisation.
2. Their main object appears to be to get as much as they can out of the Allies.
3. They are gradually becoming more and more subservient to the insidious attractions of the Soviet brand of Communism.
4. We all felt that they would willingly kill us for a gold sovereign, a watch or a pistol.
5. Their word is seldom to be trusted even in small matters.

These are harsh words. But there is a good deal of truth in them and it is a wonder, therefore, not that there were so many misunderstandings, but that so much good work was done. Those observations also throw some light on the character and nature of the Partisans with whom we worked in

Albania. They were strange and troublesome people sometimes, yet they were often extremely brave and kind.

I could not help being interested in them. I liked their rough and simple way of life. I recognised them as rogues but somehow never felt they were inherently evil. Backward they certainly were, but they had for me a certain charm. I know I was let down, I know I was cheated and deceived, but still they fascinated me. I loved their rugged, wild, undeveloped country. Some of it was very attractive.

By Western standards the people were by no means civilised. Sanitation was a word unknown to them. Honesty was one with which they were barely acquainted, and then only in some weird interpretation of their own. They lived on their wits, for the produce of their eroded soil was never likely to let them grow fat. Few of them saw beyond the hills on the horizon, and cared less than nothing for what went on over the other side.

Their chief attraction for me was that they were humble, ingenuous and patriotic but they also had a less attractive side to their characters. They were sharp, they were sinister and capable of cunning duplicity. They lived in the utmost squalor, and were dreadfully hard to the unfortunate Italians who had been abandoned in Albania after Badoglio had come to terms with the Allies.

These Italians virtually existed as slaves. Some fought for the Partisans because they were needed as technicians, but the majority of them were mere serfs, devoid of any personal rights or freedom. The Albanians had stripped them of their belongings and their warm clothes. They barely fed them, and they drove them to death, starvation or disease. I came across many of these Italians, and could only feel sorry for them. Theirs was a tragic lot, and they would have given their souls just to be allowed to return home to Italy, from whence they had been transported unwillingly by Ciano. Very few escaped from their servitude unless perchance death brought them relief.

In spite of the Albanians' savage disregard for the conventions of humanity there was some goodness in them. Some of the more intelligent Albanian peasants appreciated their own shortcomings and nursed a passionate, if ineffective, desire to improve their way of life. I think many of them were obsessed by their hatred of the type of monarchy which they had experienced under King Zog; as a result they were unbalanced in their determination never to allow their country to be ruled again by a handful of powerful men. They therefore never quite knew what particular breed of political state they were seeking, and thus drifted inevitably into communism.

It is sad to think that such was the case. The peasants were too disinterested ever to oppose it, or too ignorant to understand its dangers. What a pity they never did, for I believe they must now be both fundamentally unhappy and unsuited to the executive methods and the curtailment of individual freedom which are features of communist control. I got the impression that the whole conception of it was strange to them, as they were essentially liberal by nature.

I avoided political conversation as much as possible while in Albania, but I know I came away with the belief that democracy would be ultimately established if the people were prepared to make some sacrifice to regain it. Unfortunately, they did not care sufficiently and all too quickly the power of the Partisan communists gained too strong a hold.

Our main operations in Albania were designed to cut across the German lines of withdrawal from Greece. But before these moves were carried out there were other small tasks which fell to us.

Captain John Olivey—who had been captured on Leros—had escaped in Athens and then gone home to Rhodesia for a short spell of leave. How well he deserved that leave! For nearly three years in the desert he had commanded a Patrol. He was a good leader, and quite fearless. His had often been the task of transporting David Stirling and his Special Air Service parties on their forays into enemy-occupied airfields.

Then when we left the desert, and went to reorganise at the Cedars in Lebanon, John Olivey became second-in-command in the Squadron which I was then commanding. This meant irksome administration, and juggling with the whole tiresome range of military proformas. John disliked this kind of soldiering, and the forms suffered in his rather haphazard care. Very soon he was back in charge of a Patrol, which was the life he loved and understood.

After being taken prisoner on Leros he escaped twice before finally reaching Athens. With 1,500 prisoners from Leros he was shipped to Greece. They were marched through Athens lustily singing *Tipperary* till the Germans quietened them, but their progress was a sign for the Greeks to show where their sympathies lay. Some women were in tears, while others threw fruit and cigarettes to the men as they went. In this confusion John took his opportunity and dived down a side-street. He remained in hiding in the neighbourhood of Athens for over four months until he eventually made his way out to Cairo.

Very shortly after his return from Rhodesia he was sent in to the south of Albania to find out about the enemy positions across the Llogara Pass. This was on the coast road running south to Greece from Valona. It was hoped that a Commando raid could be launched against the position, and thus open up that stretch of the road for the free movement of Partisan transport in the area.

Olivey had little excitement except the misfortune of capsizing their rowing-boat off the shore after they had been disembarked from a motor torpedo-boat. He found the Pass had been evacuated a few days before his arrival. He spent one or two rather uncomfortable days in the area before we could withdraw him. The local Partisans for some reason resented his presence, and they attempted to remove the weapons from the men of his Patrol.

Stan Eastwood was dropped into the south of Albania on 9 August. We had been asked to make a reconnaissance of the areas north and south of Durazzo. Unfortunately, there were strong defences and minefields along that part of the coast, so we could not put Eastwood's party in by sea. Nor had we a suitable area into which we could drop them near enough to their target. We considered every possible way of getting Stan in, and it seemed that it would pay us to let him drop into a friendly area farther south. Here he would be able to obtain all the help he might require to make his way north to Durazzo.

Stan can hardly have expected when he left Italy in early August that he would not return until December, four months later. A lot was to happen to him during those weeks, and his men travelled hundreds of miles on foot.

His first task on arrival was to go to see Enver Hoxha, whom the Partisans styled a General, and whom they selected to be their leader in Albania. He later became their President. Alan Palmer was with Hoxha, and so Stan had the benefit of all the advice the former could give him. There was little Alan did not know about the country, and Stan was extremely lucky to be given such a good start.

Alan obtained the necessary guides and mules for Stan's journey north. With him went Major Hare, who was one of Alan's British liaison officers and who also knew the country well. He had already been there for over a year. For the next three weeks Stan and his party pushed on to the north. They moved mostly by day, and did some very long marches.

At the beginning of September Stan himself caught malaria very badly and was decidedly ill for several days. But he recovered slowly through the ministrations of an Italian doctor who did as much as he could for him. In the middle of September he reached a place called Pajandra. The few farmsteads to which the name was given were about fifteen miles south-west of the capital—Tirana—and a similar distance south-east from Durazzo. So far, apart from occasional brushes with the enemy, Stan and his men had not had much trouble. They had, however, covered a great deal of ground in a country where movement was never easy.

The first signs of general withdrawal by the enemy from Greece occurred in early September, and I saw great opportunities for us. I therefore stopped Stan from going on northward, as I hoped I could use him to receive and operate offensively with other Patrols which I planned to drop to him.

The Germans were being hard-pressed everywhere at this stage of the war. The Gothic Line had been forced on the east coast of Italy, and we had reached Rimini by the middle of September 1944. All seemed set for the Allied armies to press forward into the valley of the Po.

Bucharest had been entered by the Russians, and the Ploesti oilfields were in their hands. Bulgaria had been overrun, and the Russians were beginning to advance into Yugoslavia. In Western Europe the 1st Airborne Division had landed in Holland, and General Eisenhower's armies had breached the Siegfried Line south of Aachen. Luxembourg was in our hands, and the line ran southward to include Metz and Nancy.

With these reverses the German High Command could not possibly continue to maintain large garrisons in the Balkans. They could not be allowed to withdraw them with impunity for use elsewhere. Small as our own efforts to disrupt their plans might be, this was just the kind of opening we were waiting for, and no time could be lost in taking it.

Once the German withdrawal began in earnest I wanted to be able to drop every possible man into Albania to strike across the enemy's routes. I argued that the Germans' static defences along these roads must become disorganised, and the retreating enemy less vigilant in their desire to get on hastily to the north. At the same time I argued that the Partisans in Albania, who had been fighting for years, would be tired, and would be anxious only to speed the parting guests with as little inconvenience to themselves as possible.

I could not see them trying to delay the enemy and kill him in the confines of their own country. Far better to let the Germans go unhindered, undelayed, and not tempt them to take further reprisals. Such an attitude was parochial but very understandable, for the Albanians did not seem to be able to hate the enemy with the same ardour as the Greeks and Yugoslavs. It was difficult to make them understand that every German who lived through his exit from Greece and Albania meant another German to fight in Yugoslavia or Austria and so on as they went back to Germany.

The reaction of the Albanians after years of oppression was beginning to set in. I was very anxious to see their morale lifted as high as possible for this final stage. It happened that I had Alan Palmer on my side, and one of his officers at his base headquarters in Bari—a Major Eliot Watrous, who also saw how much there was to be gained in bringing this operation about.

The first thing to do was to sell my idea to the Balkan Air Force. To them it would mean an additional commitment for aircraft over Albania, and would thus reduce the effort in Yugoslavia. I went to see Brigadier George Davy and told him of my plans. There was little new in my ideas, for they were conventional. I wanted to reinforce the Partisans with moral courage and with arms so that they would really fight the Germans and destroy as many of them as possible. Surely, for the lack of a few aircraft to support us, we were not going to let the German withdrawal through Albania go largely unhindered? Surely no one could believe that the RAF alone could wreak complete and devastating havoc on the enemy? They couldn't possibly fly all day and all night and be damaging all the time. Surely a little extra help on the ground might have some effect, for it mattered so much about every single German who lived to fight elsewhere?

I was worked up over this plan, because it seemed to be one that would contribute most to the efforts of the Allies on the main fronts in Europe; one that would cost us little, and might pay big dividends.

I needn't have got quite so heated about it, for George Davy was quick to realise what a great chance there was. I remember him saying:

'Yes, I quite agree with all you have said but supposing we find we cannot guarantee the aircraft to supply your parties dotted all over the place?'

'They can live off the land, sir, as they have done before,' I replied. 'You never quite know what you might find to eat next, and that adds a bit of excitement to it all.'

I went on to say that if necessary we would have to feed only when we could capture something from the enemy, and that if we did this we couldn't help doing it without killing some of them. This reinforced my argument just a little, for George Davy agreed with the policy that every dead German in Albania would lessen their fighting strength in Yugoslavia. He also saw how necessary it was to encourage the Albanians, who might otherwise be content to see the Germans go quietly, while retaining their arms to fight the internal political battle for the supremacy of communism.

I began my detailed planning on 12 September. Ken and Moir worked even harder than usual, for there was a good deal to arrange and they would have to see the plans through from Italy. From the start I had every intention of going in myself to command the whole project, which was given the code name 'Lochmaben'.

For the first few days all went well with our plans. I intended to drop three more Patrols to Stan Eastwood. With this force I hoped to ginger up the Partisans in that area, and induce them to block the roads for as long as possible.

Very soon the inevitable political complications appeared on the scene. The Partisans had not been slow to grasp that if more British troops arrived it would mean increased bloodshed and destruction on their soil. These were the very things they wanted to avoid. I could understand but not sympathise with this very short-sighted and selfish view. I believe also that they feared a British occupation of their country—or rather their Soviet masters could not tolerate such a possibility.

For some reason which I could not quite understand at that time Stan Eastwood was also opposed to my plan. I later learnt that he was under pressure from the Partisans with whom he was living, and who were misleading him with gloomy and false intelligence.

Luckily, Field-Marshal Alexander's headquarters appreciated the military necessity for quick and effective offensive action and took a firm line with the Foreign Office. The latter in their turn made strong diplomatic representation to Hoxha.

On 16 September some agreement had been reached. Unfortunately, at that moment John Olivey's disagreement with the Partisans at the Llogara Pass was becoming increasingly acute. Hoxha then became even more unwilling than before to let us go in. All this while Alan Palmer was employing his most persuasive and diplomatic efforts with Hoxha, with whom he was fortunately on fairly intimate terms.

On the 18th September I feared we should be too late. Ten thousand German troops with their vehicles broke through Zervas's Greek forces in Epirus and began to pour into Albania. This was the precise moment at which we should have been in position and ready to strike. There was no time to be lost, for even when we had arrived we could not function at once. Inevitably a few days had to be spent making contacts and plans as well as reaching our targets.

On 20 September Hoxha was still playing for time, and I saw no alternative but to attempt to force his hand. I felt the only way to clear up the whole situation was to go in myself to see Stan and his local Partisans. I would then convince them of the need to fight and kill Germans as they went through the country. Once I had done this I would persuade them to convince Hoxha of the same thing.

George Davy accepted this argument, and agreed that I should go in the following night. There was a plane taking food and ammunition, among which it seemed convenient for me to tumble down to earth.

On 21 September I left Bari for Brindisi. When I arrived there I was handed a message to say that all was well, and Eastwood was ready for me. The message added, 'You may be interested to know that Whynne, who dropped into Albania last night, broke his leg on landing.' I was interested, but scarcely encouraged.

I took off from Brindisi at 7.45 p.m. that evening, not feeling greatly confident in the American crew of the aircraft. They said they had never done such a job before, and didn't know much about it. However, they assured me that 'it looked a piece of cake'. I don't think they liked my saying that cake or no cake it wasn't quite as easy as all that and would they mind telling me their plan.

As I feared, there was no plan. They thought they would fly over the water, then 'just stooge around looking for the light of Eastwood's fires'. They resented my questioning them about the height at which they proposed to tip me out. This wasn't important, they reckoned.

Despite my misgivings I felt on top of the world. I was perhaps a little lonely in the back of the Dakota, where I had been practically stacked among heaps of mortar bombs and ammunition cases. I wasn't quite alone, for there was also a Yugoslav who was to act as the dispatcher. He was a morose and sullen fellow who spoke no language known to me and did not help to make up for the confidence I lacked in the pilots of our machine. Yet I somehow didn't mind very much. I felt I was setting off on what was for me a new and fascinating adventure. I was also glad to be going for several rather selfish reasons.

I was terribly tired, and wanted to escape for a bit from the endless conferences and long hours of work which the last few months had entailed. I had rarely been to bed before 1.00 a.m., and each and every night I was wakened by the arrival of messages from the Patrols.

I also sensed that it was high time for me to go on a parachute operation. As CO it was not enough just to have done a series of training jumps. Coupled with this was the natural reluctance for parachuting with which some of the men were beginning to become obsessed. I always felt very strongly about these things, which I had inherited to a lesser degree from Jake Easonsmith, who would never send his men on any job which he himself would not willingly undertake.

There were also at this time some horrible rumours about the fate of parachutists found by the enemy in occupied territory. Although the men at the time never knew of Hitler's notorious order that they should be summarily shot, I wanted to show my disregard for such wild and disquieting stories as were beginning to circulate.

Perhaps most of all, I wanted to taste that spice of thrill and adventure which were the antidote for overwork. Although I was often supremely frightened behind the lines, I also derived a great deal of excitement from it. Much of the thrill may have been in the planning, and it was probably accentuated in retrospect, but I nevertheless enjoyed the sensations and anxieties of the unknown, the unexpected, the rough and carefree life—these were intoxicating attractions to me. Nobody loves his comfort and the good things of life more than I do, yet I can equally well enjoy an existence without them, provided I am not bored or inactive.

My thoughts were mixed as at last we lumbered away into the night. I lay down to rest as best I could on a sack of flour with my head on a bale of Army boots. Soon I was nearly asleep. But the flight across the Adriatic was short, and before long I was shaken from my reverie by the thunderous bark of gunfire.

There was no door on the aircraft, and as I looked down, through the gaping void where it should have been, I could see the harbour of Durazzo. We were flying at two thousand feet—hardly a suitable height at which to come in over a defended enemy port.

Then I saw red and green coloured tracer coming up toward us, but did not mind this so much until the searchlights caught us. These held us in their beams, and the whole aircraft became suddenly lit up inside. It seemed a long time before the pilot began to twist and dive or climb. After some terrifying aerial antics we shook off the searchlights and flew on over Albania. I was not quite certain where we were, and nowhere could I see Stan's welcoming fires. The pilot and crew began to get a little nervous, for they feared the German night fighters. I had some difficulty in persuading them to stay over the area at all.

After about an hour of fruitless search the pilot readily accepted my decision that there was no point in just flying around. I was also pretty certain that he had no idea where we were. There was nothing for it but to return ignominiously to Brindisi.

Charles Hall, who was my second-in-command at that time, sent me thirty years later the pencilled note that I had sent to him in Rodi when I got back to Italy. It confirms everything I have written about this episode, except, perhaps, that my descriptive powers were possibly a little more dramatic. It records also how frightened I was when I wrote that 'I thought of better ways to die and finally lit a cigarette; but thank goodness there were only mortar bombs to see how scared I was!' I went on to say that it was 'all quite an entertainment but doesn't help the war much'. I was feeling pretty bitter then about the aircrew's failure to get me there.

I fell asleep as we returned across the Adriatic. I did not wake until we bumped heavily in the dark on the tarmac strip at Brindisi. As we ran along the strip I could see flares rushing wildly by us at intervals. These were the markers to guide us in on our landing, and they were ghostly sights because I had not yet adjusted my senses, which were confused by the speed of the evening's events.

I was not sorry to climb down out of that aircraft. I drove straight to Bari, where I heard from Stan that he had been quite unable to light fires for my reception as he was being shelled at the time. I thought this was prudent of him! During the day we at last received permission for our whole party to go in. There were thirty-six of us altogether, and we would jump from six aircraft at intervals throughout the following night. With us we would take as much stores as we could load into the planes.

That night I dined with Rufus Montagu, and had an excellent dinner. There could have been no more contrasting experience. Twenty-four hours previously I had been keyed up to drop into enemy-occupied territory. The following night I was in the comfort and security of Rufus's flat in Bari, where I gave few thoughts to what had gone by. My mind was able to dwell on other things in normal surroundings. The conversation was always entertaining, and the fare exceedingly good. The evening passed quickly and happily. What a tonic those evenings were!

Next day we all went to Brindisi and drew our parachutes. Once more we were to be frustrated, for that night the weather was too bad for us to drop. We therefore spent a quiet day, and amused ourselves at a very average ENSA show that evening.

On 24 September the weather was right; the aircraft were ready; the Partisans were happy, and so were we. Our first aircraft was to leave at 7.45 p.m., and I had decided to go in it. The other five planes would follow at hourly intervals.

In the afternoon I got the whole party together and told them details of my plan. This was our invariable custom. Normally only the officer in charge of a Patrol knew early where they were going or what they had to do; the others were never told until the last minute. Nevertheless, our security was always good, because I think everyone realised the necessity for it. They knew that if they talked they might endanger the lives of their friends as well as their own.

That evening I dined at the Officers' Club in Bari. Ron Tinker, Robin Marr and Tiny Simpson were the three officers coming with me. We had a good party, and laughed a great deal in the kind of forced way that one does when one is feeling a little nervous. Ken Lazarus came to dine with us and to check up on any last-minute requirements. Rufus Montagu was also there to wish us good luck, and to bring good wishes from the British Minister in Bari.

It was a lovely evening as I climbed into our Dakota with Sergeant Saunders and four men of Robin Marr's Patrol. We waved goodbye to the other parties and rumbled off down the runway towards the sea. I remember nothing of the flight until we arrived over Albania. Then I began to look through the door to try to spot our dropping ground and the fires which Stan was to light down there for us on the ground.

Below us there was little to be seen save the occasional headlights of a few cars or lorries as they wound their way laboriously round the mountain passes. I knew the Germans in them could not hear the noise of our aircraft above the sound of their own vehicle engines, but I hoped that they were moving in terror of the Partisans. Every now and then I could also pick out a river or a lake as we flew over. Otherwise the earth below looked dead and uninviting.

Inside our aircraft the men were talking cheerfully and greedily inhaling their last cigarettes before they jumped into the darkness. This time one of our own men was there to dispatch us, and he was busily fixing our static lines to the parachutes on our backs. He was also getting all the bundles of stores as near as possible to the door so that no time would be lost in their dispatch.

While all this was going on I was scanning the gloom below for the reassuring signal which Stan had been instructed to make. I pictured him standing by a heap of firewood, anxiously looking at his watch and listening for the welcome sound of our aircraft engines. He would be excited, for it was always a joy to receive news and friends from a world from which he must have felt cut off.

Soon I saw the fires arranged in the agreed formation. As we flew round them I adjusted my parachute and wished the others good luck. I began to think we were a bit high, but had little time for argument as the light by the door told me to get ready. Then I stood in the doorway; both hands firmly grasped its sides as the night air and the aircraft's slipstream roared past my face.

I felt a little cold, as a tremor half of fear and half of thrill ran down my spine. My eye was on the red light, which had warned me to take up my position. Soon this light would turn to green, and then I must hurl myself into that forbidding rushing wind.

Behind me stood the other five. I had no time to look at them, but knew that there was now no way back. This was a comfort and encouragement. Then as we came in to run straight over the fires which Stan had lit below I stood tense for a second until I saw the green light, and thought no more. I threw myself out into the night.

I was first to go and looked up to see some others follow me as I floated down silently to earth. I remember muttering aloud, 'Thank God, the thing has opened', and I began to watch for the ground coming up towards me. My first fears had been realised, for I stayed in the air an uncommonly long time—we had been dropped about two thousand feet higher than the one thousand feet at which I had asked to be dispatched.

At last I saw the earth moving up towards me, and I lit my torch. I wanted to see where I was landing. It was a perfect but damp evening as I dropped unharmed into a bush. I am hazy as to what happened next. But I remember realising that I had been dropped some way from the appointed place, and I was anxious to hurry over to join Stan. I slipped out of my 'chute and strode forward into the night.

The next I knew was some hours later when an Albanian found me at the foot of a deep ravine. I was in some pain, and felt a lot of blood about my face. Beyond that I can't remember much, except that my saviour tried to drag me up the steep sides of the place where I had fallen.

Throughout the night the other parties arrived. By 4.00 a.m. the next morning all the aircraft had delivered their goods and the men began to collect everything together. This process went on throughout the following day.

We had been spread over a very wide area. Our pilots had dropped us all too high, and it was only because there was practically no wind that there were not more casualties. Robin Marr and two other men were hurt in the drop, but happily not seriously. Of the thirty-six men who landed that evening only one man fell on the selected dropping-ground—and he damaged his ankle. I later learnt that Major Hare, who was the British liaison officer at Pajandra and was on the ground with Stan, had felt so strongly about the poorness of the dropping that he sent the following signal to Bari:

'Miracle that damage was not greater. Consider pilots are quite unfit to drop bodies and it would be criminal to let them do it again.'

These were harsh words, but then Hare had had a lot of experience over the last eighteen months. I agreed strongly with his opinion.

To be fair to our American pilots, I should say that it was a tricky place over which to drop people. The field on which Stan had hoped we would land was situated between two high hills, which made manœuvre of the aircraft difficult and probably dangerous. It was never easy for pilots to drop bodies, because they had to be ejected at such a low height as to ensure that they did not drift too far off the dropping zone. Stores were a different matter, because it was not very important where they landed, so long as the enemy did not get them. The pilots we had that night had only once before dropped bodies. At the time there were no other more experienced men available, and we had to accept this element of risk.

The gods were certainly with us that night, for we might easily have had many more men injured. My own misfortune was certainly not directly attributable to any fault on the part of the pilot who had dropped me out. I had plunged over the edge of a ravine after landing safely, and fallen thirty feet in the dark.

Our first day in Albania was a fairly miserable one. It rained heavily most of the day, and we had little cover except what we could make from our parachutes.

I was utterly disconsolate. I had obviously damaged my spine, for I could not move, and I felt wretched at this failure. It was only because of the kindness of everyone that life was bearable at all. One or two of the men stayed by me all the next day and night and looked after me. I lay under a shelter, which Hare had kindly given over to me. Nothing that he could do was too much trouble, and he gave me every possible comfort that his ingenuity or that of others could devise.

There were with us two or three RAMC medical orderlies who did what they could for me. But they could obviously do no more than their training or their equipment allowed. So I lay resigned to helplessness, and handed over my command to Ron Tinker. I had brought him as my second-in-command, for I always felt that I might have to leave this operation and go back to Italy to see to affairs there.

Ron at once took control, and splendidly he did it. He also wirelessed back to Ken, and together with the medical orderlies he gave a fair diagnosis of my condition. Those in Italy were able to guess from this that I had fractured my spine.

During the day an Albanian doctor came to see me. I believe he thought I was a fraud, for he practically told me not to be so wet and to get up and walk. As any attempt to do so was a failure, he prescribed a good dose of castor-oil or some equally revolting medicine and departed cheerfully back into the hills.

Back in Italy Ken and other good friends had left no stone unturned on my behalf. At the time Michael Parsons was still with us as our unit medical officer. He was at Rodi when Ken rang him up and warned him to be ready to jump that night. Poor Michael hated jumping anyway. But he didn't hesitate, and was probably glad he hardly had enough time to think until it was all over. He spent the morning collecting equipment and plaster in which to strap me up. He then drove the eighty miles to Bari, and just had time to see Ken before driving on again another sixty miles to Brindisi.

At Brindisi he was not encouraged. A special Halifax aircraft had been arranged for his journey, and it had a picked crew, but the weather reports were extremely bad. However, the pilot said he would certainly have a try, and keep on trying, till they got Michael to me. He even volunteered to do the job by daylight if he could not drop Michael that night.

I wish I had met that pilot. All I know is that he belonged to 384 Wing of the Royal Air Force. I should like to have told him how grateful I was for his courage. In foul weather he flew in very low that night and dropped Michael in to my assistance.

It was a very brave effort by them all, and certainly saved me from getting considerably worse. Michael stayed with me and looked after me most carefully for the next few weeks. No sooner had he landed than the weather broke, and it would have been quite impossible to have received any aircraft for some days.

My own troubles were over. I somehow have a childish faith in doctors, and in Michael it was not misplaced. He soon had my spine in plaster, and he patched up my badly cut and battered face. In his haste he had not forgotten to bring anything that might be needed. He worked quickly and cheerfully, all the while amusing me with descriptions of his jump, which he quite candidly admitted had been simply terrifying. Luckily, he could laugh about it.

Ron Tinker was making plans, and very soon sent one of the Patrols under Tiny Simpson to make preparations for attacking the Elbasan–Tirana road. Stan Eastwood was still pretty sick with malaria, so he stayed at our base camp for a bit. This we established under some trees on the bank of a dried-up river-bed. Our parachutes made excellent tents, and these were covered with branches and mud.

We were lucky in having a strong character in the local Partisan commander. His name was Myslim Peza, and he was universally respected. For the last ten years he had fought against the Italians occupying his country. Everywhere he was regarded as a fine and brave fighter. He was a rugged, friendly man whom we were shortly to lose when he went to join Hoxha in the south. It was a pity that he was removed from the bandit's life at which he was a master. He was too simple to understand politics, and, I thought, too naïve to be seriously involved in them. I was very wrong, for he later became Vice-President of Albania.

A few days after we had arrived I was visited by a local Partisan brigade commander. He was in a terrible state, and said that his force was being seriously threatened by the Germans a few miles to the north of our base. He implied that unless I sent all available help not only would his brigade be decimated but the Germans would be free to wipe us out too. He saw my helpless state, and hoped to frighten me. I won't deny that he did, but I was firm.

It was no part of our plans to get involved with the Germans in set battles, and I had no intention of sacrificing my Patrols in frontal attacks against prepared positions, so I said I was sorry but I did not see how I could help. Two days later the enemy withdrew, and all was well. Our base was now fairly secure, so I sent Eastwood and his Patrol off to the Elbasan–Tirana road. Here they joined Tiny Simpson. Very soon they began their attacks together with a rabble of Partisans who joined them. The results were most encouraging, and I cannot do better than quote a note Eastwood sent to me on 7 October. It was our only means of communicating at any length, and we worked up an excellent courier service.

Stan's note read:

We have kept this Elbasan–Tirana road closed since the night of the 4th—nothing has got through. Yesterday morning three trucks and a tank tried to get through. We destroyed them all. All the Huns in the truck were killed.

Later they brought troops up from Tirana and put in two ground attacks against us. The first had about two hundred men and there were less in the second. Both attacks were beaten off. There was a convoy waiting at either end of these actions hoping the road would be cleared.

At dusk last night we blew the road in a second place and as the first one has not been fixed yet it should remain closed for some time.

We have been taking it in turns up on the road and it was Tiny who had all the fun yesterday.

Result of yesterday's battle:-

Hun. 80 killed.

NO prisoners were taken.

Following equipment captured:-

   1 Mortar and bombs.

   4 L.M.Gs.

   30 Rifles.

   20 Revolvers.

   Plenty of clothing, boots, etc.

We have pulled out for a rest and to await any explosives you can send us. Our chaps are all O.K. but we have been worried a bit by mortars and machine guns. My Partisans are as keen as mustard but are terribly badly equipped. It is a crying shame. They would love a letter of congratulations from you.

I wrote at once and received a wonderful reply in return. After greeting me with the conventional 'Death to Fascism' and 'Freedom to the Peoples' the letter concluded with the writer's 'hearty greetings to me and the British Armies under me for their day after day successes in all fields of battle'.

We had made a heartening start, and I hoped this could continue. But we were short of explosives, and badly needed all we could obtain. I had sent signals back with a request for more, and on the first clear night we received a supply from Italy. With them also came Captain Paddy McLaughlan, another New Zealand officer whom General Freyberg had allowed to rejoin us. It was excellent to see him, particularly as he brought us some mail and other good things. He even brought me a bottle of whisky, which Rufus Montagu had thoughtfully sent in for my twenty-seventh birthday.

A few days later I had another report from Stan. It was to say that the road was still cut, and that the only vehicle which had attempted to get through had been destroyed, and its party of eight Germans killed.

Not far from Stan's position was a German observation post on a high part of the road. Just below this was a barracks where an enemy company was stationed. The whole served to protect that part of the road, and was a constant source of irritation to Stan's force. He therefore decided to support a Partisan attack upon it. This little battle was also a considerable success. The RAF sent over some rocket-firing Spitfires at Stan's request, and did a lot of damage.

The attack began at 10.00 one night and went on till 1.00 the following morning. As described to me by the Partisans

the battle was fierce and the climax was reached when a small number of Partisans jumped over the barbed wire and shot some Germans. They then succeeded in burning one of the Barracks and all the Germans inside were burned to death. We killed thirty-six Germans and two Partisans were slightly wounded. We captured three thousand rounds of ammunition and much clothing.

The accent on all these actions was the amount of ammunition and clothing captured. I also noticed that prisoners were seldom taken. The two tied up together. The Partisans were pitifully short of clothing, boots and all equipment, and therefore had to strip the Germans of everything they could lay their hands on. It was savage and crude; but it was a cruel war, and much was at stake.

Very soon I began to be able to get about again, and wanted to leave to see Stan. Ron Tinker had already departed to see how things were going.

At this time our main worry was shortage of food. We had brought in with us two weeks' supply for our party, but very soon we found that we were feeding many times that number. Our diet became very limited, for there was little we could buy or obtain from the peasants. Turkeys were the only thing we could get plenty of, and we all lived on these for a week or two. I began never to want to see a turkey again. We had to pay good gold to get them, and then we had them for breakfast, lunch and dinner. At one time we became so short of food, and so impatient because there were no aircraft available in Italy to send it, that I told Ken that unless he could see any prospect of supplying us, 'I recommend that we return to Italy. We are bloody hungry.'

This was blackmail. It did the trick, however, though the food did not arrive until we had almost exterminated the local breed of turkey!

Gold was the only currency of any use, and of this we could never have enough. We bought dozens of splendid little mountain ponies to carry all our equipment; we bought *rakia*, the local and very intoxicating liquor; we bought turkeys; we bought guides; and we bought information. Without our supply of gold I don't know what we would have done. I realised its value, and how tempted the Albanians were by it. I never felt really safe while I was carrying anything up to five hundred gold sovereigns.

Since he no longer had to devote all his time to me, Michael Parsons had begun to work wonders with his very limited supplies and equipment. He found that practically no medical arrangements existed for the Partisan wounded. There were two so-called hospitals. One of these was in a vermin-infested house and the other in non-waterproof tents. At neither of these places was there any attempt at sanitation. With these establishments as a basis Michael set about clearing up some of the mess. Whenever he could leave me he would ride off to visit them, some considerable distance away. He would operate where he could, and dress such wounds as he had dressings for.

He tried to organise the elements of sanitation and to teach the local doctors. But it was an uphill struggle, and he had to be very firm. The Albanians appreciated his efforts, but they resented his outspoken criticism of their squalid habits. Still, he achieved an incredible amount. Beds were made, Partisan girls were turned into nurses and parachutes were cut up into sheets.

He would come back to me at night absolutely worn out. Travelling in Albania was no rest cure, for the mule tracks were rough and in October of 1944 it rained nearly every day. On top of this Michael had many operations to carry out. Some of these he did by night, with only an oil lamp for light. In one such operation he removed both eyes from a Partisan, and it is a tribute to his effort that this particular patient was out of danger and active again in five days. It also speaks highly of the man's courage. Wherever he went Michael was greeted in a friendly way. I often wonder if any of them would remember their gratitude now if he went back to that sad little communist country.

When I felt strong enough I went off to see Stan on the main road. He asked for Michael Parsons to come along too, as one of his men had bad malaria. There were also two Partisans with him, both of whom had been badly wounded.

It was wonderful to leave our base, where I had felt very restricted. I also felt a long way from the battle. I was kept pretty busy, for although Ken was running all our operations back in Italy, he sent me daily details of everything that was going on.

Michael wanted to go by a devious route to visit various sick people on the way, and also had some medical supplies to distribute. After two days our little party of four or five and a couple of ponies arrived at Stan's position. I cannot pretend it was a comfortable walk for me. My back was by no means right, and I had lain on it for the past ten days or so. However, with Michael's assistance and encouragement we covered about thirty miles without mishap.

I found Stan a few hundred yards from the road, and hidden from it behind a hill. It was nearly dark when we arrived, and a few shots rang out as the Partisan day patrols withdrew to their night positions. Otherwise all was quiet, and after an excellent dinner of the inevitable turkey I talked to all Stan's men. They were in very good form despite the discomfort and danger in which they had been living.

During the night we were jolted by a rude awakening. The Partisans had suddenly decided to up sticks and move off from the road. I was woken from a supremely deep sleep, and with Stan did my best to knock some sense into them. Nothing would move them—or rather stop them moving. They had had their orders to go, and go they would. It didn't matter to them that the Germans would once more be able to open up a road which we had kept closed for over two weeks.

It appeared that the Partisans had been ordered to move towards Tirana. In fact at this stage all the Partisans in Albania were slowly moving towards the capital. They all wanted to be first to enter and to grab the loot which the Germans might leave. From then on there was little balance in their minds; they forgot all their former intentions and plans and flocked towards Tirana.

Stan was left to hold the road with only twenty men. He could not possibly do this for any length of time, and I decided the only thing to do was for me to go off at once to the local Partisan Brigade Headquarters at a place called Arbana.

So with Michael and a small train of hangers-on we walked throughout that day. We reached Arbana in the evening, and I endeavoured to contact the commander. As so often happened, he was not to be found. I was instead taken to the Commissar. This individual I disliked from the moment I met him. He was pompous and most unhelpful. All he could do was to ask me to help him in attacks against Tirana. I explained how useless this was; that the Germans on the roads were the main objectives, and that before long the enemy would evacuate Tirana anyhow. I then thumped the table and said that I did not propose to do all his dirty work for him on the roads while he waited outside Tirana to be the first to get in and seize the loot.

The results of my efforts were negligible. We were given a house in which to sleep the night, and departed the next morning. All I had succeeded in doing was to pick up some of the fleas and bugs with which our sleeping-place was profusely infested. This made me more angry than ever!

There was no point in leaving Stan and his party where they were, so I ordered them all back to our base for a rest and to get some much-needed food. They therefore had to leave the road which they had kept so completely closed for just on three weeks. Every attempt to open it had been defeated.

Meanwhile Ron Tinker with Paddy McLaughlan and Robin Marr's Patrol had been operating against the Elbasan–Struga road. They had blown one very effective crater which they planned to cover by fire, and thus prevent the enemy from repairing. But Tinker was with a poor lot of Partisans who never seemed anxious to engage the enemy. They did not want to provide troops to cover the crater, and withdrew, leaving Tinker to do his best with the few men he had with him. This he did without any Partisan help for the next week. He was then driven off by a strong German attack in which at the last moment some Partisans graciously consented to join and assist him.

He then planned a more effective method of blowing the road. At the place he selected a river ran alongside it. Ron hoped to burst the banks of the river and cause it to flow through five great craters which he was to blow. This enterprising plan only just failed.

For six hours Ron's men worked to bore five large holes each six foot deep. Into these he placed his main charges. Paddy McLaughlan was with him, and as a Sapper he revelled in this job. The result was impressive, but they just failed to initiate a large-scale overflow of the river. This activity did not go unheeded by the Germans, who brought up more troops to force Tinker's party back into the hills. After a vigorous battle he had once more to withdraw.

Ron was constantly being frustrated in his efforts. Either he had not enough explosives for his plans or the Partisans refused to help him. This happened so often that his patience was sorely tried. He was never one to suffer fools gladly, and least of all fools who would not fight the Germans. He lived for action, and was a master at the art of fighting. I know that he had many maddening problems to overcome, and it was only due to his strong personality and drive that he succeeded as he did. When there was no more that he could do in Albania he was withdrawn in the last days of November.

Stan spent the rest of November chasing the enemy where he could. He had considerable success before the end. The RAF were able to answer several of his calls for help, and the retreating enemy was constantly harassed. One of his more spectacular achievements was the result of a splendid little bit of co-operation with the RAF.

Stan had received information of a big German convoy moving from the south to reinforce Tirana. He therefore decided to halt it by blowing a bridge where the road crossed a river. When he had done this he called the RAF, who sent over a large number of aircraft and together with the ground forces completely destroyed a convoy of '1,500 men, a few tanks, guns, M.T. and horse-drawn vehicles'. This action once more established Stan's reputation with the Partisans, and the earlier frigid relations between them melted.

Tirana fell on 17 November 1944. By this time there were considerable Partisan forces outside the city. Stan Eastwood's primary role was to call up the aircraft they needed to support their attacks. The RAF did not let him down, and for three successive days sent over as many aircraft as they could spare to attack targets Eastwood had indicated. On the last of these days they sent twenty-eight rocket-firing Beaufighters in strafing attacks against barracks and gun positions. It was perfect co-operation, and the Partisans were exultant at this action.

Stan was just outside Tirana when it fell, but was forbidden to enter the city. Next day he disregarded this absurd and unjustifiable order, and his men reached the goal which for months had seemed so far away. They spent the next few days preparing the airfield for the arrival of aircraft. Mines were lifted and rubble was removed. At the end of November the airfield was ready for use.

In early December Stan Eastwood and his Patrol left Albania—they had been dropped in during the first fortnight of August.

It has not been possible for me to relate details of all they did, for they did so much. I have had to cut short or even omit accounts of many of the occasions when they engaged the enemy. Also I have not been able to give a complete picture of the fluctuations of Partisan co-operation.

This was the hardest problem for the Patrols in Albania, for they never really knew where they were. When they felt inclined to fight the Partisans fought like demons, but often, and with little warning, they would refuse to fight at all. Such change of face was all very baffling to understand. It can never have lightened the worries which any young officer already had on his shoulders, when he had been dropped by parachute and been ordered to operate offensively against the enemy in the territory he occupied.

However, this whole operation had been an unqualified success. The enemy had certainly been severely delayed in his withdrawal, and had suffered quite a number of casualties, which after all had been the intention of the whole undertaking.

For the part that he had played in the weeks he had been in Albania, Eastwood's sergeant—Andy Bennett—was awarded a Military Medal. He had shown great courage and initiative in the actions in which he had been involved.

Bennett had previously distinguished himself on Leros, where he had been a private soldier with Olivey. Since then he had been with Eastwood as a corporal on Corfu and during the raid at Orso Bay. During each of these operations he had thoroughly proved his worth. Later he was promoted to be the squadron sergeant-major of the Rhodesian Squadron. His meteoric progress through the ranks was in some ways a tribute to his great character. He was a man of a type seldom met with in the ranks of the Army, and was respected and liked universally. I knew few so reliable, willing and ingenious. He served the Long Range Desert Group extremely well.

I myself left Albania at the end of October. Together with Michael Parsons, and with Signalman D. C. Jones to operate my wireless set, I trekked south across the Shkumbin river, and from there towards the coast.

There was much for me to do in Italy, and I felt that the end was in sight in Albania. For three weary days we moved towards the coast, and travelled many miles. Then when I knew we had only a short distance to go I sent a signal to Italy asking for a boat to collect us that night. I was sad to leave Albania, and we were given a royal send-off. We arrived on the beach at dusk and settled down to await the craft which we were to expect at midnight.

It was a cold night, but our escort of Partisans lit a good fire and we huddled round it to warm ourselves. They cooked the inevitable turkey and supplied us with quantities of raw and vicious *rakia*. We had a happy evening. The Albanians sang some of their songs, and we endeavoured to reciprocate by contributing in our discordant turn. They made speeches lauding our greatness and were able conveniently to forget the difficulties of the past. We were equally insincere, and said a few feeble words.

Not long before midnight we began to flash the agreed signal of recognition. An hour later as I peered into the darkness through my glasses I saw a small naval craft glide towards us. I watched them put a boat over the side, and waited as this rowed towards me. Charles Hall, my second-in-command, leapt ashore to greet me.

We bade a fond farewell to our escort, duly paid them a quantity of sovereigns and with a parting fusillade of shot from them we left those entrancing shores.

We quickly boarded the Italian motor torpedo-boat and warmed ourselves with rum. Charles Hall had brought Sergeant Morley with him, and I was delighted to see him again. A month ago he had been missing in the islands with Gordon Rowbottom, and I was pleasantly surprised to see him safe and sound.

A few hours later in the cold and very grey light of the Italian dawn we sailed into Brindisi. I drove at once to Bari and had breakfast with Rufus Montagu. As always, he offered me the hospitality of his flat, and I bathed and shaved with him as my host. It was wonderful to feel really clean again, and I tremble to think of the fleas and filth of which I divested myself in Rufus's spotless and ordered household. Somehow he never seemed to mind at what hour or in what state of squalor I arrived.

Next day I saw Brigadier Davy. He first ordered me to report to hospital to obtain a certificate of fitness. Without it he forbade me to parachute again or to go on any further operations. I felt fit enough, and was reasonably confident of the outcome. I therefore went to the 93rd General Hospital at Barletta.

I was X-rayed, and waited a while for the specialist to examine the negatives. Soon he came and told me that I must come into hospital at once, as I had done serious damage to my back. After some persuasion it was agreed that I could come back in two days. There was so much to clear up at Rodi, and I was grateful for the respite.

Two days later I returned to hospital, and was put into a room with two other lieutenant-colonels. One was Arthur Boyce of the Hampshire

Regiment. It was his unfailing humour and great zest for life which helped me through the next few trying weeks. He had recently been severely wounded while commanding his battalion, and had won a well-deserved Distinguished Service Order in the action.

I was told that the X-ray showed a badly fractured spine. As the injury had occurred nearly five weeks before, some deformity had set in. There was no alternative but to put me into a plaster jacket from my waist to my neck.

I asked how long it would take before I was free to move out of this straitjacket. Six months was the reply; it nearly made me weep. But worse still was the news that I would have to be invalided home, and that I could not possibly be fit for military service for a very long time.

It was not that I did not want to go home, for there was nothing I should have liked more—if I had felt free to go. I had left England with my regiment to serve in Palestine in 1938. I was still overseas six years later. My father was very ill in hospital, and I knew how lonely my mother was without him.

Yet somehow I felt certain that my duty lay in Italy. It was likely that the war would be over before too long, and I thought I should stay there to the end. Besides, if it was really necessary for me to go home I should be sent home without further question. Obviously I was only a borderline case. I did not know what to think. I could only realise that my going would have meant the end of my long, happy service with the Long Range Desert Group.

A day or two later they operated on me. Major McEwen was the orthopaedic surgeon, and he did the job beautifully. I felt very uncomfortable for a few days, but McEwen was very kind and sympathetic to me; I am sure I was a rotten patient, as I felt so very frustrated.

The days passed slowly, but I soon began to mend well. By the middle of November I was fit enough to face a medical board with a good chance of being passed fit enough to stay on in my job. All worked out as I had hoped, and after facing the board for one and a quarter hours I felt that I had convinced them. At the end of it all they told me that they had recommended me for six months base duties.

I therefore saw no reason why I could not go back to Rodi. There I could live in comparative comfort, generally keep an eye on our operations and be near enough to the hospital to pay occasional visits.

Major McEwen agreed to this suggestion, and almost exactly a month after I entered hospital I was back again with the unit. That was all I wanted, and I knew that once I had something to do again I would soon recover very quickly. I remained for another two and a half months in the uncomfortable plaster jacket. But it was only an inconvenience, and did not prevent me from carrying on with my day-to-day business. Through a series of long delays I was not re-examined again by a medical board until I was absolutely fit. They had no alternative but to pronounce me so.

It was through no fault of the staff of the 93rd General Hospital that I had not enjoyed the few weeks I was in their care. Everyone was most considerate to me. The Commanding Officer—Colonel Ward—was a veteran of the First World War, and during it had been decorated with the Distinguished Service Order and the Military Cross. He was extremely tolerant of my impatience, and I always felt that he sympathised with my dislike of enforced inactivity.

The medical officers and nursing sisters were also very kind, and I often wondered how they were able to work the incredibly long hours that they did and still remain patient, sane and sympathetic. Their devotion was selfless, and nothing was too much trouble for them. I found the same spirit, the same passionate generosity, in all the many military hospitals that I either visited or in which I was a patient during the war.

While I was in Albania several other parties had gone off on operations. Ken Lazarus was still responsible for the planning at Bari, and Charles Hall held the fort at Rodi. Between them they carried on the good work exactly as before. Although the responsibility was theirs they kept me informed of what was going on elsewhere. Each day in Albania I had been sent a summary of the activities of the other Patrols, and thus I knew, and could retain general direction over, the plans and control of all operations in progress. Later, when I was fit enough in hospital, I was never far away from Ken, and he could consult me when necessary. In fact, he seldom did, for he was quite capable of getting on with things on his own.

In this way I was able to watch the movement and successes of Moir Stormonth-Darling near Florina in Greece. He had at last been permitted to go himself on operations, rather than suffer the tedium and anxiety of controlling them. I know it was hard to hold him back for so long, but officers of his worth were hard to replace. His experience was invaluable, and I could not risk losing him.

# CHAPTER 18

# Operations in Greece and Northern Albania

As the end of the war began to come in sight men like Moir became impatient, and wanted to fire just one more shot in anger. It was difficult to restrain them, nor would it always have been wise.

So off he went like a happy schoolboy on his half-term holiday. He took with him two Patrols of his Squadron under Gordon Rowbottom and Jack Clough. He also took Bill Armstrong, the Sapper who had volunteered for the Brenner Pass exploit which I mentioned earlier, and who could help him with any major demolition tasks he decided to take on. They were parachuted into the area of Florina with orders to harass the enemy on their withdrawal through Greece. This was in early October 1944.

Their arrival was not an easy one, for Moir did not know whether he would be jumping to the welcome of a reception party or not. As always, it was a tricky operation throwing men out blind over enemy-occupied territory. We now tried to ensure that there was normally someone on the ground to see that everything possible was done to make the landing of parachuted parties reasonably safe.

As it turned out in Moir's case, all was well, and those he hoped would be there to greet him had not been forced to move as he had suspected. But speed at that time was essential, and the risk of a haphazard landing had to be accepted.

This party achieved considerable success against the rapidly retreating enemy. It was not a picnic, for German columns were still well organised and in some considerable strength. Without a high degree of imagination and leadership Moir could never have succeeded as he did.

Numerically the best results were obtained in an action Moir's party fought against a convoy of vehicles. His few Sappers under Bill Armstrong had mined two culverts on the road. The charges were to be set off by a length of fuse which ran into some sparse cover about a hundred and fifty yards from the road. Here Armstrong himself was concealed with a box of matches to ignite the fuse. The rest of Moir's men were in position behind

202

boulders up the hillsides which flanked the road. They lay there waiting for a suitable target.

After a time a convoy of tempting size approached. Armstrong then bided his time until he could cause the maximum chaos. When he had two vehicles almost on top of the culvert and one more on the second he fired the fuse. The effect was perfect, and such as we used to dream about. All three vehicles completely disintegrated and a fourth, which was between the two culverts, had its wheels blown off. Complete chaos ensued. There was a perfect road block, and the stage was set for the second act of this little drama.

Moir's men opened fire with every weapon they had. They went on bloodthirstily until their ammunition was exhausted. Before the Hun had time to collect his few remaining thoughts he had lost over fifty killed and wounded. Moir wasted no time in getting away, and disappeared into the hills as quickly as he had arrived. He was too wise to risk being involved in a pitched battle.

Then in a response to a call from Moir the RAF arrived, and they were able to complete the carnage. Our communications were so good, and our liaison with the Balkan Air Force so well established, that it was often only a comparatively few minutes before our aircraft would be over to answer a call for support.

John Olivey was also in Greece commanding a Patrol of Rhodesians mounted in Jeeps. He had been put ashore in the Peloponnese with a party of the RAF Regiment to seize and hold Araxos airfield, from which the enemy had been reported to have withdrawn. John's secondary task was to provide the reconnaissance element for George Jellicoe's Special Boat Service, which was also to come in some strength to assist in hastening the German withdrawal.

Soon after being landed John's Patrol was in action near the Corinth Canal, which they crossed after some opposition. Then they swept on into Athens, to be with the leading troops to re-enter the city. We were all glad that this triumphal task should fall to John, who had escaped in Athens nearly a year previously. He could not stay in Athens, though, and had to push on through Greece, maintaining contact and harassing the enemy where he could, until finally he joined forces with Moir and his party near Florina. They returned together to Athens, where I imagine there were some fairly hilarious parties during the two days before Moir had to come back to Italy.

Olivey's party had covered a lot of country in their ten Jeeps. They had also quite a lot of fun en route, though they had been unlucky in losing two men killed on the way. One died accidentally when sorting through a lot of odd weapons which had been captured. The other was blown up on a mine near Corinth.

The latter was Corporal A. Tighe MM, of the REME. He had been the fitter with my Yeomanry Patrol in the desert, and had been with me on all our sorties in those earlier days. He had won his award for a series of gallant actions on several Patrols. He had earned it over and over again.

Tighe was a quiet, shy, unassuming man who was a master at his craft. I believe also that no unkind thought ever entered his mind. I certainly never heard one pass his lips in the years when I had lived close to him. His reputation in the unit stood high, largely because he had been a survivor of a party of men who had been attacked in the desert south of Kufra in 1940. This epic of endurance and fortitude had become a legend among the more recent arrivals in the unit. Tighe was quite rightly given the tribute such a hero deserved. That he should have been killed on a mine, so near the end of the war and after suffering and enduring so much, was a twist of fate which was hard to understand. His death was a great loss to us all.

John Olivey had to stay in Athens, for the civil war was just beginning. Once more the old warrior was in the thick of it. But it was war of a different sort: sordid, deadly and ruthless. Yet John was as good as ever at the art, and once more he showed exemplary courage and disregard for his own personal safety.

Shortly after the trouble began he was patrolling a street in Athens in his Jeep when he was fired at by a sniper. His driver was severely wounded in the mêlée which followed, and the Jeep was damaged. In a courageous attempt to rescue his wounded partner John himself was wounded in the head and arm. He did not give up, and managed to drag the driver away from the Jeep. Unfortunately, in the attempt the driver was shot dead by further bandit sniping and John himself only just escaped to fetch assistance from a near-by armoured car. He was evacuated to hospital in Italy.

He had travelled much of Greece with his few Jeeps. We were not often able to get new ones, and many of ours were veterans of the desert. We could never have kept so many on the road for so long without the work of our Light Aid Detachment. This was a small party of REME and RAOC technicians who maintained all our vehicles, our guns and our heavy stores. They were also not beyond looking after the engines of our Waco aircraft and the diesel engines of our two Schooners and other smaller craft that we operated.

It was not often that they were able to find excuses to get themselves on operations, and so their efforts were seldom recognised as they should have been. Yet we could never have gone without them; they kept all our highly varied machinery in action. Captain Joe Braithwaite was in charge of the Detachment, and his inventive brain and genius for improvising something out of nothing was one of our most valuable assets.

While Moir and John Olivey were in Greece there were other parties still operating in Albania. David Sutherland had taken in a force of his Special Boat Service in order to disrupt enemy movement on the eastern borders of the country. This party had some successes, but were thwarted all the while by the vagaries of petty political feuds. The frightful intrigue and treacherous dealing was hard to stomach when such fine opportunities were presenting themselves.

Jack Aitken was also in Albania, but he was in the north. His role was to destroy the retreating enemy on the road from Milot to Scutari and Lesh. With him he took two Rhodesian patrols under Jackson and Savage.

Aitken was another New Zealander who was a born leader of men. Nothing rattled him or confused or worried him save one thing: and that was dishonest dealing.

Unfortunately, this was what he found in Albania, and it made him impatient. Full co-operation from the Partisans was never accorded him, and he was frustrated from the very start. Yet despite the unwilling attitude of the Partisans he led his force in harassing operations against the enemy's main line of retreat. He was in the country for three weeks, and certainly produced results beyond my expectation—knowing, as I did, the difficulties with which he had to contend.

Aitken's whole task was complicated by the internal political situation in Albania. In order to get him to the right area we had no alternative but to land him on a part of the coast held by Abas Kupe. The latter was an inveterate royalist who had set himself up in opposition to the communist Partisan organisation. At the same time he was struggling hard against the Germans.

Abas Kupe's day was nearly over, and he only held control over a small area where Aitken had landed. The British Government had maintained a small mission with him under Lieutenant-Colonel Billy McLean, but McLean had been withdrawn on the vessel which had put Aitken's party ashore. Aitken could only leave Abas Kupe to his fate, and he moved off into the hills to contact the Partisans. Neither side trusted the other, and Jack Aitken was constantly let down.

Jackson, who was with Aitken, distinguished himself by gaining an MBE on this operation. He added this to a Military Medal which he had won as a sergeant in the desert. He was ordered by Aitken to make a reconnaissance of some German positions near a place called San Dovani. Aitken hoped to carry out a raid if Jackson's information showed that the target was a suitable one. In order to approach these positions Jackson had to swim the Drin river. Its banks were patrolled by the enemy, who could cover its width with small-arms fire. At the place where Jacko decided to cross the river it was two hundred yards wide.

In November the rains in Albania are heavy, and the river was swollen and flowing dangerously fast. Jackson set off across it with two men, and being a strong swimmer he soon reached the far bank. His companions got into difficulties and shouted to him for help. So he dived in again and brought one of the two men safely to the bank. This was Sergeant Ryan, another Rhodesian, who had been with Jacko and the unit for a long time.

Almost exhausted, he swam back at once to try to help the other man, but the river's current was too strong and the poor fellow had already been drowned and swept away. There was no more Jacko could usefully do, and so with a heavy heart he continued with the task which he had been set.

He could only get really close enough to the enemy by moving through a minefield three hundred yards deep. That the mines were only sparsely laid Jacko of course did not know. It was incredible luck which brought him safely through to obtain the information Aitken required. He had lost his field glasses while he had struggled in the river, and he therefore had to approach his objective far nearer than was healthy.

This incident was an example of fine personal courage. I remember commending Jacko at a later date for it; and I honestly believe that he meant what he said when he replied, 'Oh! it was nothing, but it was jolly cold for a time.'

Yet cold and damp were not the only discomforts we, or any other soldiers, faced. There were also the irritating persistence of fleas or lice; the sores which would not heal because they were never clean; the nights of extreme cold when one lay, if one was lucky, on the concrete floor of some wretched farmstead or perhaps among the rocks under the shelter of a tree; there were days of intense heat when the weight of our rucksacks pressed ruthlessly on our weary shoulders, or the nights when we would stumble and crash through the darkness over rocky passes or find ourselves inextricably entwined in the thorny thickness of an interminable patch of scrub.

We could not always know where the enemy was lying across our paths, nor could we always tell whom we could trust among our new-found friends. In many cases the lure of financial gain or privilege was too great a temptation for the country people. In others the fear of reprisals was a deterrent to the free expression of traditional hospitality to a traveller.

After all, the local people often had everything to lose in giving us their support. What was there to gain except the intangible prize of self-respect and the possibility of a reward promised after the war? Is it not understandable that we were sometimes shunned or treacherously given away? It would not have been human nature if there had been only Good Samaritans among the Balkan peasants we encountered. Yet in my recollection there were comparatively few cases where even the poorest would not willingly give of what little they still possessed. Seldom did they ask for or expect anything in exchange.

In little mountain farms, where the families seemed to live only on their wits and little else, we would usually find a bed—or at least a covered space to lay our heads—for the night. They would even produce a few eggs, some bread and a little wine. They would dry our clothes and darn our socks. They might even stay awake the whole night through to watch for sounds which they knew to be alien. Then in the morning, when we woke from a stuffy slumber passed in an atmosphere of pine-savoured smoke, they would harness our mules and lend us their few implements with which to cook a meal.

As dawn broke our funny little caravan would move off over the hill, leaving behind us a family who must have been strangely bewildered. I often used to wonder what their thoughts had been as they gave succour and shelter to soldiers of a race most had never even seen before. Of a sudden in the night we would come along—a tired, dishevelled, cheerful crew of ruffians. We would steal nothing and make no threats. Our behaviour was quiet and our needs were simple. It must have been a weird contrast for these backward peasant people. There were times when we could not even converse with them, and yet somehow there was a sympathy between us born of mutual respect.

In the late autumn when, perhaps, the rain was falling and the skies were unsettled by a thunderstorm we would sit inside some tenant farmer's little house. In the corner of the room a frantic signaller would try to coax some sympathy from his lifeless wireless set. Outside the charging engine would throb in a way which never failed to madden me. The rich smell of bully stew would contrast with the smoky atmosphere which hung thick in clouds above our heads as we squatted on the floor. Every now and then a wild little child would come, look at us quizzically for a few moments, and then dart off again to the squalor whence he had emerged. His departure would be hastened by the raucous rasp of his scolding mother's voice.

Sleep was frequently fitful, for either there was the arrival of some messenger with outside news or a signal would come in from Ken in Bari. Perhaps there was a scare of the enemy's imminent arrival, or the rumble of near-by gunfire. Sometimes the sentry would report the sound of movement along the rocky paths or announce the approach of a friendly Partisan conspirator.

Yet in spite of these interruptions we usually slept well. We were healthily tired, and we were existing on the minimum of sleep. A few hours would be all we could expect, and this was sometimes more than we ever got. There were nights on end when we were on the move, or alert or in action. Then we could only snatch sleep as and when we could, and it was all the more blissful.

It is easy to magnify the dangers and aggravations with which we were faced. It would be only fair to sum up too our advantages.

Firstly, we practically never suffered the horror of a heavy barrage, the menace of a bombing raid or the carnage of the infantry overrun by tanks. We did not live with constant gunfire, in touch with an enemy a few hundred yards away. We seldom had to traverse minefields or move helplessly in columns of transport advancing or retreating in equal haste. Our battles were usually fought on ground, and at a time, of our own choosing. No one depended on us save ourselves. Our failure would reflect on us alone. We could move largely where we wished, and not just in conformity with some wider plan. There was no front line for us, because we were always behind and among the enemy.

Secondly, we were free to make our own decisions of space and time.

We were given general directions from our base and then left to work out the details for ourselves. This freedom of action gave us an opportunity to devise our plans and to adjust them as the situation demanded. There were few restrictions, and these were created for our own safety—or sanity.

Thirdly—and this is no exaggeration—we were comparatively safe. True, there was always a danger, but it did not often materialise. We would go for days without seeing a German—but we smelt and sensed them all the time. When we did see them we could usually avoid them when they did not interest us. We were trained and equipped to move in the mountains into which they seldom ventured. If they did penetrate them they were usually hampered with all manner of impedimenta.

Lastly, there was the satisfaction of something achieved. I know our efforts were only flickers of fire in a total conflagration, yet we experienced the sensation of a success which was out of all proportion to the expenditure or the resources involved.

From my own point of view there were also tangible advantages. I was served by officers and men who were of my own selection. If they were a failure for any reason I could readily dispose of them and replace them from the many who never failed to volunteer to fill our ranks. For no other reason did they leave, and I was never confronted with the constant demand for officers or men required to fill appointments on some superior staff.

I was helped also by the priority we were accorded for the selection of men and for the provision of unconventional equipment. Without it we would never have obtained some of the strange little items we required; marine engines for our launches; bagfuls of bullion for our purchase of goods, intelligence or human lives; cameras to record or support the information we collected; skis for our parties isolated in the mountains of the wintry Balkan scene; or perhaps a special band of frequencies on which to operate some wireless set, where the operator had knowledge to pass on, and which might well be worth the complications it involved.

All these and many other things we were granted. Sometimes we had to struggle for them, but when our case was good there was no doubt that we would obtain them in the end.

# CHAPTER 19

# Working with the Navy and RAF

The LRDG was fully occupied with operations in the Dalmatian islands, Istria and Croatia during the last three months of the war. By this time the German counter-offensive in the Ardennes had been crushed and their forces had been driven back to the frontier of Germany. The Russians were less than fifty miles from Berlin. Belgium had been liberated.

In Italy Field-Marshal Alexander's armies had been cruelly weakened to sustain other fronts, and it was not until early April that they could move forward again and debouch from the Apennines into the valley of the Po. The Russians had overrun Bulgaria, Roumania and most of Hungary, and were then virtually halted by stubborn German resistance until they were able to drive westward on to Vienna in the spring.

I have already touched on the difficulties which had arisen with Tito's Partisans. These had been nothing to what was to come. They were mere inconveniences compared with the dangers and indignities to which we were later exposed by their political spite. It is hardly believable that such things could have happened between allies. It is even more incredible when the British had given so freely of their short supplies and had exerted themselves to the very limit to assist and keep alive the Tito movement.

Yet the time came when our Patrols were even put under arrest by the Partisans; they were thrown into squalid gaols, and deprived of the means of communicating with their base.

But more of that later. The events that led up to those incidents were frustrating but often supremely successful.

At the end of January 1945 two factors became apparent. The first was that until the operations of the Allied armies had reached the north of Italy there was little use for our Patrols in the north of Yugoslavia and in southern Austria. When the battle surged on towards those areas our chance would come again, and we should meanwhile train for operating in those higher altitudes.

Secondly, there were not sufficient tasks available in Istria and the northern Dalmatian islands to keep both my Squadrons fully employed..

With some regret I decided to withdraw Moir's Squadron from operations. They were to be trained in mountain warfare, and would gain further experience in the arts of ski-ing, rock-climbing, mule-management and the general technique of moving and living in snow conditions.

Obviously Moir was disappointed at this development, as were his men. It was bad luck that they should be pulled out after they had waited so long to start on operations. They had done very well already, and they obviously wanted to go on with what they had begun. But there seemed a good chance that they would be required at full scale later on in northern Italy and Austria. I chose that Squadron because the other one was committed more deeply, and it would have been difficult to extricate it. On top of this the Rhodesians knew the Dalmatian coast well and had made many contacts there.

The only consolation to Moir was that he was delighted to get back to the mountains and snow that he loved. He moved his Squadron in the middle of February to Terminillo—Mussolini's ski resort about fifty miles north of Rome. Here they installed themselves comfortably in one of the showpieces of Fascist luxurious hotels—the Caserma M. They were taken under the wing of the Mountain Warfare School, which was being run there by Lieutenant-Colonel Jimmy Scott.

After a time the School closed down, and Moir obtained permission to move his Squadron to the Gran Sasso. Here there was another hotel which had been in the news eighteen months earlier as the place in which Mussolini had been incarcerated after his capture by the Partisans. They had taken him to the Albergo Campo Imperatore—an imposing Fascist edifice at the summit of a 3,000-foot funicular.

Not long after his arrival a small German force, under Captain Otto Skorzeny, had landed by glider and overcome Mussolini's guards. Then with a light aircraft they had flown the Duce away from under the very noses of his incredulous captors. It was a great enterprise, which because of its pure daring deserved its success completely.

I remember seeing the remains of the gliders when I went with Moir to look over this mountain resort, and I realised what a bold and imaginative feat Skorzeny's had been. The only possible place to land gliders was limited in size and strewn with boulders. It is remarkable that any of them landed safely, and even more astounding that the small aircraft could land at all, let alone fly away with Mussolini and his rescuer—also a formidable figure of a man. There is no doubt that Skorzeny could never have carried out this extraordinary operation unless he had been a man of great personal courage and determination and a master in the art of turning up in the most unexpected places.

We found that it was a splendid place for further mountain training. Moir moved his Squadron there on foot. Each Patrol covered the fifty miles from Terminillo as part of their operational training. The only snag to the whole project was their complete dependence on a very temperamental funicular. Up this all their stores and rations had to be transported. It worked like a dream for twenty-four hours, and then one of its two motors broke irrevocably. There was no alternative for the men but to carry on their backs every item they needed up the three thousand feet to the top. Speed on this ascent became the object of great rivalry, and the record was set up by a man who did it in one hour and twenty-five minutes with a 40-lb pack on his back.

The enthusiasm of these men at such a late stage of the war was always a source of wonder to me. They entered into their training with the same spirit of zest and adventure as they had done before we came to Italy over a year earlier.

I know they all hoped to operate in Austria and on the northern borders of Italy. This would have been a new experience for them, in territory where none of them had gone before. The lure of fresh fields and new endeavour was as strong as ever. But it was not to be, and just before the war in Italy ended I decided to withdraw this Squadron back to the unit at Rodi. The snow on the Gran Sasso had nearly all gone, and it became obvious that they would not be required again to fight in the Italian theatre of war.

On the day war ended Moir was faced with moving everything his Squadron possessed from the hotel to the transport waiting three thousand feet below. The funicular still failed to function. They spent that historic day going up and down the mountain carrying everything, from beds to boxes of ammunition, on their backs.

For the last months of the war the remaining operations were carried out by Ken's Rhodesian Squadron. By the end of January 1945 the port of Zara had been occupied by the Partisans. It soon became clear that the best way of controlling and co-ordinating our future operations would be from an advanced base in Yugoslavia. Zara was the obvious place. It had a good harbour from which light naval forces could operate, and a reasonable airfield at Prkos, about twenty miles from the town.

What could be better? Here we could be within easy striking distance of our targets, and would have the Royal Navy and the Royal Air Force close at hand. This conception became even more closely knit when it was decided to set up a small Combined Operations Headquarters at Zara. Together the Navy, Air Force and Army would plan and execute operations, working together in one building to give each other maximum support.

There were two main objects behind the future plans of the Combined Headquarters at Zara. One was to give every possible direct help to the Partisan forces; the other was to disrupt the efforts of enemy light naval forces, which were proving an increasing threat to our shipping in the north Adriatic. For the first, the RAF was most directly concerned. They would be called upon for supply-dropping sorties on an even bigger scale than before, and would also be in a better position to provide immediate air support for the Partisan forces on the ground. For the second, we had our small part to play in assisting the Royal Navy with intelligence on shipping movements.

The Army element of the Combined Force at Zara was called Land Forces Northern Adriatic. It consisted originally of a Squadron of the Special Boat Service and our Rhodesian Squadron. Some guns of the Raiding Support Regiment were later added, as well as a unit of the RAF Regiment. The former had been raised to provide the support weapons for Partisans and others who were working in enemy-occupied territory. David Sutherland commanded this force in the early days until I took over from him after a short period of leave.

We were given as directions the task of 'harassing the enemy in the north Dalmatian islands and on the mainland of Istria and Croatia'. Our targets were given to us as enemy shipping and their crews, radar installations and other targets indirectly assisting the enemy naval position in the area. We were also enjoined to avoid destruction of basic utility plants—I don't think we ever destroyed any, but I was never quite sure what they were!

Ken Lazarus, who had served so diligently and long in Bari, was released from there and went himself to Zara. He had done a wonderful job of work in Bari, and it was high time he should be allowed to get out again into the fresh air. He had planned and controlled more than sixty operations. Of these only about five had been failures, and those through no fault of his. There is no doubt that the constant strain of waiting and hoping had taxed him heavily, yet he never showed it or lost his composure.

In Zara he set up his headquarters aboard MFV *Kufra*. She was the latest addition to our fleet, and was named after the oasis in central Libya where we had been based in the early days of the war. The *Kufra* was an 80-ton schooner which Dick Croucher had converted into a mobile headquarters. It was a comfortable small craft with very good accommodation, and Dick was justly proud of his command. The sea was in his soul, and he brought up his crew the hard way. There was never anything slipshod or lax about them or their work. In emulating the tradition of the Navy, Dick did not fall far short of their standards. This was no small achievement with his music-hall crew of flatfoots—I hope they will forgive me for this comparison with the Senior Service, with whom, as I say, they vied, and not unsuccessfully!

Tim Heywood had fixed the most elaborate and ingenious communicating system aboard the *Kufra*. Ken was in touch with Bari and our headquarters at Rodi. He was also able to intercept all messages to and from any Patrols which might be operating.

At the end of February 1945 the enemy in the coastal areas of Yugoslavia still occupied the area northward from Karlobag inclusive. They also maintained garrisons on the islands of Pag, Rab, Losinj, Cherso and Krk.

212

The head of the Adriatic had been extensively and effectively mined. German shipping was moving by night practically free from interference by our aircraft, and comparatively safe from attack by our naval craft. The elimination of this sea traffic was an essential part of the offensive programme devised by the Combined Headquarters.

Ken therefore proposed that he should send his Patrols out where they could observe this shipping. By day it was hoped that they would find the places where enemy craft were lying up, and then get the RAF to strike. For this purpose aircraft were kept ready at Prkos airfield to take off the moment information was received. By night we planned to communicate direct to RN craft lying a few miles off-shore. I have already described the method which we evolved for this particular type of aggression.

The first Patrol to go out on this task was under Mike Reynolds. He had a staunch party of men with him, and this was just the sort of job he really liked. As a wireless operator he again had Signalman Metcalfe, who had been with Mike on all his previous patrols. It was largely because of Metcalfe's efforts that this party met with as much success as they did. He was a first-class operator, and no amount of discomfort or interference ever seemed to upset him.

It must be remembered that we had to start again in the islands. After the Partisan volte-face of a few months before we had been forced to withdraw nearly all our Patrols. This time we knew the ropes, but there was all the same anxiety to be gone through and the contacts to be built up among the Partisans.

Mike left Zara during the night of 23 February 1945. He was away until the 17th of April, when he was forced to leave Istria. He was landed by sea on the east coast of Istria, not far from the Arsa channel. Here there was a jetty at which enemy shipping loaded large quantities of coal which forced labour was mining inland. He was soon able to set up a suitable observation post from which he could watch movement in the channel and at its mouth. For the first week he reported a good deal of shipping, and the RAF showed their appreciation of his intelligence efforts on the 3rd of March by sending over eighty bombers to strike at the coal jetty. Unfortunately, the weather had closed in by the time they arrived, and they did not even waste their bombs.

I think the best way of describing what this Patrol was able to do is by quoting extracts from Mike's diary, written after the event from notes he kept at the time.

| | |
|---|---|
| 4th March. | Hurricanes and bombers get hits on S.S. "Italia". |
| 5th March. | Hurricanes with rockets set fire to tramp and sink 500-ton coaster. |
| 6th March. | Three Motor Torpedo Boats attack three 'E'-Boats and one tramp. Tramp sunk. |
| 7th March. | 800-ton vessel damaged and 100-ton lighter sunk by Mustangs and Hurricanes. |

| | |
|---|---|
| 9th March. | 700-ton coaster sunk. |
| 10th March. | 800-ton vessel sunk. Walked along beach and could see no ships afloat. |
| 13th March. | Three Motor Torpedo Boats engaged and damaged 'F' and 'E'-Boats as they entered Arsa channel. On three occasions the Motor Torpedo Boats drove back enemy vessels trying to leave Arsa. |
| 14th March. | 0230 hours. Our three Motor Torpedo Boats leave. 0300 hours. Three lighters leave for Fiume. 0400 hours. Ten boats enter Arsa but recognition difficult. 1100 hours. Hurricanes sink two 'E'-Boats. |
| 20th March. | 0200 hours. Three Motor Torpedo Boats engaged and sunk a schooner. |
| 22nd March. | Hurricanes beach three lighters. |
| 23rd March. | Capture spy in our camp and hand him over to Partisans. |
| 26th March. | German patrol 100 strong beating bush near our camp. Uncomfortable. Our watchers over jetty nearly captured. |
| 27th March. | Germans still trying to find us. |
| 31st March. | Hurricanes damaged a lighter and coal installations. |
| 1st April. | 56 Liberators bomb and cause great damage to coal installations. One 100-ton vessel sunk. |
| 5th April. | Three Motor Torpedo Boats lying off shore are attacked by midget submarine which was sunk. |
| 7th April. | 200-ton vessel and 100-foot barge sunk by Hurricanes. |
| 8th April. | Germans searching for us. |
| 9th April. | Hurricanes damage 100-foot vessel. Germans still looking for us and come very close. |
| 10th April. | 0200 hours. Three Motor Torpedo Boats lying off us engaged by four 'E'-Boats. Coast defence guns also open up. Our craft suffered some damage. |
| 11th April. | Germans fire mortars and sweep bush near us with machine gun fire. |
| 13th April. | We are tricked by Partisans and placed under arrest. |

From then on until he was evacuated Mike was kept under arrest. But that is another story, about which more later.

The extracts from his diary I have quoted above speak for themselves. They show some of the successes achieved and some of the dangers encountered. But they don't tell the whole story. It would not be fair to claim that every strike by the RAF was the direct result of immediate information from Mike's Patrol. Nevertheless, by a quick system of communication which Tim Heywood had devised, and with first-class organisation by the RAF, they were able to get their aircraft over the target eighty miles from their base within half an hour of the moment that Mike had observed his prey.

What chance had the poor unfortunate enemy got? His shipping could barely move by day, nor was it safe when in hiding. Similarly, it could only move by night after about 2.30 in the morning, when our own ships were on their way home.

Such was the measure of some magnificent co-operation between the three Services. Everyone praised our efforts highly, but we realised that the sticky end of the job belonged to the other two Services whose task it was to complete the slaughter. They were most thrilling days as each new result was flashed back to us.

No wonder the Germans disliked the treatment they were being given. It was little surprise to us that they would do everything possible to trace the source of this destruction. They knew Mike was somewhere about, and did everything they could to find him. It was the avoidance of their search parties which was his real triumph, for the Germans gave him less peace than his diary shows. They employed well-paid Fascist spies who were only too keen to earn the rewards the Germans offered them. They used dogs, and they would send out heavily armed patrols to fire the bush where they thought he might be hiding.

Yet in spite of this and the reprisals which were meted out to the unfortunate civilian population the locals gave Mike every help. They supplied him with bread, meat, milk and eggs, and even organised a laundry service for him. Nor was that all, for they used to send a barber at dead of night to cut the hair of Mike's Patrol. I often wondered what the results of this nocturnal trimming must have been like!

These and other services were given by the peasants at the risk of their lives. Perhaps they knew at that stage of the war on which side their bread was buttered, but even in Istria buttered bread was no consolation for a prematurely slit throat.

There was an occasion when Mike suddenly saw the enemy surrounding the hilltop from which two of his men were observing the Arsa coal jetty. At the same time he saw two young women making their way to the top of the hill. Later he heard that these brave girls had hidden his men in a disused well while the Germans combed the area. Such was the friendly treatment he received at first. How different it later turned out to be!

While Mike was in Istria we sent other Patrols to do similar tasks. One of these was under Tiny Simpson, who had been with me in Albania. He was landed by sea near Mike so that the latter could give him all the latest information. This was a lucky arrangement, for on arrival Simpson found that his wireless was out of order. Fortunately, he had with him a small walkie-talkie type set with which he could talk to Mike, so that he was able to carry on until a new set could be sent up for him through the latter's agency.

This replacement set was duly delivered. Stuart Hamer, who was Tim

Heywood's deputy, had taken the set to Mike. The story goes that Stuart used to wear a blue fisherman's jersey and some equally unmilitary trousers. He was a good-looking man, and there is no wonder that a certain Amelia—the village belle—fell heavily for the 'escaped Russian naval captain'. When he was picked up again a few days later the story goes further that he fell into the sea in boarding the craft which collected him. The gossips said that he could not leave Istria quick enough! Many hearts were broken!

Mike sent two of his men off with the new set to Simpson. The two—Corporal Waller and Private Edwards—set off, but never reached their destination. Three days later reports were received that they had been captured. Then there was a series of alarming stories about their fate. We heard that they had been shot; we heard that they had been tortured and hanged. Neither tale seemed unlikely, for the Germans would not take kindly to anyone found in that neighbourhood with a wireless set. We then heard no more until many months later.

I found myself in a very difficult position over these rumours. I knew that Hitler had issued an infamous order that all parachutists should be shot without trial. I knew that recently a large number of the Special Air Service had been summarily shot in France.

It therefore seemed that this was to be their answer to what we were doing. After all, it was probably a very effective means of dealing with our operations, for it was bound to curtail them if the enemy were ruthless enough. We would be forced into risking lives only on targets which were absolutely vital, or on tasks where the risk of capture was small. At least, that must have been the way the Germans argued, and it gave me a good deal to think about.

Now I was faced with one or two alternatives. Either I should say nothing to any Patrols and throw them in, myself alone knowing the risks which they were facing if they were captured, or I should tell them the facts and give them the option of withdrawing. As yet my fears were only based on rumour, and I had no definite confirmation of the fate of Waller and Edwards.

It was a tricky decision. I wrote to George Davy and asked his advice. He in turn felt he should seek higher opinion. This he did, and I was authorised to tell the men the facts. I felt relieved about this, for it did not mean that I would have to send men into action under what amounted to false pretences. I had never done that, and did not want to have to start at that stage.

The outcome was interesting. Firstly, there was not one man who gave a fig for any German threat. No one considered the risk as one not worth taking. Not one man. Secondly, some time after the war was over I heard from Waller and Edwards from Rhodesia House in London. They had both been taken prisoner, had been treated quite reasonably and had made their way home at the end of the war.

Their story was interesting. They had left Mike Reynolds at 3.45 a.m. on the 22nd of March. With them they had one Partisan as a guide. About an hour later they entered a village called Pavici.

Here they were hoping to contact friends before moving on. Instead they were stopped by a sentry who in the early light of dawn they suspected to be a Partisan. While they were talking to this man and getting no reply they noticed two others converging on them. Behind these two came some more.

Quickly they realised their mistake, but it was too late, and they were soon under arrest. They were taken to Pola, and all three were thrown into Nazi detention cells. The next day they were moved to Pisino and put into the civil gaol. Here they were interrogated. They realised that the Partisan guide would be worked on, and they therefore instructed him to tell some tale which would not throw any light on the activity of Reynolds or Simpson. This story was duly extracted from the Partisan, and for some reason it was accepted.

A few days later they were moved on to Trieste and given three days' solitary confinement before their next interrogation. They were then told that the Partisan had broken down completely and regaled his captors with the full story of Mike Reynolds's activities. At the same time they were confronted with some notes which they had been carrying from Mike to Simpson. These they had thrown away before being searched, but they had later been retrieved by the enemy. On the interrogator's table was a reference pamphlet giving a picture of the Long Range Desert Group cap badge and a description of our organisation. Waller and Edwards offered complete silence to their exasperated questioner.

The next day a German lieutenant called and told them that 'as a matter of form, the Gestapo had been advised about us. The former were apparently not prepared to accept us as prisoners of war and advised our hasty dispatch.' Waller then made a statement in his defence saying that he was a British soldier in uniform, and was therefore entitled to the protection of the Geneva Convention. He explained that a German soldier landed to watch shipping in the Thames Estuary would be accorded prisoner-of-war status. This remark was received incredulously.

Nothing further happened for the next eighteen days, which they spent in solitary confinement with very little food. They were then told that they would be treated as prisoners and were put together into a cell. Soon after they were handcuffed and marched through the streets of Trieste on their way to a prisoner-of-war camp in Austria. Very shortly after this they were released when the Allies overran their camp. They wasted no time in making their way across Europe to England and home.

I never got to the bottom of the original rumours that had been put about concerning their fate. It was probably a clever piece of propaganda on the part of the Germans, who hoped they would frighten us into inactivity. Or maybe it was just another bit of Machiavellian trickery in which the

Partisans were beginning to indulge in order to discourage our Patrols from setting foot in Istria.

The capture of Waller and Edwards did not deprive Simpson permanently of his wireless set. When he heard that these two men had been waylaid he sent a Partisan into Pola to buy a replacement for the damaged part of his original set, and very soon he had his own set working.

Meanwhile he was able to contact the naval craft which lay offshore at night. For this he used a walkie-talkie. On his second night in Istria he directed the ships to an enemy barge, which was soon sunk. All the next day Simpson had to lie very low while several German patrols passed by him.

The next two nights they were prevented from remaining in useful contact with our ships as the Germans had patrols along the beach.

A day or two later when they were expecting Waller and Edwards they suddenly heard people crashing through the scrub towards them. As only two Partisans knew their exact position in the thick bush, they were surprised to find some Germans almost on top of them. A few shots were fired, and Simpson withdrew safely into hiding.

For the next two days Simpson was kept pretty constantly on the move. Each night he passed what information he could to Mike Reynolds, and they exchanged experiences. All this was done on the walkie-talkie. No code was used, as Mike and Tiny spoke to each other in the Chisona language, which was a Rhodesian native dialect common to them both. It was a fair bet that there were few Chisona-speaking Germans in Istria at that time!

The Germans gave this party no respite. They were even more doggedly hunted than was Mike Reynolds, and it became obvious that if they were to be given no rest it would be impossible for them to carry on. So at the end of March we withdrew them, but not until they had managed to collect a large amount of information about an area of which very little was known.

Another Rhodesian Patrol was active in Istria at the same time. This was commanded by that indomitable character John Olivey. It was he who had refused to cease fighting after the surrender of Leros; and it was typical and fitting that John should command the last Patrol to return to the Unit base after the war in Italy was over.

He left Zara for Istria on the 8th of March and eventually returned to us on the 12th of May. In this time he had passed right round the head of the Adriatic, through Trieste and after joining the Eighth Army in Italy came back along the western shores of the Adriatic.

I would not hazard a guess at John's age. He had the capacity for fun and the high spirits of a man in his early twenties. Everything he did was carried through with enthusiasm and humour. He was remarkably fit, and could compete with any of us. Yet I am sure he was nearer forty than thirty. He gave to the Long Range Desert Group a very great deal of himself, his courage and his sympathy over four years of war. At the end of it all he returned to his farm at Umtali in Rhodesia, and it was a great joy for me to meet him again in early 1963 when I went to Rhodesia. This was the last time I saw him, for he died some five years later.

His tasks in Istria were generally the same as those given to Mike and Tiny Simpson. We were after shipping down the east coast, and we also wanted to locate suitable targets for David Sutherland's parties from the Special Boat Service.

Olivey and his men were landed safely to a reception party from Mike's Patrol. This arrangement was a good one, as it meant that the chances of capture on landing were considerably reduced, but it also hampered the work of the receiving Patrol to some extent. Consequently we only used it when really necessary, and when there was worth-while information to hand over to the incoming party. Olivey's Patrol set up their watch in the Fianona area, and sent back some excellent information. But they encountered a lot of difficulty in a neighbourhood which was fairly heavily populated, and where tongues wagged.

In early April we decided to send John farther north to watch movement on the road between Fiume and Trieste. So Stan Eastwood's Patrol was sent in to take over from Olivey. Eastwood arrived on the 8th of April, and Olivey moved north to the high ground just west of the road and about fifteen miles west of Fiume.

It was a few days after this that the trouble which had been brewing with the Partisans finally came to a head. We had four Patrols in Istria at this time. Mike Reynolds was at Arsa, Eastwood had taken over from Olivey when the latter went farther north and Jackson had been landed in the Pisino area. These four Patrols were under the overall direction of David Sutherland, who had been put in command of all troops on the ground in Istria. He also had with him about fifty all ranks of the Special Boat Service.

On 12 April 1945 I had gone over to Italy in a motor torpedo-boat which was sailing to Ancona. Ron Tinker—who had until then resisted the wiles of women—was to be married. I was met by Tony Browne, who had my car with a wireless set in it so that I could keep in touch with Ken at Zara.

On 14 April Ron was married to a very charming New Zealand nurse who was serving at the New Zealand hospital near Ancona. It was a very good wedding, and Moir, Tony Browne, Jack Aitken and a few others joined us for an excellent stag party the previous evening. I can only remember that this went on till five o'clock in the morning of the day of the wedding. Consequently, I was in no good temper when I received the first news of Partisan treachery in a signal from Mike.

This cryptic message merely said, 'Have been taken prisoner by Partisans. Request evacuation immediately.' It was not till we got him out that I heard the full story.

## CHAPTER 20

# Frustrations in Istria

The whole time he had been in Istria Mike Reynolds had been on good terms with the Partisans, who had given him every help and assistance. They knew all about what Mike was doing, and indeed had appreciated his efforts. The local group used to come every day and discuss the situation with him. Mike was in no way surprised when eight of the usual members arrived one morning for elevenses. This had become quite a custom, as they enjoyed the tea Mike would give them. They therefore sat down and joined the party.

While this was going on the eight Partisans suddenly stood up and held up Mike and his men at the point of the gun. They were each armed with a sub-machine gun. Mike, who did not want a scene, had no alternative but to comply with the order to hand over his arms. He was told that they would be shot if they refused to obey. By good fortune the wireless operator, who was not having tea at the time, was unnoticed for a while. This short respite gave him the opportunity to send off short emergency signals, the first of which I received at Ancona. From then on he was not allowed to use his wireless until it was returned to him the next day.

Ken at Zara at once asked Mike for more news, and I returned hurriedly from Italy. After some delay he could only tell us that he could not understand the reason for his arrest. He added that whatever happened he would have to come out, as his watch had been compromised since he had been forced by the Partisans to move in daylight.

It was a most unfortunate affair. Mike had done so very well, and his information had been invaluable. To have to end it in this ignominious fashion was intolerable, but it was pointless for him to continue. I was not prepared to risk his Patrol again in an area where they had already suffered enough hunting. A few days later we withdrew him by sea.

My mind had been made up when he sent a message to say that he would 'be forcibly put on a Partisan boat and evacuated unless the Navy could send a motor torpedo-boat. I would prefer to be picked up by the Navy rather than be shanghaied by these garlic-eating bandits'. Of course, the Royal Navy sent a vessel at once, and Mike's gallant little band of men returned under the dignified protection of the White Ensign.

Mike was given a Military Cross for his exploits in Istria. The last paragraph of the citation which won him this award sums up the opinion I had of his worth. I can think of no other words in which to describe it. The citation closed:

In this, as in previous operations, Reynolds has shown complete disregard for his personal safety in the execution of the tasks entrusted to him. His courage, determination, initiative and leadership have at all times been an inspiration to his own and to other Patrols.

The next development was a message from Stan Eastwood to say that he too had been arrested, and that he could no longer continue his shipping watch. Shortly there followed a signal from David Sutherland that he and his party of Special Boat Service were also under arrest.

I was furious at all this, and sent a signal to George Davy in Bari urging that everything possible be done to effect an early release. I told him that I felt it was grossly unfair for young officers to be hampered by political interference in this way.

To me it was obvious that the whole trouble was caused by Tito's desire to have an indisputable claim to Istria. He feared that too many British troops were gaining an influence, and that we were poised ready to enter Trieste before he could reach it. What other reason could there be for such unwarranted behaviour between allies? Our Patrols were there to aid the cause only. We had no other desire. Tito did not trust our motives, and this treatment was the result.

Looking back, I am more than ever surprised at the restraint shown by everyone. I wonder how our Patrols kept their tempers. In spite of my criticisms of them at the time, there is no doubt that Allied Force Headquarters handled this dispute with considerable tact.

Balkan Air Force quickly appreciated the dangers of this situation, and worked hard on our behalf. Air Vice-Marshal Mills sent a strong telegram to Allied Force Headquarters which sums up the effect of this extraordinary affair. In it he said, among other things:

These Patrols provide information about shipping, which is quite indispensable to our successful joint operations . . . without it our Air and Sea support for the Yugoslavs will be seriously weakened . . . I think you should draw Tito's attention to this . . . he should know how serious this incident is in view of the intelligence obtained by these Long Range Desert Group Patrols which is of the utmost value—unless they are immediately released we may well be forced to consider how much assistance we should give in the way of Air Support for operations and

Air Transport for food to Allies, whose reply is to put British Troops under arrest.

Meanwhile I gave orders to all Patrols in Istria that they must obey all Partisan instructions, provided that this did not directly threaten their own security. I explained how much I understood the humiliation of their position, but that it was vital to avoid open conflict with the Partisans. They could go to the point where violence seemed imminent, and then they must give in. On no account were any of our own lives to be risked unnecessarily.

At this stage Olivey was still not under arrest, although he was no doubt being carefully watched. On 16 April Eastwood and Simpson were ordered to concentrate where Sutherland was held. At the same time a General Drapsin, who was commanding the Partisan 4th Army, expressed (to some gullible liaison officer) great regret for these incidents. He also had the impertinence to say that he was completely in the dark, and had no idea who was behind this action. He would order immediate release.

These tactics were very well known to us. The Partisans in Istria had behaved with a veneer of decency when carrying out their orders. They explained that they had been given instructions from above (4th Army), and had no alternative but to carry out their distasteful task. Yet here was higher authority denying any knowledge of what was going on.

I could only regret my weakness. The previous December when the first troubles with the Partisans had arisen I had said that never again would I send Patrols back into Yugoslavia without the written authority of Tito himself. I said that no pass issued by any local petty brigand was good for much. We must have Tito's personal authority to tell the local Partisans to co-operate. But I was talked out of this demand on the grounds that we could forget the past, and that there was a complete change of relationship for the better. In my defence I can only say that although I accepted this view, I did not believe it.

Strong protests were sent to Tito by Allied Force Headquarters. These elicited the fantastic reply that the enemy frequently infiltrated their own troops into Istria dressed in British and Russian uniforms. It was also suggested that this may have accounted for the attitude of the local Partisan commander in Istria. This excuse was put forward in spite of the fact that every one of our men in Istria personally held a pass written in Serbo-Croat and signed by the responsible official in Zara. There was also a somewhat thinly veiled accusation that we were not sharing our information with the Partisans. Nothing could really have been more absurd.

The battle now began to rage rather above my head. I was placed in no easy position. On the one hand I was given authority to withdraw all or any of the hundred men Sutherland had in Istria when I felt the situation demanded it. On the other, I could not implement my decision without referring it back to Allied Force Headquarters. This was because the whole matter had become a major political issue of prestige and bargaining.

During the evening of the 18th of April David Sutherland told me that the attitude of the local commander was getting very ugly. He added that he personally felt that he could not see how it would 'ever be possible to resume normal relations with these ridiculous people'. He strongly advocated evacuation. With this I entirely agreed, and arranged to send craft to pick up all Patrols except Olivey.

A few hours after this decision Sutherland himself asked for it to be cancelled. He hoped to be able to carry out one operation before being forced to withdraw. He felt that it was worth hanging on, as feelings were running slightly less high.

I was glad of David's change of view. I felt all along that my duty lay clearly in supporting him and accepting his advice, which was based on his personal experiences. I could not hope to know how tricky the situation was really becoming from the point of view of violence. No sooner had I heard David's latest views than I had a strong telegram from George Davy in Italy countermanding my orders to evacuate Sutherland.

Davy's view was that the worst that could happen to Sutherland's party was that they should be locked up or marched off and bundled aboard Partisan schooners. He felt that because of the clear rights and wrongs in this case we should accept these inconveniences. Unless we did it might have appeared that we were tacitly accepting the Partisan right to order us out of Istria.

Here there was a firm divergence of view between myself and my superior commanders. There was much to be said on both sides, but I felt strongly that I must support the man on the spot—Sutherland. The situation was also confusing, because I had been given the ultimate say in ordering evacuation, yet I was not allowed to implement it.

Air Vice-Marshal Mills happened to be in Zara that day. He gave me every encouragement, and himself doubted the logic of George Davy's argument.

Luckily, Sutherland's improved position solved the problem. But it only solved it temporarily, and I asked George Davy for further instructions. I told him that I doubted the good faith of the 4th Army orders for release. These had certainly never materialised. If they did not come, and Sutherland still requested pick-up, I proposed to arrange this unless he ordered me to do otherwise.

Once again Air Vice-Marshal Mills, who was still at Zara with me, supported me by giving me orders to act in accordance with his own views. These he outlined in a further telegram to Italy in which he said, 'I am certain we would lose less face by leaving Istria under our own steam and with some dignity (if position becomes impossible) than by having our men manhandled by a gang of ghastly garlic eaters.' He added that he could not agree that being bundled into Partisan schooners was a mere inconvenience from Sutherland's point of view. Nor could I: but it was easier for an Air Vice-Marshal to say this to a Brigadier than for me to do so!

I know George Davy was only passing on the broader views of Allied Force Headquarters. He never held this difference of opinion against me, nor did he ever resent my not accepting his views without argument. He was better able to appreciate that Allied Force Headquarters was in an extremely difficult position. He was in constant touch with them by telephone, and therefore heard all the arguments. I was only presented with cryptic instructions and told not to argue.

All the 19th of April this kind of argument went on. Poor David Sutherland had a very heavy responsibility to bear, and he carried it wonderfully on his young shoulders. Towards evening the situation was considerably easier.

However, on the 20th of April Sutherland signalled as follows:

'Impossible carry on. Must be re-embarked tomorrow night without fail.' He was hoping to bring out everyone except for Olivey, who was playing the idiot boy and thoroughly exasperating the Partisans in the north. This was John Olivey's most talented role. He could pretend more convincingly than anyone I know not to understand an order he didn't like. He did it by truly subtle comedy and an infectious laughter in which everyone else was soon helplessly engulfed. He must have maddened those Yugoslavs—he certainly infuriated the Germans when they had him for a time after Leros.

I told Sutherland we would pick him up if possible. I also suggested to him that Eastwood should remain if he could, on the pretext that there were insufficient craft to collect them all. I still hoped to try to maintain some hold in Istria, which was what Allied Force Headquarters also seemed urgently to want.

Only recently I was given the original of a signal which I sent on 21 April from Zara to Charles Hall in Rodi. This said that I had

recommended the withdrawal of everyone except Eastwood and Olivey. Latter playing idiot boy with great success and undoubted charm. Decision as to whether sanctions will be imposed rests with Alexander now. Hope to avoid court martial but this unlikely and an inconvenience I must accept. Tell Stormonth-Darling to buy Hansard as study of diplomatic language will be most useful weapon in future operations.

I was obviously finding everything pretty exasperating! I may have been lucky to avoid a court-martial too.

The RAF commander at Zara was Air Commodore Hallings-Pott. Throughout this contretemps he had given me every possible help and advice. He now lent his weight to my decision to evacuate Sutherland, and reported to Italy that it was asking too much of him to continue to 'hold the baby' while negotiations continued. On top of this it was quite impossible, as David Sutherland had so rightly pointed out to us, to tell when the Partisans were likely to go completely sour on him.

The issue had now been translated to such a high diplomatic level that we both felt that everyone had begun to forget the feelings, dangers and humiliation of the men actually involved.

Late on the 21st of April we received agreement to our arrangements. However, fate intervened. The weather became too rough, and we were quite unable to send any craft to collect the parties.

The next day David was told by the Partisans that unless the Navy came the following night he and his men would be forcibly marched off towards Fiume. Air Commodore Hallings-Pott and I then went to see the naval commander in Zara. Between us a plot was hatched to pick up Sutherland in daylight, with the RAF giving the Royal Navy craft the maximum cover.

This plan was just about to be put into action when it was all once more stopped. A further telegram came from Italy, reporting that profuse apologies had been received and orders to release everyone had been given. This being so, Allied Force Headquarters insisted that Sutherland should not come out until he had carried out one worthwhile operation. Once more I had to signal a change of plan to David, who was more than forbearing with me.

During this considerable delay the worthwhile targets had been diminishing. The enemy was slowly moving out of Istria, and David rightly reported to me that he would have to move north to comply with Allied Force Headquarters' wishes. He added that he fully realised that the matter was out of my hands, but that he 'could no longer endure being a pawn in this fantastic international chess match'.

Despite all assurances, the situation on the spot remained unaltered. No apology had reached Sutherland. During the afternoon of the 23rd of April he told me that unless they were evacuated that night violence was more than probable the following day. All I could do now was to tell him to acquiesce in any order, however ignominious or unattractive. Allied Force Headquarters were adamant that he should remain.

This being so, they (AFHQ) would have to accept full responsibility for any bloodshed that ensued. I could no longer guarantee restraint. Although I knew that Sutherland himself was nearly at the end of his tether, I did not know how near some of his men might be to taking action on their own against those who had tricked them. Such an incident might so easily have set light to a flame which mere diplomacy would have found hard to extinguish.

On 24 April Allied Force Headquarters unexpectedly changed their minds. They finally agreed that there was no point in our remaining in Istria, and that the Patrols could come out. The next day Sutherland said that he had at last received the promised freedom of action, and that he would move north at once to operate offensively. By that time craft were on the way to pick him up, and it was decided that this plan should go through. Sutherland was therefore ordered not to operate in Istria, and he returned very disconsolately to Zara during the night of 25 April.

Only Olivey remained in Istria. He continued with his original task until the war ended. Then, as already related, he returned to our base at Rodi through Trieste and down the east coast of Italy. A splendid round trip.

In the whole history of war there can surely have been few more extraordinary clashes between allies. It would be foolish to pretend that incidents do not happen, for they do. But when it comes to arresting and depriving an ally of free movement, then there is something very strange in the relationship between those allies.

For many months the Yugoslavs had co-operated and fought alongside us. Together we had suffered hardship and privation. We had known the joy of success against a hated enemy, and we had known the fear of their vicious retaliation. Setbacks and victory we had shared. All these things had bred some sort of trust and respect one for the other.

Then what happened? When communism grips a country—as happened in Yugoslavia in 1945—fine, brave individuals, become poisoned overnight. Everything is subjugated to the common cause—the furtherance of communism for Moscow. Past alliances meant nothing, past agreements still less. All that mattered was that Yugoslavia should retain this territory by fair means or foul. Yugoslavia must have control of Trieste—that was the prize they wanted, and they would go to any length to attain it.

It would be unprofitable to dwell on the military handling of this affair. I had certain views, which were based primarily on previous operational experience. Neither myself nor my officers knew much (or ever really bothered much) about the political intrigue and interplay. We didn't understand it. It was never part of our job. It is therefore no wonder that we failed to appreciate it when we found ourselves playing a significant part in a game we abhorred.

I would like here to record my appreciation of George Davy's tolerance, for he was often driven far beyond his judgment by the enthusiasm of our ideas. He understood when I disagreed with him. He was never acrimonious when he disagreed with me. I am grateful to him for his patience and understanding. It was only that I felt so acutely the futility of subjugating our immediate war aims to those of longer-term foreign policy. I was impatient with anything which deterred us from killing Germans; I found it hard to believe that there was ever any reason good enough to stop us. Surely, I thought, we—the Western Allies—can call the tune to any little puppet Balkan power who tries to twist our tails?

Often among ourselves we debated such controversial subjects. Time sometimes lay heavily on our hands. There were periods of excruciating boredom when we were just lying under cover waiting; waiting for signs of enemy movement or watching for his reactions. Necessarily our own ability to move was restricted so the hours had to be spent somehow. We may have talked or read or just lain listening to the wireless. Or we may have written a few notes or cleaned our guns or repaired our equipment. Whatever we did, we usually talked as well unless we slept.

I used to enjoy spending an hour or two listening with my men while one of them talked. All sorts of ideas and all sides to men's characters came out when there was unlimited time for unrestricted conversation. Some used to talk about their homes, their wives and families; they would make us laugh with all the usual run of music-hall banter. Such comedy always raised a laugh—and always will, because there is nothing quite so funny as homely pathetic truth.

While the operations in Istria which I have already described were going on there were other Patrols out on some of the Dalmatian islands.

Lt George Pitt had been landed on the Croatian mainland at a point south of Karlobag. Here he was sent to pinpoint certain gun positions which had been troubling the Partisans. After completing this task he was later sent to the island of Rab, where he had an extremely uncomfortable time. The enemy were all over the island, and undoubtedly knew of Pitt's presence. As a result he was never left alone for long. He played hide and seek for days on end, but by dint of judicious dodging he was never caught. All the while he was getting a great deal of good information, and the RAF were really enjoying the targets he produced for them. He later joined the Partisan force which attacked the German garrison on the island.

Lieutenants Savage and Saunders were on the islands of Krk and Olib respectively. Savage obtained a lot of useful information, and later provided guidance to the Partisans when they retook the island. Saunders was withdrawn after a while because there was not sufficient enemy movement to justify his remaining on Olib.

There is one other incident of some interest which occurred in these islands earlier on in the year. We had set up a small post on the island of Ist. Here we could gather information of enemy troop and shipping movements between the neighbouring islands. This post had become one of comparative safety, where very little had happened for a while. I suppose the vigilance of our men became less acute, as it so often does when there is little to sharpen it.

Our small party were living in reasonable comfort in a house on the island. In one of the rooms they had set up their wireless station, with which they kept in touch with Bari. Signalman Kenneth Smith was the operator. He slept in an adjoining room with the other members of his Patrol. In other rooms of the house the women and children of the owner slept.

On the night of 10 January 1945 a party of enemy saboteurs landed on the north-east corner of the island. They obviously had complete information of the whereabouts of our party. That night a Partisan was taking his turn as sentry. The enemy crept past him unnoticed (or, perhaps, with his connivance) and laid a time bomb on the table just inside the open window of the room, where Smith kept his wireless set. They also put bombs in one or two other houses.

At this moment some shots were fired, and Smith woke up. One of the men in the house saw the bomb, which apparently had a ticking mechanism. This was in full operation, and it was reasonable to suppose that the thing would go off at any minute.

Smith realised that there was no time to be lost. There were some of his comrades and women and children in the house. Without hesitation, he dashed in to remove the device which he intended to hurl to a safe place behind a wall outside the house.

He had gone only a few yards when the bomb exploded. Poor gallant Smith was blown to pieces. It was a very brave action, which undoubtedly saved many lives. His courageous and unselfish deed was not without its reward, for not only were the lives of others saved but he was himself honoured posthumously by the award of the George Cross—the highest award which could be won for an action which was not directly in the face of the enemy.

The last few weeks of the war had not been easy ones. They were frustrating beyond measure. I hated to watch all our endeavour and ideas fizzle out in the damp of a political fog. It was bad for everyone, and was something to which we had never been accustomed in the past.

Yet in spite of it all the spirit of all officers and men never flagged. Each new task seemed as thrilling as though it was their first.

It was only when it was all over in Europe that a reaction set in and men's thoughts began to turn toward home, their wives and families. For a time they forgot that the war in Japan was still to be won. But only for a time.

We had been together for many years, and the thought of breaking up had never seriously occurred to us before. However, something had to happen. Either we were to go on and fight in the Far East or it was the end and we would be disbanded as a unit. Admiral Mountbatten's Headquarters had asked for us to go out there in November 1944, but Allied Force Headquarters could not spare us at that time.

As it turned out we were disbanded, though not through any lack of a desire to see the war through. In July 1944 I had made a case out for our future employment. In early 1945 I had discussed the whole problem with General Laycock, who was Chief of Combined Operations. In May, after the war was over, Allied Force Headquarters had recommended that we should go on as a unit to the Far East. I had also discussed all this with the Rhodesian Government which was prepared to support us as splendidly as they had done in the past.

What was more important was the number of men who were behind me in my proposals. At one time I had over three hundred men who were keen to go on to South East Asia. Of these over half were willing to defer their release in order to go. Their only proviso was that we should go together as a unit. I was not going to suggest to them that they should go in any other way.

However, our fate was to be otherwise. On 16 June 1945 Allied Force Headquarters told me that the War Office had definitely asked for us to return home to England as a unit. Here we were to regroup and have some leave before going on to Asia. Less than a week later I received a signal telling me of the War Office decision to disband us.

I can't pretend that this news was anything but bitter and disappointing for me. Yet in some ways, perhaps, I was glad.

I felt that many of us were tired and needed a rest from operations behind the lines. We had been at it a long, long while and some had been through enough. Anyway, there was nothing I could do but accept the ruling, which left us all with mixed emotions and a sudden emptiness and lack of purpose.

On the 21 June 1945, I assembled the unit to break the news to them, and the next six weeks were spent in carrying out the intricate business of a disbandment order.

There was much paper work to be done, and details to be tied up. I was helped magnificiently in all this by my Adjutant—Captain Leo Capel. Under his care men, vehicles and stores were dispatched to various depots, until by the 1st of August, 1945, no more of anything remained—only the vivid, wild and happy memories which we all of us retain.

During the last few weeks many letters of commiseration and congratulation were received. We were most proud of those we had from two very great friends and soldiers—Field-Marshal Alexander and General Freyberg. Both had done a great deal for us, and to both we owed a debt of gratitude which we could never repay.

Five years and fourteen days after its formation in Cairo, the Long Range Desert Group ended its active career. I believe that its days in the desert have made some mark in military history, but few people realise that our story did not end until over two years after that campaign was won.

# Select Bibliography

**Long Range Desert Group**  W. B. Kennedy Shaw  Collins  1945
**Eastern Approaches**  Fitzroy Maclean  Jonathan Cape  1949
**The Desert My Dwelling Place**  David Lloyd Owen  Cassell  1957
**G Patrol**  Michael Crichton-Stuart  William Kimber  1958
**The Campaigns of Wavell 1939–43**  Robert Woollcombe  Cassell  1959
**Hidden Heroes**  Trevor Constable  Arthur Barker  1971
**The Special Air Service**  Philip Warner  William Kimber  1971

# Index